T0182092

Software Development Measurement Programs

Miroslaw Staron • Wilhelm Meding

Software Development Measurement Programs

Development, Management and Evolution

 Springer

Miroslaw Staron
Department of Computer Science and
Engineering
University of Gothenburg
Gothenburg, Sweden

Wilhelm Meding
Ericsson AB
Gothenburg, Sweden

ISBN 978-3-030-06308-5   ISBN 978-3-319-91836-5   (eBook)
https://doi.org/10.1007/978-3-319-91836-5

Printed on acid-free paper

This Springer imprint is published by the registered company Springer International Publishing AG part of Springer Nature.
The registered company address is: Gewerbestrasse 11, 6330 Cham, Switzerland

To our families. . .

Foreword by Tom Gilb

Engineering Metrics Are a Necessary Tool for Software Development

The biggest and longest-lasting problem in software development is that we constantly fail to live up to our own promises and stakeholder expectations.

There is a simple explanation. We have in the past six decades seen an explosive growth in size, complexity, and the need for integration with other disciplines. At the same time, it takes a long time, decades to centuries, to develop successful cultures to handle such complexity, and we have not had enough time; by a long shot. In fact the nature of the problem seems to still be changing, faster than any time scale we would need to master, and cope with, the complexity and growth.

Some organizations, such as my own clients, Ericsson, IBM, HP, Intel and Boeing, have had to face size, complexity and change earlier than many others, and this is where this book has a role to play. This book incorporates many of the experiences and fruits of efforts to try to cope with the problems.

Not really surprisingly the answer to these problems, as in ages past (think Roman engineering, Egyptian pyramids), lies in the discipline of engineering. It is no accident that almost all of organizations such as the above-mentioned ones, have had a strong engineering culture, before the arrival of "software" as a component. And they have learned to apply engineering numeracy to the software domain.

The key tool in engineering, as in science, is *numeracy*. Quantification, measurement, feedback, learning, adjustment: a fact-driven culture. An 'evidence-based' culture. Too much of software culture today is based on the *craft of programming*, not the engineering of software (the *term* 'Software Engineering' was coined in 1968). The craft does not scale!

"Those who cannot remember the past are condemned to repeat it." (Santayana, 1905)

This book is *advanced, practical and useful* to potential readers, both industrial and academic.

Your own organization and problems are no doubt different from the organizations at the root of this book. But you can still select key ideas and practices, and adapt them to your current needs. You can be inspired to take new and advanced steps forward.

I certainly would recommend this book to people who want a deeper insight into the software metrics of today, and the trends toward tomorrow's software measurement.

With tools like these to build on, we might some time catch up with the complexity of the software development problem. It is not the whole answer, but we cannot afford to re-invent this wheel; we must learn from it.

Oslo, Norway   Tom Gilb
www.Gilb.com
February 2018

Foreword by Alain Abran

In both public- and private-sector organizations, huge amounts of money are spent on software, competing for scarce organizational resources: how do you ensure that such amounts are spent wisely and efficiently?

In engineering and in business, as well as in all applied sciences including medicine and social sciences, measurement is a fundamental tool. However, unlike these traditional fields, which have access to mature measurement programs based on international standards, the software community at large is still looking for evidence of well-designed software measurement programs with proven value. In the software domain in particular, there is a large variety of software metrics proposed in academia and by tool vendors for monitoring software development and evolution; however, many of them have fairly weak foundations and many will not withstand the test of time. Implementing software measurement programs in an organization therefore requires addressing a number of issues, including: Which software metrics options to choose? In what contexts should they be used? And what are the conditions of success for the design and deployment of software measurement programs? Such are the issues discussed by the authors of this book.

Staron and Meding share their years of experience from collaboration between industry and academia in the design of software measurement programs and their successful deployment and use as decision-making tools. The authors have structured their measurement programs based on the wealth of accumulated knowledge in mature fields of measurement, including the International Vocabulary on Metrology and the ISO 15939 standards for software measurement programs. They also share their expertise on how to assess the quality of the measurement programs themselves, and what tool sets are available for deployment in industry.

Software organizations of all sizes must acquire such **know-how** about the design of software measurement programs and how to deploy them for the benefit of their stakeholders. In this book they will find effective strategies for improving quantitative software management, along with numerous industry examples for the application of best practices in designing and deploying software measurement programs.

The recommendations offered here will help software organizations design and implement efficient software measurement programs as a basis for decision-making.

Montreal, QC, Canada   Alain Abran
January 2018

Preface

When a scientist and an engineer measure something, they focus on two different things. The scientist focuses on the ability of the measurement to quantify the measured thing (called the *measurand*). The engineer, however, focuses on finding the right qualities of measurement given the designed system (e.g. correctness), the quality of use of the system (e.g. ease of use) and then the efficiency of the measurement process. It happens all too often that these two focuses, seemingly contradictory, lead to a lack of consistency between the academic and industrial views on software measurement. In this book, we argue that both focuses are necessary and complementary. We argue that we can focus on the exact quantification and efficiency at the same time. We, finally, argue that industrial measurement programs need to combine both accuracy and efficiency to provide software development teams, project managers, product managers and quality manager with the right measurement methods, tools and instruments.

We, the authors of this book, come from academia and industry, where we worked together for the past 12 years. Our work has always been driven by the need to satisfy information needs of our stakeholders—product owners in the beginning and recently empowered software development teams. We have worked with both small and large software development organizations, as both researchers and as measurement engineers, measurement program leaders and even teachers. We have seen a number of measurement initiatives fail and equally many succeed, all too often depending on small things. These small things could be automation of measurement processes, combining of objective measures with subjective judgement or continuous evolution of key performance indicators in organizations.

Based on our experience we set off to organize and document our experiences. The result of this documentation is the book which you, dear reader, hold in your hand now. We wrote the book to help you define, implement, deploy and maintain a company-wide measurement program—a set of measures, indicators and roles which are built around the concept of measurement systems.

We organize the book as a gradual progression from theories of measurement (yes, you need theories to be successful!) to practical, organizational, aspects of maintaining measurement systems (yes, you need the practical side to understand how to be successful). Whenever possible, we provide anecdotes and examples from our experiences to help you realize what is important and what the common pitfalls are. We start the book with Chap. 1, where we introduce the need for measurement and how modern science looks upon major concepts like measurability; we also look at major differences between the academic and industrial view on measurement. In Chap. 2 we dive into details of the theoretical foundation of measurement—metrology and standards like ISO/IEC 15939 (Software and Systems Engineering—measurement processes). In Chap. 3, we introduce the main characters of this book—a measurement system and a measurement program. These characters stay with us for the rest of the book and guide us in the next chapter—Chap. 4. In Chap. 4, we explore the question *How do I know that my measurement program is of a good quality?* In particular, we describe the reasoning which we experienced throughout our collaboration—what makes some measurement programs successful and what makes other programs fail. We uncover such jack-of-all-trades tricks like how to find a good stakeholder and how to reduce the cost of measurement in an organization. In Chap. 5, we uncover other tricks related to the tooling for quantification (i.e. measurement instruments), data processing and analysis, and finally visualization. Once we have provided the examples of tooling, we can share some of the experiences on which measures/indicators work and which do not (and why!). Chapter 7 is no longer about our experiences, but about what we see as the future of software measurement—machine learning and flexible counting algorithms. From what we see today, it is these areas which will shape the field of engineering software systems and therefore we have to understand the principles of how a machine (an algorithm) "understands" numbers. In Chap. 8 we dive into the topic of deployment and maintenance of measurement programs in large software organizations. Based on our experiences from introducing over 40,000 measurement systems in more than a dozen companies, we share the tips and tricks on how to do it in the most painless way possible.

We hope that you will enjoy reading this book and that it will help you to understand how to become a successful scholar and practitioner in the area of software measurement!

Gothenburg, Sweden   Miroslaw Staron
January 2018   Wilhelm Meding

Acknowledgements

First and foremost, we would like to thank our industrial partners and colleagues, who have contributed to our work and learning over many years.

In particular, we are grateful to Micael Caiman from Ericsson, who has actively supported and believed in our work for over a decade. This book would not exist if it were not for his support and encouragement.

We thank our colleagues from Software Center (www.software-center.se), who helped us to understand the complexity of industrial work on many levels, in particular: Prof. Jan Bosch, Dr. Anna Sandberg, Kent Niesel, Anders Henriksson, Christoffer Höglund, Ola Söder, Magnus Bäck, Anders Caspar, Gert Frost, Sajed Miremari, Peter Ericsson and many, many more. There would be no measurement theme and measurement projects if it were not for them.

We are very grateful to Tom Gilb, who has provided us with ideas to improve the book and contributed directly to it, in particular, for letting us see a bigger perspective of measurement programs and for helping us to address a wider audience.

We thank our colleagues from the department of Computer Science and Engineering at Chalmers/University of Gothenburg, who contributed through discussions about measurement and metrics over the years.

We are also grateful to our many colleagues from Ericsson, who supported us over the years. In particular we thank Karl-Johan Killius for his decisive support, as well as Jonas Bjurhede, Tommy Davidsson and Per Sundvall. Without their commitment, engagement and extraordinary technical skills there would have been no state-of-the-art, fully automated infrastructure.

We would like to thank our publisher, Ralf Gerstner, from Springer, who supported us in writing and constantly provided us with invaluable advice.

Finally, we are indebted to our families, for their unconditional love, support and understanding. There would be no book, no research and no fun, without them in our lives.

Contents

Chapter 1
Introduction

Abstract In this chapter we introduce the problems which are addressed by software measurement—e.g., providing quantitative insights, and we describe the possibilities which open up when we have software measurement of products, processes and enterprise in place. We discuss the possibility of quantitative fact-based management, customer data-driven development and using artificial intelligence (or machine learning) once we have a solid measurement program. Towards the end of the chapter we outline the concept of a company-wide measurement program and introduce the content of the book.

1.1 Academic and Industrial View on Software Measurement

Measurement is a great activity that engineers love to do; it makes the discipline of engineering so elegant and structured. Software engineering is no exception to that. We can program and create software, but it's really difficult if we cannot measure properly. Because, if we can't measure our activities and products, how do we know that we're on the right track in their development.

Together with the ability to process large data sets—the so-called Big Data systems—measurement has gained a strategic value for modern enterprises. Regardless, whether we consider a large software development company with distributed projects or a small agile team developing a mobile game, measurement is strategic. The large companies need the measurement to capture the market's requirements and to quantify the complexity of their large software projects (or their large number of small projects). The small software development companies need the measurement to assess whether the company's choices are right for their customers; the small companies need to show to their customers which assets they have and how to cash in on them.

Measurement is also strategic in today's enterprises because of the ability to use data for complex decision models and complex algorithms [ASH⁺14, ASM⁺14]. We can see that modern cars are using the data to autonomously drive and to provide a completely new experience for their customers. We can also see that advanced machine learning and artificial intelligence can take advantage of measurement and provide new values for customers. One of the applications which we are used to is stock market software trading agents, which trade stock every fraction of a second based on such measurements as stock price, the price's predicted development and risk.

If you have even encountered problems on how to measure one of the following, then the book is for you:

- Quality of your software product.
- Size or complexity of your software product.
- Availability, reliability or maintainability of your piece of software.
- Performance of your software development/maintenance/management organization.
- Progress of your software project.
- Release readiness of your product.

These aspects are so common that almost all software engineers encounter them and you are not alone. Luckily, we are here to help you.

Our book has been written as a result of a long-term (over a decade long) cooperation between academia and industry [SPA11]. It started with a pragmatic need from one of our industrial partners; it started with a question: "What should we measure?" The academic answer to that question, at the time, was quite pragmatic— give us 2 weeks and we will tell you. Unfortunately, even after the decade-long research project, we still cannot answer that question. Why? Simply because the reality around us changes so fast that our answer is out-of-date already at the moment when it is given.

This "give me 2 weeks" answer shows the challenge and the need for common language between academic innovation and industrial practice. What's easy to draw on paper (theoretical solution) is often very hard to realize in practice (practical realization of the solution). Therefore, we set off to write a hands-on guide for practitioners and academics on how to establish a measurement program.

1.2   What a Measurement Program Is: A Brief Introduction

A measurement program is a socio-technical set of measurement systems and their users. The notion of a *measurement system* is crucial for this work and we introduce it properly in Chap. 2. However, for the sake of discussion, we can see a measurement system as a software program which collects data about a number of attributes (e.g. size of a program, quality) and displays it to a stakeholder (a person who has the mandate to monitor and act upon the data displayed by the measurement system).

It is exactly here where we see the first challenge—the need to simultaneously work at two levels: the technical measurement systems and the social stakeholders and their organizations.

Based on our experience, this distinction, between the technology and social aspects of measurement programs, provides an efficient framework to separate the concerns of how, what and why.

The social part of the measurement program provides the meaning for the measurement and designates its value. We could say directly that a measure without a stakeholder is a waste of an organization's scarce resources and should be abandoned as soon as possible. We could also say that the higher the value of the measure, the more strategic it is for the company.

The technical part of the measurement program provides the process of data collection and management to arrive at the measure of the "what." We see these two parts as inseparable and essential for the success of the measurement program.

The measurement processes, used in the measurement programs, apply to *values*, *qualities* and *management objectives*, for products, systems and related organizations. We need to initially analyze our product and system environment, then determine the many critical stakeholders in that environment. We then need to determine the critical needs of those many stakeholders. The "critical needs" need to be specified in a disciplined manner [Gil05], with well-defined "scales of measure" and well-defined levels of future performance levels. This value specification is a logical prerequisite for at least three things:

1. the time of delivery prioritization of the required levels of performance,
2. the clarity of input to the architecture or design phase, and
3. the selection of one or more practical measurement processes, so as to manage and confirm delivery of the planned performance levels.

The measurement processes are our best cost-effective choices for getting feedback information about the progress of improving, or failing to improve, our critical values and objectives. In advanced engineering cultures measurement processes are in fact an engineering design decision based on many requirements and constraints. Most real cultures select measurement processes by default, by culture or by ignorance.

A single product value might employ several different measurement processes during its life-cycle, for example in early stepwise deliveries, in handover to the market, and in operation. However, these processes need to be carefully planned, executed and evaluated; thus we need to understand how to assess the quality of the measurement processes and their overarching measurement programs.

1.3 What a Successful Measurement Program Is

There are many definitions of what a "successful" measurement program is in this context [SM16, SM11]. For us, a successful measurement program is such a program that optimizes the usage of resources for measurement and the value delivered to the stakeholder of the measurement program. For example, it operates using minimal resources (both human and computer), maximizes the value of measures to their stakeholders and can be quickly adapted to the evolution of the organization and its products. This book is structured to address these items.

Measurement programs that are unsuccessful, to the contrary, are such programs as those that:

- use significant amount of resources, competing with the product development for these resources,
- require specialized competence, competing with the product development for the competence,
- provide "carved in stone" measures, making it hard to follow the evolution of company's products, processes, strategies,
- ignore the needs of their stakeholders, making the measures in the program useless and leading to parallel, unofficial measurement programs, or
- use off-the-shelf, one-size-fits-all measures to benchmark the company's specific business, leading to wrong business and technical decisions.

The view of measurement programs has changed over time. We can see that many of the modern enterprises today can be characterized by:

- focus on customer value rather than technology for its own sake [Sta12],
- rapid response to the evolving market [SMH$^+$14],
- operating in an ecosystem-based software development environment [Bos16],
- operating in a rapidly changing markets, where disruption is common [Col01],
- relying on empowerment of their employees for innovation, development and maintenance of their products [Tes14, RGMR16],
- relying on innovation to find new market niches for new products and constantly evolve [kim],

The book is primarily for the companies that expose at least two of the above characteristics, although every company in the software business will find parts of the book valuable and important for their measurement programs.

In order to better understand the novelty of this book, let us go through the historical developments in the area of measurement programs.

1.4   A Brief History of Software Measurements

One of the first books about software measurement was Gilb's *Software Metrics* from 1976 [Gil76]. Although the area of measurement has been around before, the book opened up the area for practitioners. In particular, the book introduced such fundamental concepts as, for example: (1) all variable attributes (qualities, values and costs) can be expressed quantitatively, (2) for any defined scale of measure, it is possible to define one or more methods for practical and economical measurement (and more than one measurement process might be useful and economical at any given time).

The measures presented by Gilb, used to monitor quality, qualified the product directly. In 1979, Albrecht presented another way of measuring software—by combining multiple measures to provide more direct support for decisions [Alb79]. The method presented there laid the foundations for size measurement using function points. This area is still being actively developed with certification programs and wide adoption in industry.

In the 1980s, the area of object-orientation developed, and so did the related measures. In particular, the object-oriented measures by Chidamber and Kamerer appeared, although these were published in 1994 [CK94]. Boehm's Constructive Cost Model (CoCoMo, [B$^+$81]) introduced an alternative to function point measurement, and further popularized the idea of measurement for estimation of project costs. In 1986, Motorola popularized their Six Sigma approach [Har94]. Six Sigma introduced many of the concepts of statistical quality control, still used today. The example of these concepts were statistical inferences, confidence intervals, and time series.

A lot happened in the area in the 1990s. The development of Team Software Process by Huphrey (TSP, [McA00]) popularized the control of quality on the team level and on the individual level. TSP popularized concepts similar to Six Sigma, but with lower granularity, balancing statistical methods, manual data collection, reporting and documenting, with the benefits of quantitative management of projects and products.

Standards like the ISO 9126 were approved and the standards in metrology were introduced into software engineering [oWM93]. These standards provided the industry with reference points in the area of measurement. The ISO/IEC 9126 provided the first standardized way of documenting measures, which "lives" in the new editions of these standards like the ISO/IEC 25000 series.

The book by Fenton, *Software Metrics: A rigorous and practical approach*, marked the importance of both theoretical and empirical measurement validation [Fen96]. The book bridged many of the practical aspects of measurement (e.g. definitions) with the academic view on measurement (e.g. validation of measures).

It was also the end of 1990s when software development companies used software measurement programs to a large extent. Almost all large companies had some sort of measurement program. The major characteristics of these programs, however, was their limitation to either quality assurance (descendants of Six Sigma) or cost estimation (descendants of function point measurement).

To widen up this view on measurement, in the 2000s, such standards as the ISO/IEC 15939 were introduced (originally approved in 2002, revised in 2007). These standards defined the way in which measurement processes should be established. This popularized the notion of measurement programs even in smaller enterprises. Together with the introduction of efficient presentation of information, dynamically on web pages, this popularized dashboards and measurement at all levels of organizations. In contrast to the centrally managed measurement programs of the 1990s, the 2000s measurement programs can be characterized by agility, team involvement and measurement of multiple properties of software products.

In 2010, the book of Abran [Abr10] updated the view on measurement by providing metrological foundations to modern software measurement. In particular, it advocated the importance of using etalons in software engineering for calibration of measures.

Currently, in the late 2010s, the measurement programs have evolved to entities which support organizations in large-scale data collection. Usually, this data comes from customers using software products (e.g. dating back to the first, large-scale, error reporting of MS Windows 95), where companies use the data to improve their products and provide new services. All modern enterprises, successful in business, have this kind of measurement programs in place.

1.5   Measures in Decision Processes

The purpose of this sub-section is to help stakeholders to understand how to use measures in an effective way in the decision process. We use the measure-decision dependency model, based on the principles from our previous work [Sta12]. The model is shown in Fig. 1.1. In the model we distinguish between measures and indicators, on the one hand, and system and strategic decisions on the other hand. The distinction between measures and indicators stresses the fact that indicators are important to trigger decisions (metrics push) whereas measures are used to monitor the execution of the decisions. The distinction between the system measures and the strategic measures reflects two types of stakeholders in modern companies— product-oriented and business-oriented.

The model is important for the companies as it allows them to filter out measures which are not related/used in any decision making processes.

1.5.1   Decisions-Measures Dependency Model

The decisions-measures dependency model contains four distinct types of measures that are closely related to formalizing and implementing decisions: two types have more influence on formalizing decisions, while two types are more important for implementing the decisions [Boe84].

The model lists measures that relate to the type of decision, i.e. product (e.g. memory consumption of a software product) or strategic (e.g. budget). The model lists also measures that relate to the type of the measure, i.e. base measures, derived measures, and indicators [SMN08].

Indicators often trigger decisions—when measures draw the attention of managers to the entity they measure (e.g. when problems occur), e.g. during decision meetings [FSHL13, SHF$^+$13].

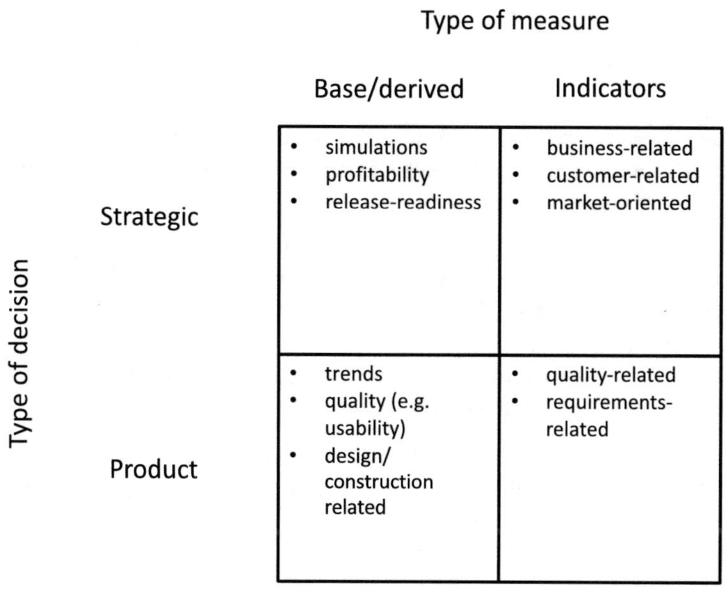

Type of measure

	Base/derived	Indicators
Strategic	• simulations • profitability • release-readiness	• business-related • customer-related • market-oriented
Product	• trends • quality (e.g. usability) • design/ construction related	• quality-related • requirements-related

Type of decision

Fig. 1.1 Metrics—decisions dependency model, adapted from [Sta12]

Base and derived measures, on the other hand, are triggered by measurement processes to make a concrete decision in the organization—when managers demand collecting new measures and/or new analyses in order to take decisions [SMP12].

Strategic decisions are defined as decisions related to stakeholder value and organization of software development [Boe84]. These decisions usually impact the software development organization directly and the development product indirectly—resource reallocation might lead to re-planning of features included in a release.

Product decisions are defined as decisions related to the product internal and external properties and impact the product directly [RS05]. These decisions are often triggered by measures related to product quality.

Triggering of decisions is caused by management indicators—when indicators show "red," things happen in organizations. Usually, managers use technical indicators to formulate decisions, complementing them with simulations using managerial measures, e.g. "What if. . ." analyses. For example, when implementing a cost reduction program, managers need to observe the actual burn rate (compared to the simulated one) and interpolate it with current product quality trends. The technical indicators often push decisions in specific directions when decisions are formulated, although they could also trigger decisions. They have also the potential to change the course of a decision already being implemented.

While implementing the decision, base/derived technical and managerial measures are of highest interest for companies or organizations. The differentiating aspect between the managerial and technical measures is the need for monitoring trends of technical base/derived measures.

1.5.2   Effective and Efficient Measures for Decision Formulation

In the dependency model, the most effective measures for decision formulation are indicators, both for strategic decisions and for product ones. These indicators should have the following characteristics:

- Clear analysis model (decision criteria for interpretation: whether the indicator shows a positive—"green"—or a negative—"red"—status).
- Compact presentation and information provision, e.g. in the form of mobile apps and MS Vista gadgets.
- Long feedback loop for the managerial indicators: ca. 1–2 years.
- Short feedback loop for the technical indicators: ca. 0–20 weeks.

This book supports both the technical and managerial decision-making processes. Managers can read about how to use measures and how to support their organizations in setting up measurement systems. Architects and designers can read about how to cost-efficiently set up measurement systems and how to collect the data needed for making decisions.

Regardless of their position in the organization, all practitioners can read about the pragmatics of how to work with measurement systems, maximize the benefits of measurement and minimize its costs.

1.6   Content of This Book

The goal of this book is to popularize the structured, standardized and accurate use of software measurement at all levels of modern software development companies. We could have a subtitle—"Hands-on instructions on how to design, deploy and maintain software measurement programs, in modern software development companies," and it would capture the focus of this book and its intentions in general. In particular, we focus on the following aspects:

1. sound scientific foundations—the measurement program should include state-of-the-art measures and the latest developments in the area of product sizing, quality management and technology adoption,
2. cost-efficiency—the measurement program should cost as little as possible,
3. standardization—the measurement program should be based on the latest standards in the area of measurement, to maximize the portability and dissemination of the program,
4. value-maximization—the measurement program should maximize the value for its stakeholders, the stakeholders' companies and their customers,
5. flexibility—the measurement program should evolve at the pace of the evolution of its companies and enterprises,

6. combining organizational and technical aspects—the measurement program should maximize the stakeholders' insight using modern technology, and
7. seamless technology integration—the measurement program should maximize the adoption of machine learning technologies to reduce the burden of measurement for the enterprise.

The book is written to support these aspects and in general to increase the automation in measurement programs. It supports the companies in their journey from manual reporting to automated decision support, i.e. from Figs. 1.2 to 1.3

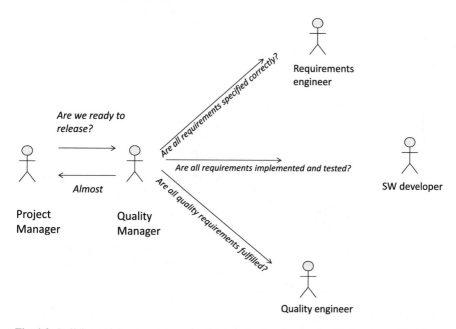

Fig. 1.2 Building opinion based on manual data collection involves multiple roles and is effort-intensive

The content of the book supports this by combining academic research and industrial practice.

1.6.1 Chapter 2: Foundations

We start by describing the theories and standards important for the modern measurement programs. We overview such standards as ISO/IEC 25000 and ISO/IEC 15939, which are needed to fill the content of the measurement programs and for structuring it.

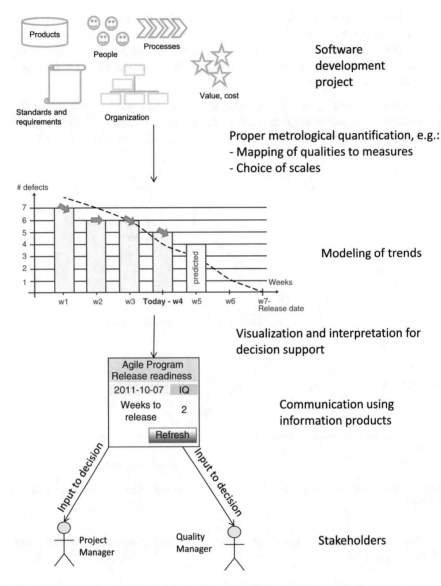

Fig. 1.3 Automation provides insight and increases efficiency of the organization

We describe also the ways in which measures should be defined and documented, based on templates from these standards. These descriptions provide the necessary foundations for further exploration of the more advanced concepts of metrology. These more advanced aspects include calibration of measurement instruments and empirical measure validation.

In Chap. 2 we provide the vocabulary which we use throughout the book and we focus, as mentioned, on foundations.

1.6.2 Chapter 3: Measurement Programs

The natural next step is to continue with the description of measurement programs in modern enterprises. In Chap. 3 we present the measurement program model, which describes elements of a measurement program—see Fig. 1.4.

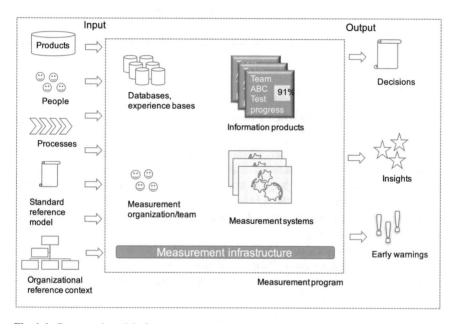

Fig. 1.4 Conceptual model of a measurement program

In the chapter we provide checklists for designing each of these elements, e.g. measurement information products.

Once we know the structure and the first-order entities of the measurement programs, we can continue to discuss the quality of measurement programs.

1.6.3 Chapter 4: Quality of Measurement Programs

The aim of Chap. 4 is to provide the foundations of what a good measurement program is. Based on the measurement program model presented in Chap. 3, we provide four views on quality of the measurement programs:

1. data quality—where we focus on the quality of the data used in measurement systems,

2. information quality—where we focus on the quality of the calculations and data flows in measurement systems,
3. information completeness—where we address the challenges of knowing how much of the product, process or organization a measurement program covers, and
4. coverage of the measurement program—where we focus on designing a measurement program that covers the minimum set of necessary aspects of modern software development.

These four views on quality of the measurement programs are important to understand how to check whether a measurement program is adequate for the purpose it's supposed to serve. However, we deliberately do not discuss the quality of the tools used in the program, as we focus on the modern tooling in the next chapter.

1.6.4   Chapter 5: Tooling in Measurement Programs

Automation is one of the cornerstones of measurement programs in modern companies. Without it, we cannot achieve efficiency and measurement programs become a burden rather than help. Based on the distinction between measurement instruments, measurement tools and visualization tools, we provide a description of measurement tools and measurement instruments used in measurement programs: see Fig. 1.5.

We provide guidelines for choosing different types of tools, structuring databases and visualizing measurement information products. We prepare for the next chapter in our book, which is about how to fill the measurement programs with content— measures and indicators.

1.6.5   Chapter 6: Measures in Measurement Programs

Filling a measurement program with content is tricky because it needs to combine the organization's needs and the existing measures/measurement instruments. Therefore, in Chap. 6, we complement the organizational need identification, described in Chap. 3, with the list of possible measures. We organize the list into categories as presented in Fig. 1.6.

We also provide examples of how to narrow down the scope of a measurement program for a specific role. We also provide examples of visualizations of measurements.

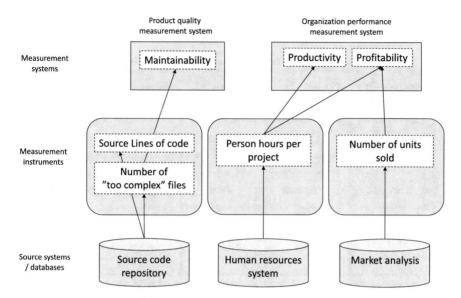

Fig. 1.5 Illustration of difference between measurement systems and metric instruments (aka metric tools)

1.6.6 Chapter 7: New Techniques

When discussing measurement programs, we should also discuss the newest developments in this area. In particular, which new techniques we can use for making the measurement programs smarter, more cost-efficient and of maximum value.

In Chap. 7 we discuss three main trends:

1. Big Data and availability of open data sets—providing the possibility to benchmark organizations, increase accuracy of measurement and exchange experiences,
2. machine learning—providing the possibility of automated decisions support, trend discovery and learning from data, and
3. measurement reference etalons—providing the possibility to calibrate measurement instruments to minimize measurement errors and maximize measurement certainty.

These techniques used to be reserved for advanced users, but thanks to the availability of new tools, they can now be used by all roles in measurement programs.

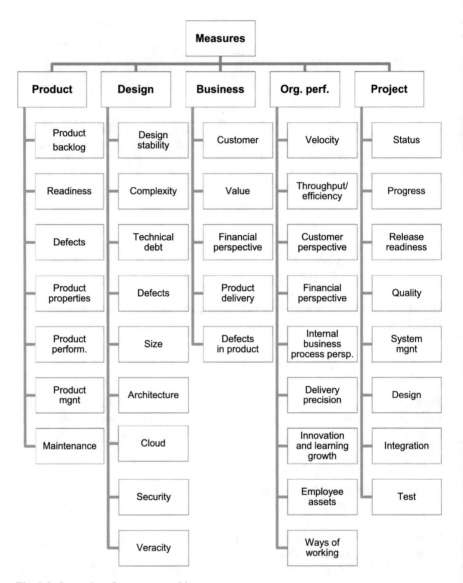

Fig. 1.6 Categories of measures used in measurement systems

1.6.7   Chapter 8: Maintaining and Evolving Measurement Programs

Sustainable, cost-efficient and valuable measurement programs in modern companies require maintenance to keep up with the evolution of organizations and technologies. In Chap. 9 we provide a number of guidelines on how to make the maintenance as painless as possible for the measuring organizations. Based on our experiences of maintaining over 40,000 measurement systems and working with over 20 different organizations, we compiled a set of guidelines and good practices, which we describe in this chapter.

1.6.8 Chapter 9: Summary and New Directions

Finally, we conclude the book by looking through the magic ball into the future and speculating on what kinds of new directions we can take once we adopt techniques and guidelines presented in this book.

1.7 So, Let's Start

This book is based on our experience of over 10 years of working together, working with different organizations and research groups. In our collaboration, we always enjoy the quantitative nature of research in software measurement and the tangible research results applied in our collaborating organizations. We hope that you will find this book valuable.

If you are interested in the nuts and bolts of measurement systems, we encourage you to move on to Chap. 2—Foundations.

1.8 Related Reading

One of the complementary readings about the foundations of measurement is Fenton and Bieman's *Software Metrics* [FB14]. This is a classical position in the area of software metrics. It's been around since 1990s and is perceived as providing the foundations of software metrics. It provides great examples and theories for measuring in general.

Another important reading is Abran's *Software Metrology and Software Metrics* [Abr10]. This is the newest position in the discipline of software engineering. It provides a very good foundation in metrology and provides some examples of modern software measures. However, the major focus in the book is on the COSMIC FP measure.

We also recommend reading *Competitive Engineering* by Gilb [Gil05], which provides a wider context for the use of software measures, in particular how to operationalize goals into measures.

If you are interested in more details in the ISO/IEC 15939 standard, we propose reading McGarry et al.'s *Practical software measurement* [McG02]. This is a very good book for practitioners who want to apply the ISO/IEC 15939 standard. The book provides a solid description of the standard which describes the measurement process, but does not add the newer standards like ISO/IEC 25000 describing measures nor discusses metrology. It is also almost 10 years old.

Another classical reading is Ebert and Dumke's *Software Measurement* [ED07]. This book is a classical position which provides solid foundations on measurement theory and estimation. It is a good starting point, which we explore more in detail with a focus on internal quality metrics (e.g. software complexity) and modern process metrics (e.g. speed of continuous integration, software development velocity) as well as product delivery metrics (e.g. release readiness indicators).

Ebert et al.'s *Best practices in software measurement* [EDBS05] presents a number of best practices of measurement. It complements our book with more details on standardization in software measurement.

Finally, readers interested in cost estimation can continue with Trendowicz's, *Software cost estimation* [Tre13] and Trendowicz and Jeffery's *Software Project Effort Estimation* [TJ14]. These books present an in-depth application of one type of measurement for estimating the project size—CoBRA and provide very solid foundations for estimations, including the foundations for statistical methods for estimations.

References

[Abr10] Alain Abran. *Software Metrics and Software Metrology*. John Wiley & Sons, 2010.

[Alb79] Allan J Albrecht. Measuring application development productivity. In *Proc. of the Joint SHARE/GUIDE/IBM Application Development Symposium*, pages 83–92, 1979.

[ASH+14] Vard Antinyan, Miroslaw Staron, Jörgen Hansson, Wilhelm Meding, Per Osterström, and Anders Henriksson. Monitoring evolution of code complexity and magnitude of changes. *Acta Cybernetica*, 21(3):367–382, 2014.

[ASM+14] Vard Antinyan, Miroslaw Staron, Wilhelm Meding, Per Österström, Erik Wikstrom, Johan Wranker, Anders Henriksson, and Jörgen Hansson. Identifying risky areas of software code in agile/lean software development: An industrial experience report. In *Software Maintenance, Reengineering and Reverse Engineering (CSMR-WCRE), 2014 Software Evolution Week-IEEE Conference on*, pages 154–163. IEEE, 2014.

[B+81] Barry W Boehm et al. *Software engineering economics*, volume 197. Prentice-hall Englewood Cliffs (NJ), 1981.

[Boe84] Barry W Boehm. Software engineering economics. *IEEE transactions on Software Engineering*, (1):4–21, 1984.

[Bos16] Jan Bosch. Speed, data, and ecosystems: The future of software engineering. *IEEE Software*, 33(1):82–88, 2016.

[CK94] Shyam R Chidamber and Chris F Kemerer. A metrics suite for object oriented design. *Software Engineering, IEEE Transactions on*, 20(6):476–493, 1994.

[Col01] James Charles Collins. *Good to great: Why some companies make the leap... and others don't*. Random House, 2001.

[ED07] Christof Ebert and Reiner Dumke. *Software Measurement: Establish-Extract-Evaluate-Execute*. Springer Science & Business Media, 2007.

[EDBS05] Christof Ebert, Reiner Dumke, Manfred Bundschuh, and Andreas Schmietendorf. *Best Practices in Software Measurement: How to use metrics to improve project and process performance*. Springer Science & Business Media, 2005.

[FB14] Norman Fenton and James Bieman. *Software metrics: A rigorous and practical approach*. CRC Press, 2014.

[Fen96] Norman E Fenton. *Software metrics: A practical and rigorous approach*. International Thomson Pub., 1996.

[FSHL13] Robert Feldt, Miroslaw Staron, Erika Hult, and Thomas Liljegren. Supporting software decision meetings: Heatmaps for visualising test and code measurements. In *Software Engineering and Advanced Applications (SEAA), 2013 39th EUROMICRO Conference on*, pages 62–69. IEEE, 2013.

[Gil05] Tom Gilb. *Competitive engineering: A handbook for systems engineering, requirements engineering, and software engineering using Planguage*. Butterworth-Heinemann, 2005.

[Har94] Mikel J Harry. *The vision of six sigma: Tools and methods for breakthrough*. Sigma Pub. Co., 1994.

[kim] *Blue ocean strategy: How to create uncontested market space and make the competition irrelevant*.

[McA00] Donald R McAndrews. The Team Software ProcessSM (TSPSM): An Overview and Preliminary Results of Using Disciplined Practices. Technical report, CARNEGIE-MELLON UNIV PITTSBURGH PA SOFTWARE ENGINEERING INST, 2000.

[McG02] John McGarry. *Practical software measurement: Objective information for decision makers*. Addison-Wesley Professional, 2002.

[oWM93] International Bureau of Weights and Measures. *International vocabulary of basic and general terms in metrology*. International Organization for Standardization, Geneve, Switzerland, 2nd edition, 1993.

[RGMR16] Tammy L Rapp, Lucy L Gilson, John E Mathieu, and Thomas Ruddy. Leading empowered teams: An examination of the role of external team leaders and team coaches. *The Leadership Quarterly*, 27(1):109–123, 2016.

[RS05] Gunther Ruhe and Moshood Omolade Saliu. The art and science of software release planning. *IEEE software*, 22(6):47–53, 2005.

[SHF+13] Miroslaw Staron, Jorgen Hansson, Robert Feldt, Anders Henriksson, Wilhelm Meding, Sven Nilsson, and Christoffer Hoglund. Measuring and visualizing code stability–a case study at three companies. In *Software Measurement and the 2013 Eighth International Conference on Software Process and Product Measurement (IWSM-MENSURA), 2013 Joint Conference of the 23rd International Workshop on*, pages 191–200. IEEE, 2013.

[SM11] Miroslaw Staron and Wilhelm Meding. Factors determining long-term success of a measurement program: an industrial case study. *e-Informatica Software Engineering Journal*, pages 7–23, 2011.

[SM16] Miroslaw Staron and Wilhelm Meding. MeSRAM – A method for assessing robustness of measurement programs in large software development organizations and its industrial evaluation. *Journal of Systems and Software*, 113:76–100, 2016.

[SMH+14] Miroslaw Staron, Wilhelm Meding, Jörgen Hansson, Christoffer Höglund, Kent Niesel, and Vilhelm Bergmann. Dashboards for continuous monitoring of quality for software product under development. *System Qualities and Software Architecture (SQSA)*, 2014.

[SMN08] Miroslaw Staron, Wilhelm Meding, and Christer Nilsson. A framework for developing measurement systems and its industrial evaluation. *Information and Software Technology*, 51(4):721–737, 2008.

[SMP12] Miroslaw Staron, Wilhelm Meding, and Klas Palm. Release readiness indicator for mature agile and lean software development projects. In *Agile Processes in Software Engineering and Extreme Programming*, pages 93–107. Springer, 2012.

[SPA11] Anna Sandberg, Lars Pareto, and Thomas Arts. Agile collaborative research: Action principles for industry-academia collaboration. *Software, IEEE*, 28(4):74–83, 2011.

[Sta12] Miroslaw Staron.   Critical role of measures in decision processes: Managerial
        and technical measures in the context of large software development organizations.
        Information and Software Technology, 54(8):887–899, 2012.
[Tes14] Bjørnar Tessem. Individual empowerment of agile and non-agile software developers
        in small teams. *Information and software technology*, 56(8):873–889, 2014.
 [TJ14] Adam Trendowicz and Ross Jeffery. *Software project effort estimation: Foundations
        and best practice guidelines for success.* Springer, 2014.
[Gil76] Tom Gilb. Software metrics. *Studentlitteratur AB Sweden*, 1976.
[Tre13] Adam Trendowicz. *Software Cost Estimation, Benchmarking, and Risk Assessment:
        The Software Decision-Makers' Guide to Predictable Software Development.* Springer
        Science & Business Media, 2013.

Chapter 2
Fundamentals

Abstract Measurement as a process is nothing new, nor specific to software engineers. As humans, we are used to measuring from other engineering disciplines. However, in software engineering, the science behind measurement—metrology— is relatively little-known, which results in low quality of measurement programs. In this chapter we describe the essence of metrology as a science, and we introduce the concepts from the most relevant standards in the area of measurement in general, and in software engineering in particular. We also show how the scientific view on metrology complements the industrial view on the same aspects.

2.1 Introduction

The questions about theoretical foundations of measurement do not pop up as the first questions for industrial measurement program designers. Since it is so easy to measure things, why should we bother with the theories and standards? From our experience, these questions come when practitioners realize that something does not work in their measurement programs. The practitioners realize that measures and indicators are not "trusted," because the practitioners cannot show the validity of these measures and indicators. Their critical stakeholders, on the other hand, feel the need to question the measures and indicators, because they want to be sure that their decisions are based on solid measures and indicators. Solid, correct, and accurate measures are therefore the basis for successful measurement programs. Standards and theories, in turn, are the foundations of these solid, correct, and accurate measures.

In this chapter, we explain the theoretical foundations of measurement programs. We start by introducing metrology—the science and standards needed to communicate measures, indicators and measurement programs in organizations. In this chapter we describe, shortly, the basic concepts from metrology which are important for solid measurements. We base our description on the general standard in software metrology ([oWM93] VIM—Vocabulary in Metrology), and describe such concepts

© Springer International Publishing AG, part of Springer Nature 2018
M. Staron, W. Meding, *Software Development Measurement Programs*,
https://doi.org/10.1007/978-3-319-91836-5_2

as mappings from the empirical world to mathematical objects (quantification), measurement error, measurand and measurement reference etalons:

- Metrology—describing the concepts needed to understand the theory of measurement.
- Mapping of real-world objects to measures—describing the process of quantification of real-world entities to numerical objects.
- Estimators and predictors—describing the basic concepts of working with estimators such as scales, allowed operations and usage of numbers in the mathematical domain.

We can conceptually put the measurement standards in between the standards of product lifecycle and decision making standards, the placement which we show in Fig. 2.1. The figure shows examples of the lifecycle standards and the maturity/process improvement standards. In practice, there is a whole plethora of standards, provided by both ISO/IEC and IEEE, but also by a number of countries, such as the United Stated Department of Defense standards.

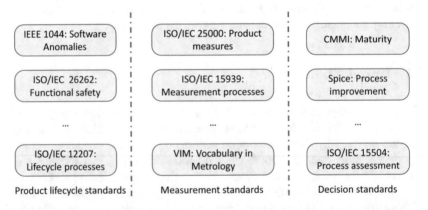

Fig. 2.1 Measurement standards are placed between the product lifecycle standards and decision support standards

In our model, we place the standards between the product lifecycle standards, such as ISO/IEC 12207 [Int08], and the decision support standards like CMMI [CMM02], because the measurement standards require solid definitions of work products, processes and products. They define the maturity of processes in modern companies. The measurement standards also have dependencies between each other. For example, the ISO/IEC 15939 standard defines such important concepts as the indicators and base/derived measures, which are used in the definitions of measures of ISO/IEC 25000 (Fig. 2.2).

The ISO/IEC 25000 series of standards define the concepts important for quality measurement, and they reuse the definitions provided by ISO/IEC 15939 for such

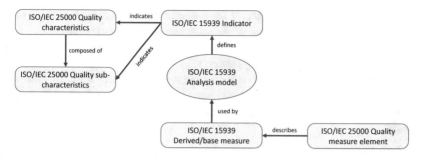

Fig. 2.2 Example dependencies between ISO/IEC 25000 standards and ISO/IEC 15939 standards

concepts as indicators and base measures, whereas the ISO/IEC 15939 uses the format for quality measure elements to describe its measures.

We can now continue, by briefly introducing the major standards applicable to software measurement. We give a short presentation of two standards—product measurement (ISO/IEC 25000 series, with focus on ISO/IEC 25023), and measurement process (ISO/IEC 15939). The concepts presented in these two standards allow us to cover the vocabulary needed for practitioners when establishing the measurement programs—e.g. base measure, derived measure, and indicator as defined in ISO/IEC 15939.

However, we need to start with the fundamental standard used in almost all engineering fields—Vocabulary in Metrology (VIM) [oWM93].

2.2 Software Metrology and the VIM Standard

Metrology is the science of measurement. It sets the grounds for quantifying physical phenomena into numbers. It is a set of rules, guidelines and principles behind the processes of how to transform a property of an entity from the real, empirical world to a number—the process commonly known as measurement. However, assigning a number to a variable, which represents the numerical model of the measured entity, is only the beginning. Metrology, as a science, provides us with the conceptual methods and tools for reasoning about such concepts as:

- measurand—a quantity intended to be measured or, as we sometimes call it, the measured property of the entity,
- measurement trueness—closeness of the agreement between the average of an infinite number of replicated measured quantity values and a reference quantity value; in other words—how close the measured value is to the observed property,
- uncertainty of measurement—parameter characterizing the dispersion of the quantity values being attributed to a measurand, based on the information used,

- measurement error—a deviation of the measured value from the real value of the measurand—a direct derivative of the uncertainty of measurement,
- measuring instrument—device used for making measurements, alone or in conjunction with supplementary device(s),
- measuring system—set of one or more measuring instruments and often other devices, including any reagent and supply, assembled and adapted to give measured quantity values within specified intervals for quantities of specified kinds.

When setting up a measurement program, we need to be able to unambiguously define, describe and document the measurand—it is important to be very precise about what it is that we actually measure. Now, this looks simple in theory, but it is not as simple in practice, which we can illustrate on the example of the LOC measure shortly.

Defining the measurand needs to be complemented with the definition of the measurement procedure, also known as the measurement method. The measurement method provides the precise description of how to take the real-world phenomena and quantify it—e.g. by counting occurrences of specific patterns. The definition of the measurement method requires us to define the so-called measurement method model, which describes the next important concept—measurement trueness. The measurement trueness defines how well our measurement method quantifies the measurand, and is therefore related to the uncertainty of the measurement, or its direct derivative—the measurement error.

This basic vocabulary provides the measurement designers a precise, common language to define, use and deploy measurement programs. We cannot stress enough how important it is to have the right vocabulary, as without this vocabulary all roles in the measurement program will not be able to communicate. For example, the line managers use the term KPI (Key Performance Indicator) whereas the designers can name the same concept as just an indicator.

Since the metrology and the VIM standard are rather large, we choose only the most important parts of them. In particular, we use the concept of mapping of measurand to a number, which is the core of any measurement process. This process can be considered fundamental, because if it is done incorrectly (e.g. measurements have too large uncertainty), then the practical value of the collected measures is low. This in turn leads to low trust in the measures and the entire measurement program.

2.2.1 Lines of Code Measure: Defined from the Perspective of the VIM Vocabulary

The lines-of-code measure is usually calculated using automated software tools, which provide deterministic results. The measure has been used in practice since the 1950s and there is a substantial body of research on it, [Boe99]. It is also used as an input variable to many prediction models—e.g. the Constructive Cost Model (COCOMO) and its newer versions [BCH+95].

LOC measure is often also called SLOC (Source Lines of Code) as an acronym and has multiple variations, for example:

1. Physical (Source) Lines of Code—measure of all lines, including comments, but excluding blanks,
2. Effective Lines of Code—measure of all lines, excluding: comments, blanks, standalone braces, parentheses, and
3. Logical Lines of Code—measure of those lines which form code statements.

The variations of the measure are used for specific purposes and can be regarded as measures of the same entity, but with different measurement methods according to the definitions included in ISO/IEC 15939 [OC07]. We can also observe that these measures are susceptible to systematic errors in different ways. For example, the number of physical lines of code includes comments which do not add to the complexity of the algorithm, but may impact the effort needed to develop the program; the logical lines of code are, naturally, not sensitive to the same type of error (i.e. comments). Figure 2.3 illustrates the difference between physical LOC and logical LOC.

Fig. 2.3 Example program illustrating the difference between the physical LOC (all lines) and the Logical LOC (the lines with numbers)

```
/* Hello World program */

#include<stdio.h> (1)
#include<stdio.h> (2)

main() (3)
{ (4)
    /* multi-line
        comment
    */

    int x = 0; (5)
    printf("Hello World1"); (6)

    printf("Hello World2"); // comment
                                (7)
    printf("Hello (8)
            World3"); (9)

    // single-line comment
} (10)
```

Therefore, we can use the ISO/IEC 25021 (Quality Measure Elements) format to describe the measure of LOC, which we do in Table 2.1.

The format of the definition of a QME from the standard provides a concise way of documenting a measure. However, it does not provide all important details, such as the measurement method or the measurement procedure for collecting the data. These procedures need to be documented using formats available in ISO/IEC 15939.

Table 2.1 Definition of the LOC measure using the format of QME from ISO/IEC 25021

QME	Description
QME category	Data size
QME name	Lines of code
QME ID	LLOC
Detail	Lines of code measures the number of non-empty lines of code (non-empty means that the line contains at least one non-whitespace character)
Input	Source code module
Documentation	LLOC defines the size of the program in terms of executable instructions and comments
Measurement scale	Ratio
Measurement focus	Internal

Although useful, these formats require us to provide information about the whole metrological chain from the base measure to the indicator, linked to the measurable concept. This linking is important, but sometimes clutters the definition of measures. Therefore, let us use that format and illustrate the differences between these two ISO/IEC standards in that way. We define LOC according to the format prescribed in ISO/IEC 15939 in Table 2.2.

Table 2.2 Definition of the LOC measure using the format of measurement construct of ISO/IEC 15939

QME	Description
Information need	Estimate the size of a software product
Measurable concept	Size
Relevant entities	Source code module
Attributes	Programming language statements
Base measures	LLOC
Measurement method	Count semicolons in the source code module
Type of measurement method	Objective
Type of scale	Ratio
Unit of measurement	Line
Derived measure	N/A
Measurement function	N/A
Indicator	Product size
Model	N/A
Decision criteria	If the product size is larger than 1 MLOC, it should be flagged that it is getting too large and should be split into a product line

When comparing these two definitions, we can see that the model used in ISO/IEC 15939 is more context-oriented. It provides links to the information needs and, what is important, to the decision criterion. The decision criterion provides the most important link to the organization, as it provides a direct reference to what should/could be done, based on the values of the newly defined measure.

2.3 Mapping of Real-World Objects to Measures

To start discussing the process of mapping of the measurand to a number, let us illustrate it on the example of the measure of logical LOC. This simple measure of size is a very nice example as it is as tangible as any quantity in software engineering can be—even though we cannot physically touch lines of code, we can see them on a computer screen and we can have an intuition of how many are too many. Figure 2.4 presents the transformation.

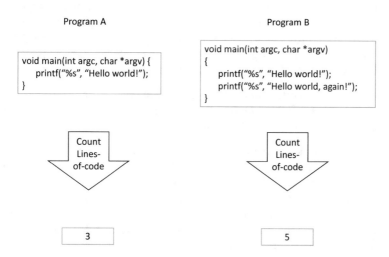

Fig. 2.4 Quantifying size of two programs with the help of LOC measure

In this transformation, the "magic" takes place in the arrows. The arrows are:

- Mappings—in mathematical terms, which means that they are specific kinds of injective functions, and
- Measurement methods—in metrological terms, which means that they quantify a property of an entity.

In contemporary measurement programs, the measurement methods and mappings are realized by measurement instruments—programs dedicated to measuring properties of entities of specific kinds.

2.4   The Concept of Measurement Error

With the introduction of the measurement information model in the international ISO/IEC 15939 standard for measurement processes, the discipline of software engineering evolved from discussing metrics in general to categorizing them into three categories—base measures, derived measures and indicators. Base measures are fundamental for constructing derived measures and indicators. The base measures are also the types of measures which are collected directly and are a result of a measurement method. In many cases, this measurement method is an automated algorithm (e.g. a script) which we can refer to as the *measurement instrument* which quantifies an attribute of interest into a number.

Since in software engineering we do not have reference measurement etalons, as we do in other disciplines (e.g. kilogram or meter for physics), we often rely on arbitrary definitions of the base quantities. One of such quantities is the size of programs measured as the number of lines of code. Even though the number of lines of code of a given program is a deterministic, fully quantifiable number, the result of applying different measurement instruments to obtain the number might differ. The difference can be caused by a number of factors, such as:

- difference in implementation of the same measurement method,
- difference in the definition/design of the measurement method, or
- faults in the measurement instruments.

Since we do not know the true value without the measurement procedure, we need to find what the accuracy (certainty) of the measured value is. When using measurement instruments, it is often not possible to explore the measurement methods in detail by analyzing the implementation of the measurement method (in practice the measurement instruments are provided as compiled code), which means that the measurement engineer needs to either accept the fact that the uncertainty is unknown or estimate the uncertainty.

Measurement error is defined in measurement theory as *the deviation between the real value of the measurand and the value obtained from the measurement process*. It is derived from the concept of *measurement uncertainty*, which is the dispersion of the values attributed to the measurand. The main definition is provided in ISO/IEC 17045 (General requirements for the competence of testing and calibration laboratories, [oWM05]) and later on used in software engineering in the ISO/IEC 25000 series of standards [ISO16a].

The measured quantity can be referred to as the *estimator*, as the true value of the measurand always remains unknown because of the finite accuracy of the measurement instruments. In general, the estimators (X) combine both the expected value of the measurement (M) plus the error (E)—see formula 2.1.

$$\hat{X} = \hat{M} + \hat{E} \tag{2.1}$$

The measurement error is a combination of two types of errors—the systematic error (S) and the random error (R)—formula 2.2.

$$\hat{E} = \hat{S} + \hat{R} \tag{2.2}$$

The systematic error is usually caused by the miscalibration of the measurement instruments and is the same for all measurements taken by the instrument. The mean of the systematic error is expected to be non-zero, and causes skewness of the measurement results. In order to minimize the systematic errors, the measurement instruments are calibrated—adjusted to show the correct results when measuring entities of known properties.

The random error, on the other hand, is different for each measurement taken. The mean value of the random measurement error is expected to be zero, and it causes the distribution of the measurement results to be wider.

In general, it seems easy to distinguish between these two types of errors, but in practice it might be very difficult.

2.4.1 Impact of Measurement Error on Predictions: Standard Error of the Estimate

Software measures are usually used within various models designed for monitoring and forecasting [Sta12, RSB+13]. When using these measures within prediction models, the other major source of errors come from estimation error. Every estimation method involves an estimation error, which comes from the simple fact that the real quantity generally differs from its estimated quantity.

Taking an example of simple prediction model with single predictor (x) and predicted variable (y) that have a linear relationship between them ($y \sim m * x$, where m = 2), two scenarios of prediction model can be shown as in Fig. 2.5.

As evident from Fig. 2.5, the prediction model A seems more accurate than prediction model B, or in other terms the estimation error is expected to be lower for model A compared to model B.

The standard error of the estimate (or SEE) is the measure of accuracy of predictions. For estimations, using linear regression minimizes the sum of squared deviations of prediction (also referred to as Sum of Squared Errors, or SSE). Thus the standard error of estimate for method of least squares (linear or non-linear models) is equal to SSE, which can be calculated as:

$$\sigma_{est} = \sqrt{\frac{\Sigma(Y_a - Y_p)^2}{N}}. \tag{2.3}$$

Where σ_{est} is the standard error of estimate, Y_a is the actual value, Y_p is the predicted value, and N is the number of observations.

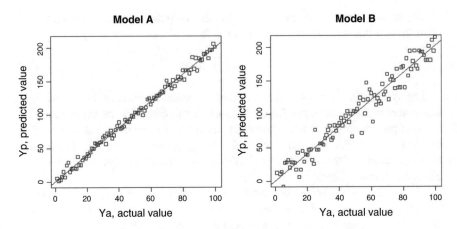

Fig. 2.5 Regression models with different accuracy of prediction

Knowing the measurement errors is an important part of establishing the correctness of the measurement program. We discuss the concepts of correctness in more detail in Chap. 4.

2.5 ISO 15939: Measurement Processes

We have a number of standards to help us with the right vocabulary and the right definitions. In Sect. 2.2, we outlined the most important concepts in metrology in general. Although these concepts are valid in software engineering, we should also note that there is a dedicated standard, derived from the VIM standard, defining the most relevant concepts. This complementary standard, ISO/IEC 15939 (Systems and software engineering—measurement processes), describes how a measurement process in a modern software engineering enterprise should look.

In order to do justice to the standard, we use the following definitions from ISO/IEC 15939:2007 throughout this book:

- Base measure—measure defined in terms of an attribute and the method for quantifying it. This definition is based on the definition of base quantity from the VIM standard.
- Derived measure—measure that is defined as a function of two or more values of base measures. This definition is based on the definition of derived quantity from the VIM standard.
- Indicator—measure that provides an estimate or evaluation of specified attributes derived from a model with respect to defined information needs.
- Decision criteria—thresholds, targets, or patterns used to determine the need for action or further investigation, or to describe the level of confidence in a given result.

- Information product—one or more indicators and their associated interpretations that address an information need.
- Measurement method—logical sequence or operations, described generically, used in quantifying an attribute with respect to a specified scale.
- Measurement function—algorithm or calculation performed to combine two or more base measures.
- Attribute—property or characteristics of an entity that can be distinguished quantitatively or qualitatively by human or automated means.
- Entity—object that is to be characterized by measuring its attributes.
- Measurement process—process for establishing, planning, performing and evaluating measurement within an overall project, enterprise or organizational measurement structure.
- Measurement instrument—a procedure to assign a value to a base measure.

The view on measures presented in ISO/IEC 15939 is consistent with that in other engineering disciplines; the standard states at many places that it is based on such standards as ISO/IEC 15288:2007 (Software and Systems engineering—Measurement Processes), ISO/IEC 14598-1:1999 (Information technology—Software product evaluation) [Int99], ISO/IEC 9126-x [OC01], ISO/IEC 25000 series of standards, or International vocabulary of basic and general terms in metrology (VIM) [oWM93]. Conceptually, the elements (different kinds of measures) which are used in the measurement process can be presented as in Fig. 2.6.

One of the key factors for every measurement system is that it has to satisfy an information need of a stakeholder, i.e. there needs to be a person/organization who/which is interested in the information that the measurement system provides. Typical stakeholders are project managers, organization managers, architects, product managers, the customer representatives [SMN08]. The indicator is intended to provide quantitative information along with interpretation, which implies the existence of an analysis model that eases the interpretation. The analysis model is a set of decision criteria used when assessing the value of an indicator, e.g. describing at which value of the indicator we set a red flag signaling problems in the measured object. The derived measures (based on the definition of the derived quantity) and base measures (based on the definition of the base quantity) are used to provide the information for calculating the value of the indicator.

2.5.1 Base Measures and Measurement Methods

To describe the model justly, let us follow it from the bottom up—starting from the measurement method and base measures. In Sect. 2.3, we introduced the concept of the mapping of a property of a phenomenon from the real-world domain to a number in the mathematical domain. This mapping is also present in the ISO/IEC 15939 standard—it's called measurement method. Its theoretical description from Sect. 2.3 can be realized, in practice, by an algorithm describing how to quantify the desired property. An example of such a manual mapping is shown in Fig. 2.7.

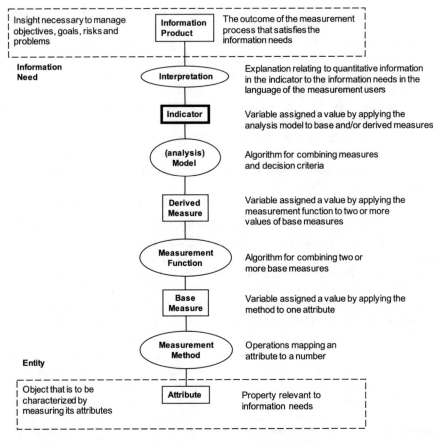

Fig. 2.6 Measurement system information model (from ISO/IEC 15939:2007)

A procedure to count the lines of code in the file:

Open the file and count all lines in the file

Fig. 2.7 An example of a manual measurement method for counting lines of code

This example is simple and it seems to be straightforward. However, it is also very ambiguous—we do not know how to handle lines that are wrapped in the editor, how to handle empty lines, lines with comments, etc. Therefore, this measurement procedure results in a base measure with high uncertainty—once we obtain the result we do not know which lines were included and which were not. We can say that we lack the metrological traceability for the measurement method here.

An improved measurement method is shown in Fig. 2.8, which shows how we can use an algorithm to describe the procedure more unambiguously.

In this example, we see that there is no uncertainty about whether to count the empty lines and comments. However, we could also pinpoint that this measurement

```
1.  Open the source code module with text editor

2.  Remove line wrapping

3.  Count the number of lines in the file,

       •   Include empty lines

       •   Include lines with comments

       •   Include the last line of the file with EOF

4.  Note down the result – it is the value of the LOC
    measure

5.  Close the source code module
```

Fig. 2.8 An example of an algorithm used as measurement method for counting lines of code

method is prone to random errors—simply because a person who does the counting can make mistakes. It is also impossible to use this procedure for large programs—imagine having to count the lines of code for the entire Linux kernel code (over ten million lines of code). Therefore, the most common measurement methods are programs or scripts. They are often referred to as *measuring instruments* or *measurement instruments*. An example of a script for counting lines of code is presented in Fig. 2.9; the code is written in Ruby.

```ruby
iLines = 0
File.open("source_code_module.cpp") do |sourceFile|
    sourceFile.each_line do |sourceLine|
            iLines = iLines + 1
    end
end
```

Fig. 2.9 An example of a Ruby script used as measurement method for counting lines of code

We can now see that using a script reduces the uncertainty of the result—the base measure.

In practice, we can see that the measurement instruments are linked closely to the definition of their corresponding base measure. This close relation is similar to the relation of measurement instruments of physical quantities—for example a ruler, shown in Fig. 2.10.

Fig. 2.10 Measurement instrument of length—a ruler; used under Creative Commons licence CC0 Public domain; author: pixabay.com

In Chap. 5 we dive a bit deeper into different kinds of measurement instruments, when we discuss tooling in measurement programs.

The result of using a measurement instrument is the base measure, which is an example of a base quantity specified in the VIM standard.

2.5.2 Derived Measures and Measurement Functions

Once we obtain our values of base measures, we can start using them in calculations. These calculations are known as measurement functions in ISO/IEC 15939. Measurement functions are formulas which combine base measures and result in a derived measure. An example of such a measurement function is the formula to define productivity—defined as a ratio of lines of code produced during this time to the effort (person-hours), as shown in Fig. 2.4.

$$\text{productivity} = \frac{LOC}{person - hours} \tag{2.4}$$

This simple formula is a standard way of calculating derived measures, and can, in theory, be used as input an infinite number of base measures. In practice, the formulas include up to ten base measures, as more base measures result in derived measures that are hard to interpret. In industrial practice, the measurement functions are often calculations embedded in scripts/code of measurement systems or spreadsheet files. The most common use of measurement functions is to provide basic descriptive statistics—means, medians and standard deviations.

2.5.3 Indicators and Analysis Model

From our experience, we could observe that derived measures are rarely in the focus of either the stakeholders or measurement designers. The measurement designers often focus on the measurement instruments and base measures, whereas the stakeholders focus on indicators and their information products.

The indicator is a measure with the associated decision criteria, which are provided by the analysis model. We can see the indicator as a number together with its interpretation. A metaphor used frequently as the interpretation is the traffic light metaphor, as shown in Fig. 2.11.

Fig. 2.11 Traffic light
metaphor; used under
Creative Commons licence
CC0 Public domain; author:
pixabay.com

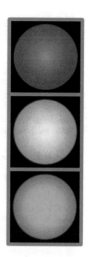

The most crucial element in the calculations of the indicator's value is the analysis model. The analysis model defines the rules of how we provide the interpretation; usually these rules are in a form or a table, as presented in Table 2.3.

Table 2.3 An example of an analysis model for productivity value

Value	Interpretation	Color
<20 LOC/week	In our organization, we expect all designers to develop at least 20 lines of code per week	Red
20–50 LOC/week	On average, we expect the designers to develop between 20 and 50 lines of code per week	Yellow
>50 LOC/week	Very good designers in our organization are able to develop at least 50 lines of code per week	Green

Although the example analysis model is a very simplified model, it shows the principle of how we map the values of the indicator to its interpretation. The example provides an important insight—the link between the organizational goals (how many lines are expected to be produced per week) and the interpretation.

2.5.4   Definition of Test Progress Using the ISO/IEC 15939 Measurement Information Model

We already defined the measure of LOC using the format for measurement constructs and we explained base measures, derived measures and indicators. Now, let us define the measure of test progress, using a graphical representation of the measurement information model of ISO/IEC 15939. We show the definition in Fig. 2.12.

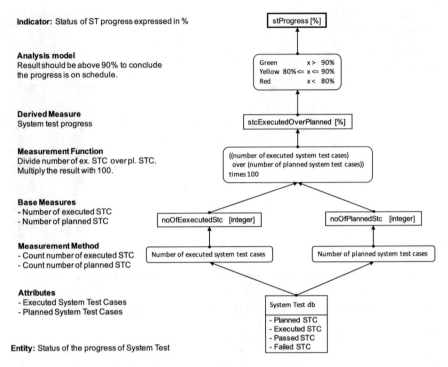

Indicator: Status of ST progress expressed in %

Analysis model
Result should be above 90% to conclude
the progress is on schedule.

Derived Measure
System test progress

Measurement Function
Divide number of ex. STC over pl. STC.
Multiply the result with 100.

Base Measures
- Number of executed STC
- Number of planned STC

Measurement Method
- Count number of executed STC
- Count number of planned STC

Attributes
- Executed System Test Cases
- Planned System Test Cases

Entity: Status of the progress of System Test

stProgress [%]

Green   x > 90%
Yellow 80% <= x <= 90%
Red   x < 80%

stcExecutedOverPlanned [%]

((number of executed system test cases)
   over (number of planned system test cases))
times 100

noOfEexecutedStc [integer]

noOfPlannedStc [integer]

Number of executed system test cases

Number of planned system test cases

System Test db

- Planned STC
- Executed STC
- Passed STC
- Failed STC

Fig. 2.12 Graphical definition of the test progress indicator

The focus of this definition is the information product, placed at the top. From our experience these information products can take many forms, but the best ones were information radiators, MS Windows Gadgets/MacOS X Widgets and dashboards.

We instantiate this definition in the example in Fig. 2.13.

As the figure shows, both the instance and the definition are structured in the same way. The structure, in turn, is based on the ISO/IEC 15939 measurement information model.

2.6   ISO 25000: SQuARE

The ISO/IEC 25000 series of standards is a family of standards, spanning from the area of requirements for quality, and quality models to quality measure elements. In the definition of LOC, we reused the table used to define the quality measure elements. In this book we use two parts of this family of standards—ISO/IEC 25012 about data quality in Chap. 3 and ISO/IEC 25023 about product performance measurement, in this chapter.

Fig. 2.13 An instance of the test progress indicator

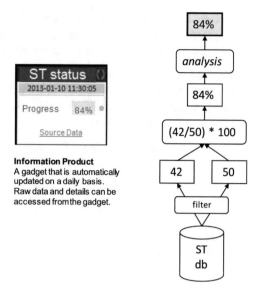

ISO/IEC 25023 [ISO16b] was approved in 2016. It defines the measures of product and system quality. The list is organized into categories (the definitions are quoted directly from the standard):

- Functional suitability—used to assess the degree to which a product or system provides functions that meet stated and implied needs, when used under specified conditions.
- Performance efficiency—used to assess the performance relative to the amount of resources used under stated conditions. Resources can include other software products, the software and hardware configuration of the system, and materials (e.g. print paper, storage media).
- Compatibility—used to assess the degree to which a product, system or component can exchange information with other products, systems or components, and/or perform its required functions, while sharing the same hardware or software environment.
- Usability—used to assess the degree to which a product or system can be used by specified users to achieve specified goals with effectiveness, efficiency and satisfaction in a specified context of use.
- Reliability—used to assess the degree to which a system, product or component performs specified functions under specified conditions for a specified period of time.
- Security—used to assess the degree to which a product or system protects information and data so that persons or other products or systems have the degree of data access appropriate to their types and levels of authorisation.
- Maintainability—used to assess the degree of effectiveness and efficiency with which a product or system can be modified by the intended maintainers.

- Portability—used to assess the degree of effectiveness and efficiency with which a system, product or component can be transferred from one hardware, software or other operational or usage environment to another.

Each of the categories have a number of sub-categories and each sub-category has a number of measures defined. Let us review a list of measures defined for one of the sub-categories of reliability—maturity measures (once again definitions of measures follow the standard):

- Fault correction—addressing the question of *what proportion of detected reliability-related faults has been corrected*, defined as the ratio

$$X = \frac{\text{Number of reliability-related faults corrected in design/coding/testing phase}}{\text{Number of reliability-related faults detected in design/coding/testing phase}}.$$

- Mean Time Between Failures (MTBF)—addressing the question of *how long the MTBF is during the system/software operation*, defined as the ratio

$$X = \frac{\text{Operation time}}{\text{Number of system/software failures actually occurred}}.$$

- Failure rate—addressing the question of *how many failures were detected during a defined period*, defined as the ratio

$$X = \frac{\text{Number of failures detected during observation time}}{\text{Duration of observation}}.$$

- Test coverage—addressing the question of *what percent of the system or software capabilities, operational scenarios or functions, covered by their associated test suites are actually performed*, defined as the ratio

$$X = \frac{A}{\text{Number of system or software capabilities, operational scenarios or functions}},$$

where A is defined as the number of system or software capabilities, operational scenarios or functions covered by their associated test suites are actually performed.

The examples of the measures, defined for maturity, show that the definitions of the measures delineate the boundaries of the measurement procedure. These boundaries are not as precise as the definition of quality measure elements presented before. Nevertheless, these measures provide guidance on how to define specific characteristics and how to operationalize them (to some extent). As the standard is targeted to all domains (automotive, telecom, web, healthcare, etc.), it cannot provide more specific ways of defining the measures.

2.7 Other Standards

Naturally, we can find measures in almost every standard, as the discipline of measurement is fundamental to engineering. However, the following standards are the most relevant ones, which any measurement designer should understand. These standards can be used as defining either measurands and the measurable concepts, or they can use the measures to make decisions.

- ISO 9126—Framework for quality measures: this standard provides a very good introduction to the concepts of measuring quality. As a predecessor of the ISO/IEC 25000 series of standards, it has been replaced by it. However, the principles still remain and these principles are very useful to understand when beginning with quality measurement.
- ISO/IEC 15504—Information technology—Process assessment: this standard provides the basics for the assessment of processes, where we can find examples of how to quantify processes by counting activities, work products and roles.
- ISO 9000:2008—Quality management systems: this standard describes how to create a quality management system covering product quality.
- ISO 9001:2008—Quality management systems—Requirements
- ISO/IEC 24744—Software Engineering—Meta-model for Development Methodologies
- ISO 12207—Systems and software engineering—Software life cycle processes
- ISO 14888—Information Technology, Product evaluation—Security
- IEEE 1061-1998—Software Quality metrics methodology

We recommend measurement designers to look closely for measurable concepts in their applicable standards, and keep a catalogue of these measurable concepts. Over time, the measurement designers should complement these measurable concepts with the base and derived measures; maybe even with indicators, if possible.

2.8 Scientific Work Provides Closure to the Standards

Metrology, as a science about measurement, defines the most important concepts and terms needed for an effective use of measures in scientific and industrial applications. However, these standards are a few years old and the discipline of software engineering moves forward. Therefore, in this section, let us explore the work in the area of metrology which is not yet standardized, but shapes the field of measurement in software engineering.

2.8.1 Types and Properties of Measures

Briand and Morasca [BMB96a] provided one of the influential theoretical foundations of measurement in software engineering. Based on the previous works of Weuyker [Wey88], they defined a set of types of measures in software engineering. Their types are:

- Length—property describing the size of the measured entity in unidimensional space, or when we are interested in only one dimension.
- Size—intuitive property describing the size of the measured entity or system (as originally defined by Briand and Morasca).
- Complexity—defined as an intrinsic property of the object, not a perceived complexity that shows how difficult the system's interaction with other systems is.
- Cohesion—defined as tightness, i.e. how well-grouped entities relate to one another.

These four types of measures provide the basis for categorization of all measures in software engineering. Deciding upon the type of the measure is necessary to properly construct the measure, its scale and admissible transformations. This typing determines what kinds of properties we should build into the definition of the measure.

For each of these types, Briand and Morasca have defined a number of properties that each measure of this type needs to have. We can generalize these properties to the following ones:

- Null-value—the value of the measure for the empty entity should be zero.
- Nonnegativity—the value of the measure should never be less than zero.
- Additivity—the sum of the value of the measure after adding two entities should be the same or more than the sum of the value of the measure for each entity.
- Nonincreasing monotonicity of connected entities—adding connections between entities does not increase the value of the measure.
- Nondecreasing monotonicity of nonconnected entities—adding connections between entities does not decrease the value of the measure.
- Disjoint entities—the value of the measure for two disjoint entities is equal to the maximum of the value of the measures for these two entities.
- Symmetry—the value of the measure does not depend on the convention used to represent the entity.
- Monotonicity—the value of the measure is the same or greater than the value of the measures for two disjoint sub-entities of the entity.
- Normalization—the value of the measure belongs to a specific interval.
- Cohesive modules—The cohesion of a module obtained by putting together two unrelated modules is not greater than the maximum cohesion of the two original modules.

Although these properties seem to be straightforward, many of the well-known measures do not have these properties. Let us take the instance of formula for

defect density, which is defined according to Formula 2.5, where *defects* denotes
the number of defects and *LOC* denotes number of lines of code.

$$dd = \frac{defects}{LOC} \tag{2.5}$$

The defect density measure is a derived measure and does not fulfill the basic
property of null-value—i.e. that the value of the measure for an empty system should
be zero. The value of the defect density measure is undefined for the system which
has 0 LOC.

We can see that from test progress measure defined in this chapter does not fulfill
this property either.

The solution to this problem is to define the measure using a conditional
statement as presented in Formula 2.6.

$$dd = \begin{cases} 0 & \text{if } LOC = 0 \\ \frac{defects}{LOC} & \text{if } LOC > 0 \end{cases} \tag{2.6}$$

Based on our previous description of the measures from ISO/IEC 25023, we
could quickly see that these definitions suffer from the same problem. This shows
that the scientific body of knowledge, and the standardization practices still need
each other to provide a holistic toolbox for measurement designers.

Table 2.4 provides an overview of which properties are required for each type of
measure, according to Briand and Morasca [BMB96a].

Table 2.4 Properties of different types of measures

Property	Size	Length	Complexity	Cohesion
Null-value	x	x	x	x
Nonnegativity	x	x	x	x
Additivity	x			x
Nonincreasing monotonicity		x		
Nondecreasing monotonicity		x		
Disjoint entities		x	x	
Symmetry			x	
Monotonicity			x	x
Normalization				x
Cohesive modules				x

From our experience, we recommend spending ample time defining the measures
together with their type and proving that the properties of the measures fulfill the
requirements of their type. This "proof" can be both formal and informal, and
it should guide the designer of the new measures away from the most common
mistakes—for example, the mistake of defining a measure that does not fulfill the
property of null-value.

2.9   Measurement Systems

Delivering measures and measurement information across organizations can be done in multiple ways. The concepts of information radiators [RS05], metric tools [FP98], business intelligence [SMH$^+$14] and visual analytics [TC06] were coined for this purpose, and each concept describes a specific kind of a measurement system.

In this book, we use the concept of *measurement system* extensively. Even though the term is defined informally in literature, the international standard ISO/IEC 15939:2007 (Systems and Software Engineering: Measurement process) introduces the concept of measurement systems. It comprises the measuring systems (e.g. instruments for data collection and visualization), the infrastructure where these operate, the knowledge bases on the use of measures and the stakeholders involved in the measurement process.

2.9.1   Architecture of a Measurement System

A simplistic measurement system can be built based on MS Excel and its scripting language VBA (Visual Basic for Applications) as presented in Fig. 2.14. The main worksheet of the MS Excel file (the grayed page at the top of the figure) contains indicators (green cells on the grayed page) as defined by the stakeholders, while the other worksheets contain values of measures. The indicators worksheet has the associated base and derived measures in other worksheets of the MS Excel file. These measures and indicators are calculated using VBA scripts (VBA for calculating measures and indicators), and VBA scripts are used for accessing the raw data from other measurement systems.

The figure contains a set of components with specialized roles. The *VBA for accessing and storing the information* is responsible for getting the data from the source systems or raw data files (i.e. files with the data exported from the source system during low load time period). This component is also responsible for exporting the calculations to the information products and exporting the measurement system to the web server once all calculations and information quality checks have been run. The *VBA for calculating measures and indicators* is responsible for the calculations of measures and indicators. Examples of the measures and indicators are:

- Number of defects reported per week, which is collected from a defect database by executing scripts that export the defect database to a raw data file which can be accessed by the measurement system. Details of the exact definition of the measure can be found in [SM09],
- Release readiness prediction, which is an indicator combining measures of the number of defect reports open and number of tests to execute, and a function of test progress. More details on the definition can be found in [SMP12],

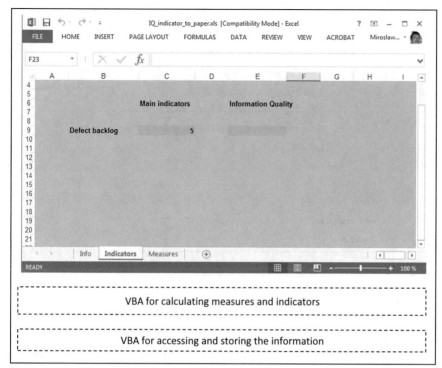

Fig. 2.14 Example of a measurement system

- Product downtime in field, which is a measure collected from the product log files reported by the customers at regular intervals; it combines the measures of time in use and downtime of a product and aggregates that per product line. More details about the definition can be found in [SM11], and
- Code stability, which is a derived measure collected from source code repositories and combines the measures of the number of code churns and their size per time unit. Details about the definition of the measure can be found in [SMH$^+$13, SHF$^+$13].

An example VBA code for the calculations is presented in Fig. 2.15. The code is executed after the VBA for importing the data stores the data in the worksheet "strProjectName."

The code is representative of the code used for calculations and, as shown, it is not very complex.

We can also encounter more complex measurement systems, but for the sake of argument, this simplistic example will be enough.

```
1      Public Function measureNumberOfRequirements(strProjectName As String) As Integer

2          Set oProj = Worksheets(strProjectName)

3          For Each SelectedProj In RQDB.Projects

4              If Not oProj Is Nothing Then

5                  For Each rqType In oProj.ReqTypes

6                      If (rqType.ReqPrefix = "FR") Then

7                          Set reqs = oProj.GetRequirements(rqType.ReqPrefix, 2)

8                      End If

9                  Next

10             End If

11         Next

12         measureNumberOfRequirements = reqs.Count

13     End Function
```

Fig. 2.15 Example of a VBA code for calculating measures

2.10 Summary

When designing measurement programs for software development companies, it is important to base them on solid theoretical grounds. Having the solid fundament makes the measurement program robust to problems with well-formedness of the program.

In this chapter, we presented the theoretical foundations of measurement programs. We presented the basics of metrology, the nature of measurement errors and the properties of different types of measures. These foundations allow us to define the measures in the right way, i.e. making sure that our measures are theoretically sound.

However, we also need to understand whether a measure is right for its purpose, i.e. appropriate for the context in which it is to be used. Therefore, we introduced the main standards in the area of measurement. We continue with appropriateness in Chap. 3, where we discuss the context of the measurement—measurement programs.

2.11 Further Reading

Abran [Abr10], in his book, describes metrology in more detail and explains its concepts in the context of function point measurement. This reading is recommended for advanced readers who want to explore the science of measurement more thoroughly.

Measurement error is discussed in more detail in our previous work [SDR17], where we examine how to calibrate measurement instruments to decrease the uncertainty of the resulting measures. By calibrating the measurement instruments on programs with a known LOC, we can decrease the measurement error by ca. 20%.

The basic concepts of measurement theory for software engineering have been redefined by Briand et al. [BEEM96]—for example the concepts of relational systems, mappings and scales. Similarly to the definition of relational systems one can define properties of software measures, which are a foundation for defining a general measurement instrument model. Such properties are defined by Briand et al. [BMB96b] based on the general properties of measures defined by Weyuker [Wey88], Zuse [Zus98] and Tian and Zelkowitz [TZ92]. Although the property-based definition of measures addresses the problem of correct definition of software metrics, it does not address the issues of uncertainty of the measurement process in practice (i.e. the instantiation of the mapping between the empirical world and the relational systems).

References

[Abr10] Alain Abran. *Software metrics and software metrology*. John Wiley & Sons, 2010.

[BCH+95] Barry Boehm, Bradford Clark, Ellis Horowitz, Chris Westland, Ray Madachy, and Richard Selby. Cost models for future software life cycle processes: Cocomo 2.0. *Annals of software engineering*, 1(1):57–94, 1995.

[BEEM96] Lionel Briand, Khaled El Emam, and Sandro Morasca. On the application of measurement theory in software engineering. *Empirical Software Engineering*, 1(1):61–88, 1996.

[BMB96a] L.C. Briand, S. Morasca, and V.R. Basili. Property-based Software Engineering Measurement. *IEEE Transactions on Software Engineering*, 22(1):68–86, 1996.

[BMB96b] Lionel C Briand, Sandro Morasca, and Victor R Basili. Property-based software engineering measurement. *Software Engineering, IEEE Transactions on*, 22(1):68–86, 1996.

[Boe99] Barry Boehm. Managing software productivity and reuse. *Computer*, 32(9):111–113, 1999.

[CMM02] CMMI Product Team. Capability Maturity Model Integration (CMMI), Version 1.1– Continuous Representation. 2002.

[FP98] Norman E Fenton and Shari Lawrence Pfleeger. *Software metrics: A rigorous and practical approach*. PWS Publishing Co., 1998.

[Int99] International Standards Organization. ISO/IEC 14598:1999–2001. *Information Technology-Software Product Evaluation – Parts 1, 6*, 1999.

[Int08] International Standardization Organization/International Electrotechnical Commission and others. ISO/IEC 12207: 2008, systems and software engineering–Software life cycle processes. *Geneva, Switzerland: ISO/IEC*, 2008.

[ISO16a] ISO/IEC. ISO/IEC 25000 - Systems and software engineering - Systems and software Quality Requirements and Evaluation (SQuaRE). Technical report, 2016.

[ISO16b] ISO/IEC. ISO/IEC 25023 - Systems and software engineering - Systems and software Quality Requirements and Evaluation (SQuaRE) - Measurement of system and software product quality. Technical report, 2016.

[OC01] International Standard Organization and International Electrotechnical Commission. ISO/IEC 9126, Software engineering, Product quality Part: 1 Quality model. Technical report, International Standard Organization/International Electrotechnical Commission, 2001.

[OC07] International Standard Organization and International Electrotechnical Commission. Software and systems engineering, software measurement process. Technical report, ISO/IEC, 2007.

[oWM93] International Bureau of Weights and Measures. *International vocabulary of basic and general terms in metrology*. International Organization for Standardization, Geneva, Switzerland, 2nd edition, 1993.

[oWM05] International Bureau of Weights and Measures. *General requirements for the competence of testing and calibration laboratories*. International Organization for Standardization, Geneva, Switzerland, 1st edition, 2005.

[RS05] Hugh Robinson and Helen Sharp. Organisational culture and XP: three case studies. 2005.

[RSB+13] Rakesh Rana, Miroslaw Staron, Claire Berger, Jorgen Hansson, Martin Nilsson, and Fredrik Torner. Evaluating long-term predictive power of standard reliability growth models on automotive systems. In *Software Reliability Engineering (ISSRE), 2013 IEEE 24th International Symposium on*, pages 228–237. IEEE, 2013.

[SDR17] Miroslaw Staron, Darko Durisic, and Rakesh Rana. Improving measurement certainty by using calibration to find systematic measurement error – a case of lines-of-code measure. In *Software Engineering: Challenges and Solutions*, pages 119–132. Springer, 2017.

[SHF+13] Miroslaw Staron, Jorgen Hansson, Robert Feldt, Anders Henriksson, Wilhelm Meding, Sven Nilsson, and Christoffer Hoglund. Measuring and visualizing code stability – A case study at three companies. In *Software Measurement and the 2013 Eighth International Conference on Software Process and Product Measurement (IWSM-MENSURA), 2013 Joint Conference of the 23rd International Workshop on*, pages 191–200. IEEE, 2013.

[SM09] Miroslaw Staron and Wilhelm Meding. Using models to develop measurement systems: A method and its industrial use. 5891:212–226, 2009.

[SM11] Miroslaw Staron and Wilhelm Meding. Factors determining long-term success of a measurement program: An industrial case study. *e-Informatica Software Engineering Journal*, pages 7–23, 2011.

[SMH+13] Miroslaw Staron, Wilhelm Meding, Jörgen Hansson, Christoffer Höglund, Kent Niesel, and Vilhelm Bergmann. Dashboards for continuous monitoring of quality for software product under development. *System Qualities and Software Architecture (SQSA)*, 2013.

[SMH+14] Miroslaw Staron, Wilhelm Meding, Jörgen Hansson, Christoffer Höglund, Kent Niesel, and Vilhelm Bergmann. Dashboards for continuous monitoring of quality for software product under development. *System Qualities and Software Architecture (SQSA)*, 2014.

[SMN08] Miroslaw Staron, Wilhelm Meding, and Christer Nilsson. A framework for developing measurement systems and its industrial evaluation. *Information and Software Technology*, 51(4):721–737, 2008.

[SMP12] Miroslaw Staron, Wilhelm Meding, and Klas Palm. Release readiness indicator for mature agile and lean software development projects. In *Agile Processes in Software Engineering and Extreme Programming*, pages 93–107. Springer, 2012.

[Sta12] Miroslaw Staron. Critical role of measures in decision processes: Managerial and technical measures in the context of large software development organizations. *Information and Software Technology*, 54(8):887–899, 2012.

[TC06] James J Thomas and Kristin A Cook. A visual analytics agenda. *Computer Graphics and Applications, IEEE*, 26(1):10–13, 2006.

[TZ92] Jianhui Tian and Marvin V Zelkowitz. A formal program complexity model and its application. *Journal of Systems and Software*, 17(3):253–266, 1992.

[Wey88] Elaine J. Weyuker. Evaluating software complexity measures. *Software Engineering, IEEE Transactions on*, 14(9):1357–1365, 1988.

[Zus98] Horst Zuse. *A framework of software measurement*. Walter de Gruyter, 1998.

Chapter 3
Measurement Program

Abstract In this chapter, we build on the theoretical concepts of measurement and discuss the notion of a company-wide measurement program. We describe what a measurement program is and the components that build it up. We go also into details on how we know if a measurement program is successful or not, and whether we need the help of expert consultants and expensive tools to build and maintain a measurement program. We look into how measurement programs can be scaled to suit different company and organizational sizes. These are some of the topics we have addressed over the years, while working with measurement programs at software intensive industry companies. The aim of this chapter is to describe what a measurement program is, how to design, implement and maintain it, and most important, how to succeed in doing so. The goal of this chapter is that you the "company," or you the "organization," will be able to do this successfully on your own.

3.1 Introduction

Theoretical foundations of measurement, presented in Chap. 2, show how important it is to design and deploy measurements properly, e.g. by proving that the measures have relevant properties. In this chapter, we focus on how to operationalize the process of measurements at a company.

The purpose of this chapter is to give an insight as to what a measurement program is, how to design and deploy measurement programs, and also, how to assess the robustness of measurement programs. Each sub-section starts by giving a description of the subject in focus, complementing it with hands-on, and easy-to-use, checklists. From our experience, we have found these checklists to be an important tool for setting up the measurement program.

This chapter is the result of (ca. 20) years of work, studies and research, at a number of different software-intensive development companies. Based on these

© Springer International Publishing AG, part of Springer Nature 2018
M. Staron, W. Meding, *Software Development Measurement Programs*,
https://doi.org/10.1007/978-3-319-91836-5_3

experiences, we found that there are three types of elements, see Table 3.1, which group key elements of a measurement program:

- Components: technical elements such as measurement systems, measurement instruments and measurement tools.
- Roles: social roles needed for the measurement program to be institutionalized, such as line management or measurement librarian.
- Rules: principles which should be followed in order to make full use of the measurement program.

These three elements have to interact and support each other, in order for the measurement program to be successful.

Table 3.1 Measurement program—components, roles and rules

Components	Roles	Rules
Measurement systems	Line management	Theory of measurement (metrology)
Information products	Measurement analyst*	Measurement-related standards
Databases	Measurement librarian*	
Measurement infrastructure	Measurement process owner*	
Measurement organization	Measurement sponsor*	
	Measurement user*	
	Measurement designer*	
	Stakeholder*	
	Database administrator	
	Metrics team leader	

In general, measurement programs are built up by the five components presented in the first column of Table 3.1. The five components are described in Sect. 3.2. In this chapter, we choose to take out the information products from the measurement system, and treat them separately. We do this to simplify things for the reader, as we explain in the next section.

There are many roles related to a measurement program, as we can see in the table. The roles with a "*" are taken from ISO/IEC 15939:2007, [ISO07]. The other roles we have come across at different software-intensive development companies and organizations. We discuss all roles and their respective purpose in the context of the measurement program in Sects. 3.3 and 3.4.

Measurement programs must rely on rules, which govern the operations of the measurement program's components, roles and stakeholders. There are, mainly, two types of rules, see Table 3.1, that measurement programs have to abide by: theory of measurement (metrology), and measurement standards, e.g. ISO/IEC 15939 and parts of the ISO 25000 family [ISO16]. The theoretical foundations are important to ensure the correctness of the data used in the measurement programs, while the standardization is important to ensure the right organizational support for the program.

The checklists that we present in this chapter come from theory, standards and also from our industrial best practices.

What does it take to successfully design, deploy and maintain a measurement program? Experience shows that *all* of the following *must* be in place:

1. Management commitment: managers support measuring financially and set the ethical boundaries related to measuring.
2. A metrics team: experience has shown, time and again, that there must be one or more persons dedicated 100% to measuring.
3. Use of measuring-related theory and standards: theory and standards provide, among other things, guidance in measuring, and a measuring specific language.
4. Automation: automation is the very foundation for a well-structured and efficient measurement program.
5. Measures that reflect the culture and core essence of the company or organization: some of the measures used need to reflect the culture/tradition/values of the company or organization.

Throughout this chapter we present and discuss what is needed to fulfill the requirements for having all of the above items, 1 through 5, in place. We come back to summarizing these bullets at the last section of this chapter, where we discuss the characteristics of measurement programs and how to evaluate them.

The structure of this chapter is as follows: in Sect. 3.2 we present the measurement program model, in Sect. 3.3 we go through the three processes that govern measurement programs, in Sect. 3.4 we discuss the important measurement program role of the stakeholder, and finally, in Sect. 3.5 we present how to assess the robustness of measurement programs.

3.2 Measurement Program Model

Measurement program is a set of well-defined components, roles and rules. The purpose of this section is to list and describe the components that build up a measurement program, so that we, in the next section, can describe the processes around measurement program, i.e. processes to design and deploy a measurement program. The processes related to the maintenance of the measurement program are discussed in Chap. 8.

Figure 3.1, which is based on our previous work on robustness of measurement programs [SM16], shows the conceptual model of an industrial measurement program. We see in Fig. 3.1 the components of a measurement program: measurement systems, information products, databases, measurement infrastructure, and the measurement organization. Let us go through these components briefly, one by one.

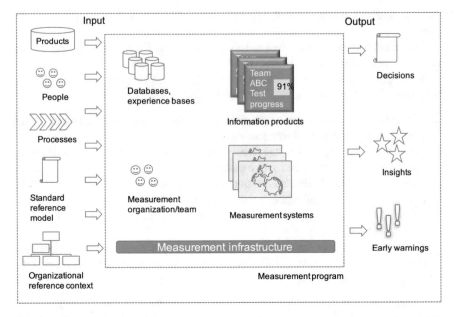

Fig. 3.1 Conceptual model of a measurement program

3.2.1   Measurement Systems

Measurement systems were formally defined in Chap. 2; in plain English, a measurement system is a technical system that collects data, performs calculations and presents the calculation results to a stakeholder. The stakeholder is the person that needs the result of a measurement in order to make decisions important for his/her work and for his/her organization. A measurement system is a set of measurement instruments assembled in order to measure a quantity of a specified type. The measurement instruments are used to measure a specific entity, for example a program or a model, and collect a number of measures from one entity. The measurement system uses the values of measures from one or several measurement instruments and calculates indicators from them. These indicators are signals for attracting attention of the stakeholder and usually are calculated from a significant number of data points. It is not uncommon that in our case there are over 1000 data points used to calculate a single indicator.

In this chapter we have chosen to separate information products from the measurement system for a reason: information products, e.g. widgets, are what users of measurement systems see. The rest of the measurement system is "hidden" in the code, stored in servers, MS Excel files or other tools. This separation makes it easier to grasp the otherwise complex nature of measurement systems. Sometimes, we can see that the distinction is not that clear as the measurement systems can be integrated with the information products in dashboards; it could also be the case that the measurement systems provide the basic visualization methods, thus integrating information products into their structure. This distinction, however, provides the possibility to discuss the collection and processing separately from the visualization.

Important to keep in mind is that each measurement system has a dedicated purpose, and that is to satisfy the information need of a specific stakeholder. This is the reason measurement systems are depicted in Fig. 3.1 as multiple entities. The information need of the stakeholder can be explained informally as the measurement information which the stakeholder should have in order to work efficiently and provide value to his or her company.

3.2.2 Information Products

Information product is the component for presenting the results of the measurement to the stakeholder. An information product consists of one or more measures, including information about how they should be interpreted. They show the information that the stakeholders need to know, the so-called information need.

The result of a measurement does not always need to be a number. Information products can also show e.g. a sign (e.g. an arrow pointing up), a diagram, or just a color (e.g. red, indicating a problem). These signs, diagrams and colors provide the interpretation and valuation of the numbers provided by the measurement systems.

Information products come in all shapes and sizes, e.g. MS Vista Gadgets, widgets, apps, SMSs, MS Excel and PowerPoint files, dashboards, e-mails, and web-pages. The shape of the information product depends on the purpose of the information product and how it is supposed to be used. The documentation of what works best in the different contexts can be found in the measurement experience base.

During the design of the measurement program, a set of decisions is made about how the information is presented to the stakeholders. The most important of these decisions is how color-coding is used to assign the interpretation to the values of base and derived measures, thus making them indicators. The colors are often the same as those of traffic lights: red for problems, yellow for attracting attention and green to show the absence of problems. Using the traffic lights metaphor is intuitive and eases the interpretation of the status of the indicators.

3.2.3 Measurement Experience Base

Measurement Experience Base is a term that is taken from ISO/IEC 15939, and is defined as:

> Data store that contains the evaluation of the information products and the measurement process as well as any lessons learned during the measurement process.

The purpose of the measurement experience base is to store measuring experiences of the company or organization, e.g. evaluation of information products, measurement processes and measures used. Studying/analyzing those documented and well-structured experiences helps companies and organizations to improve in measuring.

Examples of information stored in the base can be:

- Defect inflow data for a product during development, per week and development project.
- Level of success of the usage of a specific information product.
- How often measurement systems have been successfully updated, in percent, per month.

In order for the measurement experience base to be meaningful, the company needs to have a mature measurement infrastructure.

3.2.4 Measurement Infrastructure

Measurement infrastructure is the ecosystem that includes the measurement systems, information products, source systems, storage areas and the mechanisms necessary for the measurement program to function.

Source systems store data, which is made available via APIs. They contain information about e.g. defects, tests, finance and requirements, and are usually maintained by the IT support organization. Examples of source systems are Jira, Bugzilla and Git.

Storage areas can be servers, databases and folders in Windows Explorer.

For a measurement program to function, mechanisms need to be in place that orchestrate the execution of measurement systems and the update of information products. An example of such a mechanism is the Microsoft Task Scheduler that can be scheduled to run tasks automatically.

Let us take an example of a measurement program, i.e. a program with only one measurement system, to exemplify the measurement infrastructure. The purpose of this measurement system is show how many tickets there are on a software development project. The tickets are stored in Jira. The measurement system is built up in an MS Excel file. It is stored in a folder, in Windows Explorer. The file uses the MS Excel language VBA, Visual Basic for Applications, to access the data from Jira, and store it structured in a table, in a worksheet. The Microsoft program Task Scheduler defines how often and at what time the MS Excel file is executed. Information product in this example is the table, stored in a worksheet, in the MS Excel file, that shows the number of Jira tickets, per e.g. week.

3.2.5   *Measurement Organization*

The measurement organization is divided into two groups; those that provide the measures and those that use the measures. Most of the employees belong to the second group, while the first group are those belonging to the metrics team.

It is the metrics team that designs, deploys and maintains the measurement systems and information products; it is the metrics team that sets up and runs the measurement infrastructure. A metrics team can consist of a single employee, but is usually a team of three or more, depending of the size and maturity of the company or organization. A metrics team of four can support an organization of up to fifteen hundred employees.

The metrics team comprises the following roles, as listed in Table 3.2.

Table 3.2   Roles in the metrics team

Role	Explanation
Measurement analyst	Individual or organization that is responsible for the planning, performance, evaluation and improvement of measurement [ISO07] Everyone in the metrics team should be able to take/have this role
Measurement librarian	Individual or organization that is responsible for managing the measurement data store(s), [ISO07]
Measurement designer	Individual that has good programming skills, to build up measurement systems, and/or information products. Everyone in the metrics team should be able to take/have this role
Database administrator	Individual that is responsible for the management of the database(s), in which raw data and measures reside. Usually, it is one or two in the team that have this competence
Measurement process owner	Individual or organization responsible for the measuring process, [ISO07]. Usually it is one or two in the metrics team that hold this role
Metrics team leader	Individual that leads the metrics team. He/she is responsible for most of the administrative issues of the team, e.g. documentation, and that the team lives up to its mission and vision. The leader holds also some of the other metrics roles

There are mainly three roles outside the metrics team: the measurement sponsor, the stakeholders, and the measurement users; see Table 3.3. Companies and organizations that are mature in measuring can have additional roles, e.g. measurement process owner(s). The three main roles are important to provide the organizational decision-making context of the measurement program. They provide the justification for why we have the measurement program, when and by whom it should be used.

Table 3.3 Roles outside the metrics team

Role	Explanation
Measurement sponsor	Individual or organization that authorizes and supports the establishment of the measurement process, [ISO07]. This role should be occupied by a line manager, with relevant budget, to support the measurement program
Stakeholder	Individual or organization having a right, share, claim or interest in a system or in its possession of characteristics that meet their needs and expectations, [ISO07]. Our recommendation is to have individuals as stakeholders, not groups. This, to avoid responsibility confusion
Measurement user	Individual or organization that uses the information products, [ISO07]

Both these groups, i.e. those in and those outside the metrics team, are active parts of the measurement program, as both of them comprise roles defined both theoretically (e.g. ISO 15939) and empirically.

Measurement programs are not isolated islands; they have inputs and outputs. Though these inputs and outputs are not the main focus of this chapter, we present them here to give the readers a holistic view of the "world" of measurement programs.

3.2.6   Input

There are many inputs to measurement programs. We have chosen to group them into five main categories: (a) products, (b) people, (c) processes, (d) organizational reference context, and (e) standard reference model. Categories (a)–(c) are based on our experience; categories (d) and (e) are taken from [Abr10]. They are part of a model called the "Refined analysis model of ISO/IEC 15939 with metrological standard reference model and organizational reference context." These two categories, shown in Fig. 3.2, expand the definition of the measurement information model, [ISO07], and take into account e.g. whether a measure or an indicator is appropriate for the organization or how it should be interpreted in the organizational context.

Table 3.4 lists short explanations about these five input categories.

3.2.7   Output

There are three main outputs from a measurement program: (a) decisions, (b) insights, and (c) early warnings; see Table 3.5. These are usually interconnected, e.g.

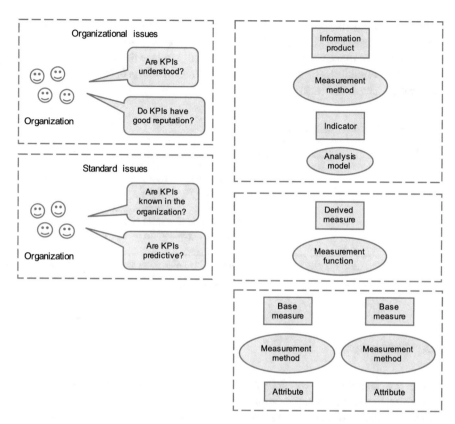

Fig. 3.2 Refined analysis model of ISO/IEC 15939 with metrological standard reference model and organizational reference context. The figure is adopted from [Abr10]

Table 3.4 Input to measurement programs

Input	Explanation
Products	Information about the performance of products; both during development and in the field, when used by customers
People	Companies and organizations are built up by humans; people. Information about organizational performance, e.g. employee satisfaction and innovation capability, is also an input to measurement programs
Processes	How people work, i.e. processes, define if, and to what extent, companies and organizations will succeed with their goals. Examples of such measures are those that relate to efficiency, lead times, bottlenecks, quality, etc.
Organizational reference context	Describes the use of indicator in the organization, [Abr10]
Standard reference model	Describes the use of indicators in the domain that is outside of the organization, [Abr10]

insights can trigger decisions, and decisions can require new insights when decisions are implemented [Sta12]. These three categories help measuring organizations to understand what to measure, and by that, drastically reduce the amount of measures used in the organization. We come back to this, in Chap. 6, where we present numerous examples of measures.

Table 3.5 Output from measurement programs

Output	Explanation
Decisions	Set of decisions, taken in companies or organizations. Decisions are taken based on facts, and among other things, decisions are based on measures
Insights	Insight is about understanding in depth how products (both during development and when used by customers), organizations (people), and processes perform
Early warnings	Measures that enable companies or organizations to be pro-active, to take measures before problems arise

3.3 Processes

In the previous section we described the main components that build up the measurement program, i.e. measurement systems, information products, databases, measurement infrastructure, and the measurement organization. We talked also about the inputs and outputs to/from measurement programs.

There are three main processes that relate to a measurement program: design, deployment, and maintenance. Maintenance is discussed in Chap. 8, as is a type of maintenance, namely the *evolution of a measurement program.*

For each of the design, deploy and maintenance processes, we show how we should use the aforementioned measurement program components, describing what to think of when designing, deploying and maintaining these components. We provide easy-to-use checklists for each of these processes and components. In the next sub-sections we give some information and hands-on checklists, to ascertain the correct design, deployment and maintenance of the measurement program components. Some checklists, or parts of checklists, reappear throughout this section. This is done so that each checklist is complete, and can be used stand-alone.

Before starting ticking off checklists for their measurement programs, we recommend the readers to first go through Chaps. 3–8, to get an overall picture/understanding of the processes and the meaning of each of the checks in the checklist.

Our recommendation is to start small and to start slow. What is absolutely necessary from the very beginning is to have a measurement sponsor, a measurement system designer, and at least one stakeholder. If these roles are in place, then the building up of the measurement program can start, given that the measurement sponsor and the measurement system designer have, above elemental measuring competence.

3.3.1 Designing a Measurement Program

Designing a measurement program is about defining how the measurement components should look. We go through the components in the following order: measurement systems, information products, databases, measurement infrastructure, and measurement organization.

3.3.1.1 Designing Measurement Systems

In this section we present how to design measurement systems, i.e. their related activities, deliverables and artifacts. Large parts of this sub-section are based on [SMKN10], complemented with our experiences from other companies.

The process of designing a measurement system is presented in Fig. 3.3. It has a V-shape, which makes the process easier to follow-up and understand, since it breaks down the design into small, well-defined steps. The horizontal lines in Fig. 3.3 show dependencies between activities, and using the V-shape visualizes these dependencies in a natural way.

To this figure, we link the checklists with items that we need to keep in mind when following the process. Each of the checks in the checklist in Table 3.6 is structured as a question. It is the measurement designer that needs to pose these questions to his/her stakeholder. Table 3.6 provides also explanations about the rationale behind every question.

Table 3.6 Designing measurement systems—checklist

Questions	Explanation
• What is it that you need to know to monitor \<your project \>? (the part in brackets depends on the information need; here we use project as a template example) • Why do you need to know it?	Elicit information need from stakeholders: the stakeholders are the primary source of information needs, as it is they who are the "customers" for measurement systems. The information needs to depend on the role of stakeholders, but the main characteristic is that the information need must be the result of one or more measures

(continued)

Table 3.6 (continued)

Questions	Explanation
How do you act based on the information provided from indicators?	Elicit interpretation[a]: once the information need is elicited, the stakeholder should be asked how the information is interpreted, including actions that are taken upon specific interpretations. The interpretation is to be used in the next step when 'color-coding' the decision criteria for the indicator
• What is the most important indicator that would notify you when there are problems with <your project >? • What other indicators help you to monitor that <your project >is according to your expectations/plan?	Define indicator: by the time the interpretation is found, several candidate indicators are usually discussed. In this activity, the candidate indicators are assessed and the main indicator (or a limited number of them) is found
• When can you say that the indicator shows problems with <your project >? • What are the values of the thresholds?	Define analysis model: after the indicator is found, the stakeholder is asked about the thresholds on the interpretation of the indicator. The thresholds are used to assess whether the indicator shows problems, shows potential problems, or shows that measured phenomena are progressing according to expectations or plans. The analysis model contains also the formula used to calculate the value of the indicator from derived and base measures. The thresholds are usually color-coded to help stakeholders quickly see whether the status is "red," "yellow" or "green," and also for non-stakeholders when interpreting the information
• Which measures are used in the formulas? Note: Not all indicators are calculated from derived measures (some can just be base measures with associated decision criteria). If this is the case, then this activity is not applicable	Define derived measures: after the indicators are found, define the derived measures, which are used in the formulas in the analysis model. These derived measures are defined in this activity
• Which base measures are used to calculate derived measures? • How are the base measures used to calculate the derived measures (what is the formula)? Note: This activity is not applicable if no derived measures are found	Define measurement function: each derived measure is calculated from one or more base measures. In this activity, the function used to calculate the derived measure is defined and documented

(continued)

Table 3.6 (continued)

Questions	Explanation
• Which base measures are needed? • Can these base measures be reused?	Define base measures: the base measures are coupled directly to the derived measures. The underlying raw data (see activities 13–14) are usually very detailed and the base measures are only an excerpt of the data (e.g. the raw data can be per team member per project whereas the base measure is supposed to be about only one team in the project—i.e. data re-configuration is needed)
• Is the measurement method correct? • Are all elements which should be measured, measured?	Define measurement method: the most important part of the definition of the base measures is how to assign the values to the base measures, i.e. how to measure. This measurement process for a single base measures is called measurement method. The measurement method is an algorithm that assigns value of a particular attribute, of a particular entity, to the base measure
• What are the entities in the measured organization/product/process (depending on the information need)? • What are the relationships between these entities? • How can the data for these entities be obtained?	Define entities: the entities that are measured need to be precisely defined since these are the main sources of information. The granularity and availability of base measures depend on the definition of the measured entities. A domain model (similar to domain models known from the Rational Unified Process, [Kru04] or Software Product Lines [CN02] can be created)
	Artifact: domain model with entities which is a part of the specification of the measurement system
• What are the most important attributes (of the entities) that are relevant for the information need? • What are the most important relationships between entities that are important for the information need?	Define attributes: each entity is characterized by its attributes and relationships. The purpose of this activity is to identify the relevant attributes and the methods to measure them. An attribute that cannot be measured should be replaced by an attribute that is easier to measure (or several other attributes)
N/A	Develop measurement system specification: after the entities, attributes, and measurements are identified, a specification of the measurement system is developed. The specification is a model of all measurements, entities, and their attributes. The model serves also as a documentation of measurements used and provided by the measurement system. The model is also important for later maintenance of the measurement system
	Artifact: measurement system specification

(continued)

Table 3.6 (continued)

Questions	Explanation
N/A	Develop measurement system architecture: the specification of the measurement system is a logical view of the measurement system. An implementation view of the measurement system is the specification of its architecture (in the form of a model): components used, e.g. files and databases
	The use of the model of components and data sources in the measurement system is important when problems occur. An important aspect of the measurement system is that it provides accurate and up-to-date information. If a problem occurs, one needs to be able to easily track the information flow in the measurement system (e.g. which files are involved in calculating each particular indicator)
	Artifact: measurement system architecture model
N/A	Identify information sources: the measurement method is directly coupled to the information sources. The information source determines how the measurement method is specified—it can be a list of questions (if an information source is a person) or a description of the structure of the database (if the database is the information source), or a procedure how to access/parse the file (if it is a text file)
N/A	Develop measurement instruments: once the information sources are identified and described, the measurement instruments are developed. A measurement instrument is an algorithm that computes how the measurement value is assigned to the base measures. A measurement instrument can be a user form in MS Excel or a webpage (if the information source is a person), or a software program integrated with the measurement system (if the information source is a database). The measurement instrument implements the measurement method specified earlier in the process
	Deliverable[b]: measurement instrument(s)
N/A	Implement base measures: once the measurement instrument for assigning the values to base measures is in place, the base measures are implemented. The implementation is creating the place where the measurement values are stored and establishing how they are accessed
	Deliverable: base measure

(continued)

Table 3.6 (continued)

Questions	Explanation
N/A	Implement derived measures: when base measures are in place, the derived measures can be implemented. The implementation includes accessing the base measures, implementation of formulas, and methods for accessing the derived measures
	Deliverable: derived measure
• Are the thresholds correct? • Do the thresholds reflect the stakeholder's perception of the situation in \<the project \>?	Implement and evaluate indicators: the indicators are to be developed and evaluated. The development is similar to the development of base and derived measures. The evaluation, however, should be done together with the stakeholder; the values of the indicators reflect the stakeholder's expectations. The stakeholders are individuals or groups of specialists whose perception of the situation of \<the project\>(or other phenomenon depending on the information need) is reflected by the status of the indicator (e.g. low or high value, "red" or "green" color). This can be done by using the historical data during the evaluation of indicators, or by having an indicator in the "evaluation" phase for a period of time when the values are recorded and discussed with the stakeholder
	Deliverable: indicators
• Where should the information be published? • How often should the published information be updated?	Deploy information product: after the indicators are validated with the stakeholder, the measurement system can be made accessible in the organization. The usual way to do that would be to create an internal webpage where the values of the indicators are displayed and explained. The color-coding helps in under-standing whether an indicator indicates problems (e.g. by being colored as red) or absence thereof (e.g. by being colored as green)
	Deliverable: measurement system (information product)

[a]Interpretation is about how the stakeholder should act, depending of the value of the indicator that is presented on the information product. One such type of coding is the traffic light analogy, where "red" indicates a problem that the stakeholder needs to address, and "green" means that the stakeholder does not need to take any action. For a formal definition of interpretation, please refer to Chap. 2 and [ISO07]

[b]One of the requirements for deliverables is that a non-metric expert is able to understand and use them, for his/her specific purposes (if needed). The main idea is that the process should be very light-weight and should minimize the amount of "paperwork" and documentation of the artifacts that are going to be used, even in the maintenance phase

3.3.1.2   Designing Information Products

Information products are the front end of measurement systems. Information products are what stakeholders and measurement users see of measurement systems. The checklist below, Table 3.7, has been developed for the designers of measurement systems and information products, to guarantee that the choice and the layout of the information product satisfies the information need of the stakeholder.

Table 3.7   Designing information products—checklist

Questions	Explanation
Is it easy for the stakehold-er/measurement users to read and understand the information presented in the information product?	Information products must be clear, succinct and unambiguous
Is the unit of the measure included in the information product?	When looking at the indicator, no one should have to guess the unit of the measure
If thresholds are defined, are they visible in the information product?	E.g. will the indicator turn red, if its value rises above or falls below a predefined level (threshold)?
Is there a link to raw data?	It adds value to the information products if one can access the raw data that is behind the measures presented
Is there an indicator for information quality?	Information quality is used to show if the stakeholder can rely on the information presented, or not. This is described extensively in Chap. 4
Is there evidence for the fitness of the purpose of the information product? [ISO07]	To what extent can the information product be demonstrated to be effective for the identified information need?
Is the information product secured from tampering?	The information product should be developed in such a way that it is protected from unauthorized tampering
Is the information product easily accessible?	Stakeholders and measurement users want to have direct access to information products, e.g. MS Vista Gadgets and dashboards on monitors (compare these to a worksheet, in an MS Excel file, that is stored in a folder area)
Do the stakeholder and the measurement users know whom they can turn to for issues regarding the information product?	If stakeholders or measurement users would like to make adjustments or updates to information products, or report malfunctions, they need to know whom to contact, and how. It is the responsibility of the designer of the measurement system (and the metrics team) to provide means of easy access, e.g. using an easily accessible web-page or a ticket system

3.3.1.3 Designing Measurement Experience Base

The measurement experience base is where experiences and lessons learned from developing and using measures are stored. Table 3.8 lists questions that relate to the successful design of the measurement experience base. The structure of the experience base is not as important as its function. The experience base can be designed as an online resource, a database or a book. The important aspect is the ability to quickly find the right experience, which requires such mechanisms as, for example, dynamically evolving cross-referencing.

3.3.1.4 Designing the Measurement Infrastructure

Measurement infrastructure is the environment that contains databases, measurement systems, information products, and the programs/scripts necessary to keep this "machinery" working. It includes also connections to source systems outside of it. A measurement infrastructure comprises the following main parts and activities:

1. Set up of access towards source systems, i.e. enabling collection of data.
2. Collection of data, i.e. collection of data from data sources.
3. Calculations, i.e. algorithms that calculate the needed measures.
4. Update of information products, i.e. technical means to keep the information products up-to-date.
5. Monitoring of information quality, i.e. if users can trust the information that is presented by the information products, or not.
6. Orchestration of the above activities, i.e. design the mechanism that will keep information products updated, on a pre-defined frequency, e.g. daily or hourly.

Listed in Tables 3.9, 3.10, 3.11, 3.12 and 3.13 are checklists for each respective activity. The checklists are to be used by the metrics team. The metrics team is responsible for the design, operations and maintenance of the measurement program, in particular its infrastructure.

Before collecting data, one needs to make sure that data can actually be collected. Table 3.9 lists questions that need to be answered, before the extraction of data can commence. The checklist helps the metrics team to decide how difficult it is to obtain the data and thus to satisfy the information needs. Answering "no" to most of the questions in this checklist indicates that a lot of effort is required to satisfy the information need in question.

The second table is about collecting data. Emphasis is put on automation, since it is an important factor for coherent, consistent, and efficient operation of data collection. Figures 3.4 and 3.5 show two different types of storage areas, a folder system in Microsoft Windows Explorer, and a server. We present this two solutions, to give the reader a brief insight into how data storage can be realized.

Figure 3.4 shows an example of a Windows Explorer data storage solution. It contains the minimum amount of folders necessary for a measurement infrastructure, i.e.:

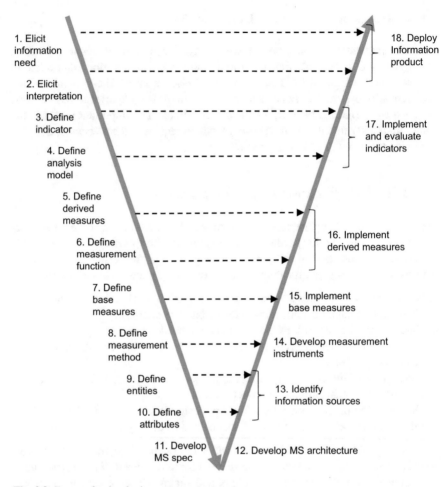

Fig. 3.3 Process for developing measurement systems

- "rawData" is the folder in which raw data is stored. Data can be stored manually and/or automatically as dumps from source systems (databases). Example of such files can be .csv, txt and .xls.
- "informationProducts" is the folder that contains the files that are either information products as such, e.g. MS Excel and MS PowerPoint files, or support for the realization of information products, e.g. JavaScript files for display on dashboards on web-pages.
- "archive" is the folder that contains files that are no longer used in the measurement program. The purpose of this folder is to store files that may be of interest in the future; for instance, compare the defect inflow or test progress between different versions of a software product during development.

Table 3.8 Designing measurement experience base—checklist

Questions	Explanation
Is the measurement experience base well defined and documented?	A document must exist describing the administrative and technical aspects of the measurement experience base
Is the measurement experience base secure?	The measurement experience base should be developed in such a way that it is protected from unauthorized tempering
Can measurement experience base be accessed programmatically?	This is not an absolute requirement, but the more it can be automated (in a measurement program) the better
Are there regular, and frequent, back-ups of the measurement experience base?	There must be a routine in place for back-ups, to secure that no data is lost
Is a person in the metrics team responsible for the structure and security of the measurement experience base?	The measurement experience base must be tied to a role in the metrics team, e.g. the measurement librarian
Is access to the measurement experience base made available for the whole company or organization?	Well defined and known means of access to the measurement experience base must be in place, e.g. via a web-page
Is it easy to access the measurement experience base?	Effort should be put to make the access to the measurement experience base easy, e.g. from a web-page. This is applicable, both for the metrics team and the rest of the organization
Is the measurement experience base future proof?	The measurement experience base will (most probably) expand over the years, as more information is stored in it. Therefore, the design of it must be such that it will allow for future expansions

Table 3.9 Set-up of access towards source systems—checklist

Questions	Explanation
Do the source systems enable access and extraction of data, by automated means?	Check with the owner of each source system, if and how to set up automated means for extraction of data
Do the source systems have well-defined and easily accessible APIs?	Check with the owner of each source system, if any special rules apply, e.g. access permission from a higher manager, custom made tools, or limit time for access
How frequently is access to respective source system allowed?	Downloading data from a source system (may) slow down its performance. Contact therefore the owner of respective source system, to check e.g. how often you can download data, and how much you can download each time (i.e. the whole database or parts of it)
Are there regular, and frequent, back-ups of the source systems?	There must be a routine in place for back-ups, to secure that no data is lost

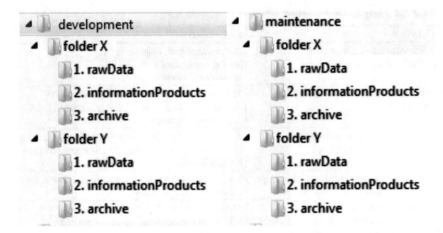

Fig. 3.4 An example of a Windows Explorer data storage solution

- "folder X" represents the generic way according to which data is structured. E.g. folder X can be the name of each product that the company or organization develops. The naming convention should be the same in both the "development" and "maintenance" folders.
- "development" and "maintenance" folders are where development- and maintenance-related data are stored, respectively.

Figure 3.5 shows a measurement infrastructure built in a database (e.g. SQL or non-SQL database). It contains the following areas:

- "Staging area" is the area where dumps from data sources are stored. The data is usually exported as-is; minor transformation of data may be allowed, e.g. change

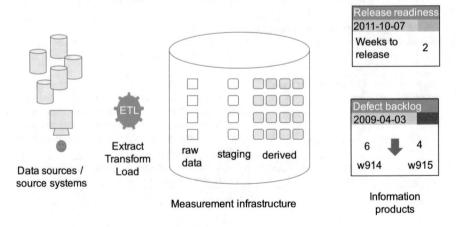

Fig. 3.5 An example of a server data storage solution

of date format. No information product accesses/reads from this area. Data is stored in data marts. The data marts can be named "staging_..."

- "Raw data area" is copied from the staging area. The same principals regarding manipulation of data apply here, as in the staging area. Information products can access and read data stored in the raw data area. Data is stored in data marts (or in views). The data marts (or views) can be named "rawData_..."

- "Derived area" is the area that contains data that is calculated from two or more raw data sources. Information products can access and read data stored in this area. Data is stored in views (or in data marts). The views (or the data marts) can be named "derived_..." The term "derived" is taken from ISO/IEC 15939.

The collection of data is important as it can be done efficiently if set up properly. The checklist in Table 3.10 provides guidance to do it in a cost-efficient way.

Table 3.10 Collection of data—checklist

Questions	Explanation
Is data collected by automated means?	The ambition should be to have all data collected automatically
Is data stored according to pre-defined structure?	Data must be stored in a structured way; see the two examples tied to Figs. 3.4 and 3.5
Can the collection of data be executed manually?	Important to have the possibility to collect data manually, when needed, e.g. when troubleshooting
Can the frequency of the collection of the data vary?	Information products need to be updated at different frequencies, e.g. daily, hourly, or on demand. Important, thus, that the collection of the data can be aligned with the update frequency need of the information products

It is not always easy to clearly (unequivocally) distinguish the activities that belong to measurement systems and those that belong to the measurement infrastructure. For instance, many measurement systems can share the same base and/or derived measures. This is the most common set-up for large measurement programs, i.e. measurement systems there are "limited" to calculating indicators, leaving everything else (i.e. collection of data, storing data, calculations of base and derived measures, and update of information products) to the measurement infrastructure. This enables an efficient measurement infrastructure, since raw data, base and derived measures are only stored and calculated once.

In Sect. 3.3.1.1 we described how to design a measurement system. Table 3.11, lists aspects that need to be taken under consideration, regarding calculations performed by measurement systems. The reason we have this checklist here is because a measurement program comprises many measurement systems; e.g. we have seen measurement programs with thousands of measurement systems. Measurement systems in a measurement program are updated in a pre-defined order; some of them may depend on others. This means that the metrics team must check that each new measurement system that is added into the measurement program can be updated in the existing measurement infrastructure.

Table 3.11 Calculations—checklist

Questions	Explanation
Are calculations performed fully automatically?	All calculations in the measurement infrastructure should be automated. This, to enable efficiency of e.g. execution of measurement systems, troubleshooting and monitoring
Can calculations be re-executed manually?	Calculations should be possible to execute manually, e.g. when troubleshooting
Are calculations efficiently optimized?	Optimization of calculations must always be part of building measurement systems. Even small measurement programs have hundreds of calculations; it is thus important to optimize, so that the execution of them is as fast as possible

The success of a measurement program depends, to a large extent, on the successful design of information products. It is this that will lead stakeholders and measurement users to use them, thus keeping the measurement program alive and thriving! Table 3.12 lists a number of checks related to the design of information products.

Table 3.12 Update of information products—checklist

Questions	Explanation
Is the update of information products fully automated?	All updates of information products should be automated. This, to enable efficiency of e.g. execution of measurement systems, troubleshooting and monitoring
Can update of information products be executed manually?	Update of information products should be possible to execute manually, e.g. when troubleshooting
Is the update of information products efficiently optimized?	Optimizing the update of information products, should always be part of the job of the metrics team. If needed, one should consider replacing the means of the information product (e.g. from MS Vista Gadget to a web-page) if it enables faster update
Can stakeholders and measurement users be notified by other means than the information product, if there are problems with the update of the information product?	When building up or maintaining measurement programs, trust is of the utmost importance, i.e. stakeholders and measurement users must be able to rely on the information presented by the information products. Stakeholders and measurement users can be notified by other means also, e.g. by automatically sent out e-mails, by informing from the main web-page of the metrics team, by having a web-page where all executions are listed as OK/Not-OK

Measurement programs handle/process large quantities of data. One question that is of the utmost importance for the users of measurement programs is whether they can trust the information presented by the information products. The trustworthiness of the information products is referred to as "Information Quality." Information quality has only two states: the information presented by an information product can be either trusted or not. All information products should therefore have an information quality indicator.

The assessment of information quality is done by checking each component and each transition in the measurement information model, [ISO07]. Information quality is handled in Chap. 4. We recommend the reader read Sects. 4.2–4.4 before continuing with Table 3.13.

Table 3.13 Monitoring of information quality—checklist

Questions	Explanation
Can all components and transitions in the measurement information model, of each measurement system in the measurement program, be monitored?	The measurement information model, [ISO07], describes all components and transitions in a measurement system. Mechanisms should be in place to ascertain the effective monitoring of components and transitions. Example of such realization is presented in Sect. 4.4.2.2
Is the metrics team notified automatically if a problem arises in a component and/or transition?	It is imperative that automated means notify the metrics team, e.g. by e-mails, about errors in the components and/or transitions. The reason for this is that it is not possible to check the performance of all components and transitions, for all measurement systems, manually
Does the information product have an indicator for information quality?	Users of the information products should be notified if they can trust the information that is presented by the information products

The metrics team should also see to that the measurement infrastructure is protected from unauthorized tampering, and the structure and the governing rules of the measurement infrastructure is documented, and reviewed by all the team members and the measurement sponsor.

The last part to design is the orchestration of all activities that take place in the measurement infrastructure, i.e. how to coordinate the execution of the collection of data, the execution of calculations, the updating of information products, and finally, the signaling to the measurement users whether they can trust what is presented by the information products.

An example of one such mechanism is the Microsoft Task Scheduler program, as we described in Sect. 3.2. This is a free, pre-installed program, available on all Microsoft PCs. There are other such scheduled tools, e.g. Jenkins continuous integration tool, described in Chap. 5. The main purpose of these mechanisms is to ensure that the measurement systems are executed at regular intervals without the need for manual operation.

Large measurement infrastructures need advanced technical solutions to handle the many, e.g. tens of thousands, activities that take place in the infrastructure. These solutions involve often the use of programming languages, e.g. C#, and/or scripts, e.g. SQL. The technical solutions are, however, not part of this chapter.

During the design of the mechanism that will handle (orchestrate) the activities on the infrastructure, we recommend the design of self-healing mechanisms. These are mechanisms that automatically correct errors during the collection of data and the execution and update of measurement systems and information products. Having this in place saves substantial amount of maintenance time. One such example is the mechanism that re-executes scripts a second time, if they failed to be executed the first time, [SMT$^+$].

3.3.1.5   Designing the Measurement Organization

There are a number of roles related to the measurement program, as we saw in Sect. 3.2. So how do you design a measurement organization from these roles?

Let us start with the metrics team. Though a metrics team can be just one employee, we strongly advise companies and organizations to have a metrics team with at least three members. In our experience, a metrics team of three can support organizations of up to six or seven hundred employees; a team of six can support up to two thousand employees. Naturally, the metrics team is needed to sustain the competence in the company and to support the measurement infrastructure. It is the automation of the infrastructure that helps to scale up the measurement program.

A metrics team must always have designers (programmers). Without this role, there is no metrics team. The reason for this is that no efficient measurement program can survive without automation, and automation requires programming. It is not only about using measurement systems like MS Excel files and its programming language VBA, it is also about having a deeper understanding of everything else that comes with it, e.g. structure of storage areas, collection of data, and distribution of information products. Without the in-house competence in programming, the metric team needs to rely on expensive consultants to develop, maintain and evolve the measurement systems.

Table 3.14 lists some aspects to take into consideration before designing the metrics team. It serves no purpose designing and planning for a metrics team if e.g. the company or organization does not have any ambition to become good in measuring.

The role of the measurement sponsor is critical and must always be present. The employee that undertakes this role should be a manager who has budget responsibility. Some companies and organizations add also to this role the managerial responsibility of the metrics team, i.e. taking the cost of the team, when it comes to both resources (number of employees) and equipment (e.g. extra computers, business intelligence (BI) tools).

There are companies and organizations where employees combine their respective roles with designing measurement systems. We advise against this as it is

Table 3.14 Designing the measurement organization—checklist for companies and organizations

Questions	Explanation
What is the ambition of the company or the organization when it comes to measuring?	The company or organization must have clear and well-defined goals about what they want to achieve with measuring
Has the company or the organization formulated, documented, and formally approved a mission and a strategy plan for the measurement program?	The company or organization must formally address its goals with measuring. There must be a stakeholder tied to each of the goals. These goals must be communicated within the company or organization, to allow them to align their measuring activities to these goals
Does the company or the organization, plan for, and takes the costs related to measuring activities?	Having a measurement program in place costs time and equipment. Unless the company or the organization is mature to acknowledge this (and acts accordingly), it is pointless to establish a measurement program
Is the company or the organization willing to undertake courses, seminars, and/or presentations, to elevate their measuring competence?	Measuring competence is not solely for metrics team. The metrics team, together with the organization, need to build up and constantly evolve their competence. The competence level of the company or organization is defined by the measuring-related goals they have defined
Has a measurement sponsor been formally appointed?	Measurement sponsor is a key role for the successful operation of the measurement program; needs to be in place!

important to have the interplay of the different perspectives; such an interplay is difficult to achieve if all roles are combined in one individual's job description. Measuring is a full-time occupation. It is better to set-up a metrics team with just one employee and take it from there. The recommendation is based on the observations we have made over the years. Companies and organizations that work like this suffer from too many measures, interpret the same measures (and same results) in different ways, have no common measuring language, and there is usually a strong distrust of the measures used and what they show. Working like this takes valuable time from the employees, and at the same time does not give the desired results.

The role of the stakeholder is an important one, and is extensively described in Sect. 3.4. However, it is important to notice the difference between stakeholders and measurement users: the stakeholders must always act upon the status of the information products. Measurement users see by information products as information providers, and they may or may not act upon the status of the information presented.

Table 3.15 lists a number of aspects to take under consideration, when designing the metrics team.

Table 3.15 Designing the measurement organization—checklist for the metrics team

Questions	Explanation
Is there a document about the metrics team in place, formally reviewed and approved?	There must be a document in place about the metrics team. Such a document should include its mission, and its management. It should also include a list to all the other documents that are written by the team, e.g. strategy plan, configuration management, and technical solutions The document must be formally reviewed and approved. The document should be approved by the measurement sponsor
Does the metrics team have sufficient resources (i.e. both personnel and equipment)?	As any other company or organizational function, the metrics team must have sufficient resources. The activities of the metrics team should always be consistent with the level of resources available to the team

3.3.2 Deploying a Measurement Program

The second process is about deploying a measurement program; an important process, equal to the design and maintenance processes. Experience has shown that this process is crucial for the successful implementation of measurement programs—in other words it's important what is deployed and how it is deployed. Both the metrics team and the rest of the company or organization forget (or do not understand) vital parts of the deployment process such as the update frequency of information products.

Let us take as an example what we have encountered many times, the deployment of information products. One would think that following theory, standards and good practices would be enough to design the "perfect" information product. What we have seen, time and again, is that stakeholders and measurement users often come back to the designer of the information products after a while, with suggestions for improvements and/or changes. This happens because designing an information product is to realize an idea, a concept. When the stakeholder sees his/her information product live, he/she has time to reflect, e.g. "Is this indicator really what I wanted?", "Does my indicator drive the desired behavior in my organization?" Measurement users may e.g. not find the amount of the information presented to be adequate to their requirements. Therefore, the designer should keep contact with the stakeholder and measurement users, at least during the first month after the formal release of the information product.

As before, we are going through all five measurement program components, one by one, talking about what to consider in general, and then listing hands-on checklists.

3.3.2.1 Deploy a Measurement System

So, the measurement system is designed, and the stakeholder has approved it. To deploy a measurement system means that it is put into the measurement infrastructure, and is being executed (updated) at the frequency that the stakeholder specified, e.g. daily or hourly.

Before the deployment of the measurement system, rigorous checks must be done to verify that it functions, as designed, in the measurement infrastructure. It is better to put time and effort before the deployment of the measurement system rather than afterwards, since "repairing" the measurement system afterwards costs (much) more effort (in total) than if done as described here. We encourage therefore the designers of measurement systems to do these checks, as described in the table below, for every new measurement system they design and deploy.

This checklist, Table 3.16, is to be used by the designers of measurement systems.

Table 3.16 Deploying a measurement system—checklist

Questions	Explanation
Has the measurement system been integrated into the measurement infrastructure, before its deployment?	The measurement system must be integrated in the measurement infrastructure before it is deployed
Has the measurement system been executed successfully in the measurement infrastructure?	Tests must be performed before the deployment of the measurement system; both manually and automatically. How many times they have to run depends on their update frequency. If the update frequency is e.g. daily or hourly, then the measurement system should be executed successfully for 8 consecutive days
Do any final updates need to be made in the documentation of the: • measurement system specification? • measurement system architecture model?	After successful execution of bullets #1 and #2, check if any updates are needed for the two documents. Please refer to Table 3.6, bullets #11 and #12, respectively
Is the execution of the measurement system transparent to the stakeholder and the measurement users?	In order to enable an efficient maintenance, and trust in the company or organization, transparency of the following must be in place: • collection of data from data sources, • storage of the raw data in the measurement infrastructure, • performed calculations, and • update of information products
Upon deploying the measurement system into the measurement infrastructure, for how long will you monitor manually the successful execution of the measurement system?	The designer of the measurement system should follow up the successful execution of the newly developed measurement system. He/she should also check the results against the information obtained by the automated monitoring means. This should be done for a period of 8 days

3.3.2.2   Deploy an Information Product

Deploying an information product means that the information product is made accessible to the stakeholder. The same reasoning as for the measurement systems, in the previous section, is applicable here.

This checklist, Table 3.17, is to be used by the designers of measurement systems.

Table 3.17   Deploying an information product—checklist

Questions	Explanation
Before deploying the information product, have tests been executed to ensure that: • the information product behaves according to defined (analysis) model? • the information quality indicator (if present) changes accordingly?	Perform tests to see e.g. that • the color of the indicator changes according to the (analysis) model, e.g. from red to green, and • the information quality indicator changes accordingly, when simulating different types of errors
Is the information product updated every time the measurement system is executed?	Obvious as it might be, this step must be checked explicitly!
Is the information product updated correctly every time the measurement system is executed?	Execute different scenarios, to see that the information product is updated correctly every time
For how long do you plan to follow up the performance of the information product, manually?	We recommend a follow-up period of eight consecutive times
For how long do you plan to keep contact with the stakeholder, to ensure the correct function of the information product?	Keep contact with the stakeholder, during the first month of the deployment of the information product. Contact the stakeholder at least twice during this period
Upon completion of the assignment, does the stakeholder know how to contact you (the designer of the information product) or someone else in the metrics team?	The stakeholder must be able to, easily, contact the designer of the information product (or the metrics team), whenever needed. The stakeholder should also receive confirmation that his/her question/request has been received, including a preliminary answer as to when the issue can be handled

3.3.2.3   Deploying the Measurement Experience Base

Source systems that are used in companies and organizations are (most often) set up and maintained by the company's IT support organization. The previous list about source systems, Table 3.9, covers most issues that the metrics team needs to check. This section focuses only on the deployment of the measurement experience base.

We have seen sometimes that companies and organizations do not know there exists a measurement experience base, or that the general perception is that the measurement experience base is something that belongs to, and is used by, the metrics team. It is therefore important that the metrics team inform the company or organization about the experience base, so that all employees can access and use the information that is stored in it.

The checklist, Table 3.18, is to be used by the metrics team.

Table 3.18 Deploying the measurement experience base—checklist

Questions	Explanation
Is the measurement experience base an integrated part of the measurement infrastructure?	To secure that the same rigorous management rules apply to the measurement experience base, as for the measurement systems, it should be an integrated part of the measurement infrastructure
Is the measurement experience base easily accessible by the organization?	The measurement experience base should be easily accessible by the company or organization, via e.g. a web-page
Is it made easy for the company or the organization, and the metrics team, to search in the measurement experience base?	Equally important that both the metrics team and the company or organization can make custom searches in the measurement experience base. Results from these searches should be able to be printed out, and exported in a user friendly format (e.g. MS Excel file)
Is information about measurement experience base formally documented and made available to the company or organization?	The metrics team should document the purpose, set-up, and how to use the measurement experience base. This document should be easily accessible to the company or organization

3.3.2.4 Deploying the Measurement Infrastructure

Deploying a measurement infrastructure means that it is in effect. This means that collection of data, calculations and update of information products, and monitoring of information quality are executed (as far as possible) automatically. It also means that the infrastructure is a solid/robust infrastructure, upon which new measurement systems and information products can be added.

The metrics team should inform the company or organization that the measurement infrastructure is now "up and running," and point them to the information product that monitors its performance.

3.3.2.5 Deploying the Measurement Organization

To deploy a measurement organization is not the same as deploying a new tool. It requires a different approach, e.g. soft issues are of the utmost importance. In addition to what is stated here, we will come back to talking about soft issues, in Sect. 8.2.

Let us start with the deployment of the metrics team. Deploying a metrics team successfully in a company or organization means a number of things, e.g. that the team and its purpose are well known, and it has a clear role in the organization, with well-defined responsibilities and authorities. It means that the company or the organization trusts and respects the metrics team; that they recognize the metrics team as an authority in all aspects of measuring.

Equally, for the metrics team, it means that it perceives its situation as adequate for its mission, e.g. that it has enough resources and equipment for the task at hand. It means also that it feels respected and acknowledged, by the company or organization as an authority in measuring.

Table 3.19 lists different aspects that the metrics team must consider to have a successful deployment.

Table 3.19 Deploying a measurement organization—checklist for the metrics team

Questions	Explanation
Is the metrics team well known in the company or organization?	It is imperative for the successful operation of the metrics team that it is well-known in the company or organization
Does the company or organization know how to contact the metrics team?	The metrics team must have means for the organization to contact them, via e.g. a metrics team web-page, e-mail, and/or a ticket system
Does the metrics team and the measurement sponsor have a good relationship?	Obvious maybe, but it is a prerequisite for the successful function of the metrics team, and the measurement program
Do the company or organization in general, and the stakeholders in particular, understand and respect the role and function of the metrics team?	Obvious maybe, but it is a prerequisite for the successful function of the metrics team, and the measurement program

It has to be clear to the company or the organization that knowledge about measuring is not only for the metrics team; they also have to understand, at least, the basics about measuring, e.g. what it means to be a stakeholder, the difference between a "simple" measure and an indicator, and that it is pointless to measure everything that can be measured.

Table 3.20 is intended for the company or organization. We exclude the questions about stakeholders on purpose, since we talk extensively about this role in Sect. 3.4.

Table 3.20 Deploying a measurement organization—checklist for companies and organizations

Questions	Explanation
• Is the role of the measurement sponsor well known in the company or the organization? • Does the company or the organization know who the measurement sponsor is?	Measurement sponsor is a key role for the successful operation of the measurement program. Important thus that both questions to the left are answered with a "yes"
Is the metrics team, its mission and function, well known to the company or the organization?	The success of the measurement program is dependent, among other things, on how well the metrics team is known in the company or organization
Does the company or the organization know how to contact the metrics team?	The metrics team *must* have means for the organization to contact them, via e.g. a metrics team dedicated web-page, e-mail, and/or a ticket system

3.4 Stakeholders

The role of the stakeholder is central in measurement programs. Measuring-related theory and standards describe what should be measured, and what to think of when measuring. They fail, however, to capture the uniqueness of every company and organization; they fail to capture each company's and organization's specific ways of working, their specific challenges, their specific culture. Stakeholders function thus as a proxy for the information that is missing in theory and standards. Going back to Fig. 3.2, stakeholders function as proxy for the two "boxes," the one that refers to the organizational context, and the one that refers to the standards.

This section describes what makes a stakeholder, a good stakeholder and the role of the stakeholder in the design and deployment processes.

3.4.1 What Makes a Stakeholder, a Good Stakeholder?

In our experience there is a great confusion and misinterpretation about who a stakeholder is and who a measurement user is. According to ISO/IEC 15939, a stakeholder is defined as:

> Individual or organization having a right, share, claim or interest in a system or in its possession of characteristics that meet their needs and expectations.

According to ISO/IEC 15939, a measurement user defined as:

> Individual or organization that uses the information products.

The definition of the stakeholder uses the term information need, i.e. information that is absolutely necessary for the stakeholder to do his/her job. How the information is used is the first criterion that distinguishes the stakeholder from the measurement user. Another way to express this is that the information presented by an information product is regarded as "need to have" for the stakeholder and "nice to have" for the measurement user.

Another aspect related to the role of the stakeholder is the mandate, i.e. if the employee has the mandate to act upon the status of the information presented. If the employee has this mandate, then the employee is a stakeholder. Let us take an example: a project monitors the "defect backlog." All project members are measurement users of this measure, since all in the project have an interest about the status of the backlog, e.g. are there many or few defects, is the trend of the backlog rising or decreasing? The stakeholder for this measure is the project manager, since he/she is the only one that has the mandate to act upon the status of this measure. For instance, if the project has many defects, the project leader can order overtime, or order new equipment for the software developers, to address the situation and reduce the number of defects. No other role in the project has the mandate to take these actions.

So these are the two criteria that distinguish the stakeholder from the measurement users; i.e. one is a stakeholder if:

1. the information that is presented by the information product is absolutely necessary to the employee to do his/her job, and
2. the employee that monitors the information product has the mandate to act upon the status of the information presented.

3.4.2   The Role of the Stakeholder in the Design and Deployment Processes

We list here the checks that a stakeholder must do during the design and the deployment processes. The focus of the checklists, Tables 3.21 and 3.22, are limited to measurement systems and information products, because these are the measurement program components that the stakeholder should be concerned with, since it is the information product that will show him/her the status of the information that he/she needs, in his/her role.

That said, it is good if the stakeholder has some basic knowledge about the measurement program; e.g. the set-up and function of the measurement infrastructure and the mechanisms behind information quality.

3.4.2.1   Design Phase: Checklist

In addition to the questions in Sect. 3.3.1.1, Table 3.6, there are a few more things that a stakeholder needs to think of; see Table 3.21.

Table 3.21 The role of the stakeholder in the design process—checklist

Questions	Explanation
Is the data flow from data source to the information product transparent?	Transparency of data flow is important for the trust of the stakeholder in the measurement systems, information product, and not the least, in the metrics team
Does the information product have an indicator about information quality?	The stakeholder should always be notified if he/she can trust the information presented on the information product or not
Does the stakeholder know whom to contact, if changes and/or updates are necessary?	A stakeholder must always know whom (and how) to contact if he/she needs to make changes and/or updates to the measurement system and the information product
Where should the information be published? Should there be any access restrictions?	"Where" addresses how wide the stakeholder needs to spread the information product, e.g. if it is just for him/her or for a whole project. Important to think also about potential restrictions of the access of the information product, if it contains e.g. sensitive financial or customer data
How long will the information product be used?	It is important that the stakeholder understand that every measure has an "expiration date!"

3.4.2.2 Deployment Phase: Checklist

During the deployment phase the stakeholder performs the final check-up, especially if the information product affects or is accessible/visible to larger parts of the company or organization. Table 3.22 lists relevant questions during the deployment phase.

Table 3.22 The role of the stakeholder in the deployment phase—checklist

Questions	Explanation
Have all questions in the design and deployment phase about measurement system and information product been ticked off?	The successful design and deployment of an information product depends on if all questions in Sects. 3.3.1.1, 3.3.1.2, 3.3.2.1, and 3.3.2.2 have been ticked off
If an indicator affects others: • have they understood the purpose of the measure? • will the indicator drive expected behavior?	If an indicator affects others, e.g. measuring organizational efficiency, the stakeholder must check and double-check that: • the company or organization understands the reason for this measure, and that they do not feel "policed" or offended by the measure, and • the indicator will drive the expected behavior, e.g. the organization will become more efficient

3.5   Summary

Setting up a measurement program is a complex task because it requires technical, social and organizational skills. It is also a complex task, because we need experience to govern the measurement program—in particular to balance the value of the measurement program with the cost of it.

In this chapter, we document our experiences from setting up measurement programs. We use a model of embedding the measurement program in an organizational context [Abr10] and complement it with the details from such standards as ISO/IEC 15939 [ISO07]. Our checklist help the designers of the measurement program to progress gradually from the simplistic measurement program for one stakeholder to a full-fledged measurement program for large organizations.

Chapter 3 introduced details about the quality of the measurement programs and Chap. 6 continues with the content of the measurement program—what measures and indicators exist for the measurement programs.

3.6   Further Reading

Robustness of measurement programs to changes in organizations is an important aspect. Traces of the challenges related to the robustness to change can be found in previous studies of such aspects as longevity of measurement programs. Kilpi [Kil01] presented the experiences of establishing a measurement program at Nokia, recognizing the importance of the proper definition of metrics and the infrastructure. However, the experiences presented do not provide a quantifiable set of factors determining the success. MeSRAM addresses this issue by quantifying the concept of robustness and providing the corresponding assessment method.

There are numerous studies describing experiences from establishing measurement programs in industry which usually address the challenges with the initial development and acceptance of the measurement program, but not the challenges related to making the measurement program able to adapt to changes in the environment. One of the studies has been done by Umarji and Emurian [UE05], who studied the use of technology adoption theory when implementing metric programs, therefore focusing on the social issues such as management commitment and support.

A complement to Umarji et al.'s study is a survey study of 200 participants, conducted by Nessink et al. [NvV01, NvV00], where the focus was on the organization (employees) and not the management, which resulted in exploring such factors as the roles which are interested in measurement data. Furthermore, Jorgensen [Jor99] has studied the longevity of measurement programs from the perspective of the reuse of metrics. As his work shows, this is not an easy task, due to the potentially different definitions of measures.

Measurement programs in industry are often associated with introducing or driving the change of organizations. Unterkalmsteiner et al. [UGI$^+$14, UGI$^+$12] provide a set of information needs to stakeholders, for successful indicators of software process improvement initiatives.

Daskalantonakis et al. [DYB90] have developed a method for assessing the measurement technology from the perspective of supporting maturity levels (compatible with the CMMI model). Their work is based on ten themes characterizing measurement processes as part of maturity assessment—e.g. formalization of the measurement process or measurement evolution.

In the case of our work we use the theories by Goodman and Dean [GBC80] to describe the introduction of the measurement program as a change in the organization. We follow their recommendations that the effect of change of a single measure should be considered separately in the context of the change. In our work we focus on the ability of the measurement program to support the organizations in conducting the changes—introducing new measures, using the measures in the decision support and providing expert competence to support measurement initiatives at the company.

References

[Abr10] Alain Abran. *Software metrics and software metrology.* John Wiley & Sons, 2010.

[CN02] Paul Clements and Linda Northrop. *Software product lines.* Addison-Wesley,, 2002.

[DYB90] Michael K Daskalantonakis, Robert H Yacobellis, and Victor R Basili. A method for assessing software measurement technology. *Quality Engineering*, 3(1):27–40, 1990.

[GBC80] Paul S Goodman, Max Bazerman, and Edward Conlon. Institutionalization of planned organizational change. In *Research in Organizational Behavior*, pages 215–246. JAI Press, Greenwich, 1980.

[ISO07] ISO/IEC. *ISO/IEC 15939:2007 Systems and Software Engineering – Measurement Process*, 2007.

[ISO16] ISO/IEC. ISO/IEC 25000 - Systems and software engineering - Systems and software Quality Requirements and Evaluation (SQuaRE). Technical report, International Standards Organization, 2016.

[Jor99] M. Jorgensen. Software quality measurement. *Advances in Engineering Software*, 30(12):907–912, 1999.

[Kil01] T. Kilpi. Implementing a software metrics program at Nokia. *IEEE Software*, 18(6):72–77, 2001.

[Kru04] Philippe Kruchten. *The rational unified process: An introduction.* Addison-Wesley Professional, 2004.

[NvV00] F. Niessink and H. van Vliet. Measurements should generate value, rather than data. In *6th International Software Metrics Symposium*, pages 31–38, 2000.

[NvV01] Frank Niessink and Hans van Vliet. Measurement program success factors revisited. *Information and Software Technology*, 43(10):617–628, 2001. TY - JOUR.

[SM16] Miroslaw Staron and Wilhelm Meding. Mesram–a method for assessing robustness of measurement programs in large software development organizations and its industrial evaluation. *Journal of Systems and Software*, 113:76–100, 2016.

[SMKN10] M. Staron, W. Meding, G. Karlsson, and C. Nilsson.   Developing measurement systems: an industrial case study. *Journal of Software Maintenance and Evolution: Research and Practice*, pages n/a–n/a, 2010.

[SMT⁺] Miroslaw Staron, Wilhelm Meding, Matthias Tichy, Jonas Bjurhede, Holger Giese, and Ola Söder. Industrial experiences from evolving measurement systems into self-healing systems for improved availability. *Software: Practice and Experience*.

[Sta12] Miroslaw Staron. Critical role of measures in decision processes: Managerial and technical measures in the context of large software development organizations. *Information and Software Technology*, 54(8):887–899, 2012.

[UE05] M. Umarji and H. Emurian.   Acceptance issues in metrics program implementation. In H. Emurian, editor, *11th IEEE International Symposium Software Metrics*, pages 10–17, 2005.

[UGI⁺12] Michael Unterkalmsteiner, Tony Gorschek, AKM Moinul Islam, Chow Kian Cheng, Rahadian Bayu Permadi, and Robert Feldt. Evaluation and measurement of software process improvement – a systematic literature review. *Software Engineering, IEEE Transactions on*, 38(2):398–424, 2012.

[UGI⁺14] Michael Unterkalmsteiner, Tony Gorschek, AKM Islam, Chow Kian Cheng, Rahadian Bayu Permadi, and Robert Feldt. A conceptual framework for SPI evaluation. *Journal of Software: Evolution and Process*, 26(2):251–279, 2014.

Chapter 4
Quality of Measurement Programs

Abstract Controlling the development of large and complex software is usually done in a quantitative manner, using measurement as the foundation for decision making. Large projects usually collect large amounts of measures, although present only a few key ones for daily project, product, and organization monitoring. The process of collecting, analyzing and presenting the key information is usually supported by automated measurement systems. Since in this process there is a transition from a lot of information (data) to a small number of indicators (measures with decision criteria), the usual question which arises during discussions with managers is whether the stakeholders can trust the indicators w.r.t. the completeness, correctness of information and its timeliness—in other words, what is the quality of the measurement program? In this chapter, we present what characterizes high-quality measurement programs—namely completeness, correctness and information quality. We base this on our previous work in the area and describe how to calculate the completeness of a measurement program based on the product and process structure. After that we continue to describe the concept which is extremely important for the trust in measurements—information quality. Finally, we present the method for assessing the breadth of the measurement programs.

4.1 Introduction

Effective and efficient use of measurements in large organizations is usually supported by automatic data collection and analysis tools used by line, project, or product managers during decision making processes. As studies show, one of cornerstones of a successful measurement program is management commitment [UE05, IM00, Kil01]. Naturally, this commitment is easier to obtain if data is used during the process of decision making. The data can be used for decision making if the managers trust that metrics data is collected and analyzed in a correct way and that the data is up-to-date—i.e. they can trust the metrics data [DPKM97, KL90]. In other words, the managers need to trust that the data is reliable.

© Springer International Publishing AG, part of Springer Nature 2018

M. Staron, W. Meding, *Software Development Measurement Programs*,

https://doi.org/10.1007/978-3-319-91836-5_4

A measurement system is a set of measuring elements (in software engineering also called metric tools) assembled together in order to measure a specific quantity [oWM93, ISO07]. Quantities could vary from application to application (or rather from information need to information need) and examples of these are: number of defects in a component, average productivity, process efficiency. A key element in the application of a measurement system is the stakeholder, who is a person (or a group of persons) who has an information need. The stakeholders are roles who need to monitor certain aspects of projects, organizations, or products (which are their information needs). An example of a stakeholder can be the project manager, whose information need is the cost situation in the project (e.g. the ratio between budget used and allocated). The information need is fulfilled by an indicator, which is a metric with associated decision criteria (e.g. cost situation indicator can notify the project manager about a problematic situation if current cost exceeds the allocated budget). The decision criteria reflect the required values of indicators—e.g. the cost situation indicator might have an "unacceptable" level defined when the cost of the project exceeds the budget and an "acceptable" level when the cost is up to 90% of the budget, leaving the 10% remaining to be the "warning" level of the indicator [SMN08].

In this chapter we present a method for assessing reliability of metrics data provided by measurement systems, a method for assessing completeness of measurement systems and a method for assessing the breadth of the measurement program. We focus on the reliability of information and its relation to ISO/IEC 15939 standard [OC07]. The reliability of the information is the focus of our paper, and it is a component of a larger concept—information quality—used as a theoretical framework.

4.2   Data and Information Quality in General

In general, data quality is defined as the degree to which it serves its purpose. This definition is aligned with the definitions of quality in general, but in terms of the data it requires more detailed specification. In particular, we need to consider two parts of data quality—the quality of the data itself and the quality of the data in its context.

The quality of the data itself, intrinsic data quality, is similar to the internal quality of software products. It relates to how the data is constructed, i.e. specified, collected and documented. An example of such an attribute is the precision of the data collection instruments. The precision depends on how the measurement instruments are constructed and the measurement methods used.

The contextual data quality (also known as system-dependent data quality) describes the external perspective on the usage of the data. In other words, a single data point can have both low and high system-dependent quality, but it always has either low or high intrinsic quality. An example of an attribute of the system-dependent data quality is the availability of the data—depending on the structure of the database (i.e. the system), the same data can be easily extracted by a single query, or it may require significant effort and multiple complex queries.

4.2.1 ISO/IEC 25012 Data Quality

The standard describes data quality in two of its sections—ISO/IEC 25012 (Data Quality Model) and ISO/IEC 25024 (Data Quality Measures). Both parts of the standard view data quality from two perspectives—intrinsic data quality and system-dependent data quality. The intrinsic data quality is the kind of quality that is related to the data itself and can be assessed without knowing the context of the data processing system. The systemic data quality describes the system-dependent data quality.

Table 4.1 presents the data quality attributes and their description. The definitions are quoted from [Int]; the detailed explanations can also be found in that standard.

The data quality attributes, defined in the ISO/IC 25012 standard, provide a good starting point for designing quality measures for these attributes. In fact, the ISO/IEC 25024 standard defines the basic measures for each of these attributes. For example, formula 4.1 provides the definition of the measure for accuracy.

$$\text{Accuracy} = \frac{\text{number of records with the specified field syntactically accurate}}{\text{number of records}}$$

$$(4.1)$$

The formula, although it gives a good guidance, still requires effort of defining the concept of what syntactically accurate means. This means that, in practice, the definitions provided in the ISO/IEC 25024 standard require interpretation and documented definitions. This imprecise definition is the largest obstacle in the adoption of this standard. From our perspective, this interpretation needs to be operationalized, and therefore we developed different methods to assess the quality of the measurement programs—to calculate information reliability at runtime, to calculate completeness of the measurement program and its robustness.

Table 4.1 Data quality model from ISO/IEC 25012

Attribute	Type	Description
Accuracy	Inherent	The degree to which data has attributes that correctly represent the true value of the intended attributes of a concept or event in a specific context of use
Completeness	Inherent	The degree to which subject data associated with an entity has values for all expected attributes and related entity instances in a specific context of use
Consistency	Inherent	The degree to which data has attributes that are free from contradiction and are coherent with other data in a specific context of use. It can be either or both among data regarding one entity and across similar data for comparable entities
Credibility	Inherent	The degree to which data has attributes that are regarded as true and believable by users in a specific context of use
Currentness	Inherent	The degree to which data has attributes that are of the right age in a specific context of use
Accessibility	Inherent and system-dependent	The degree to which data can be accessed in a specific context of use, particularly by people who need supporting technology or special configuration because of some disability
Compliance	Inherent and system-dependent	The degree to which data has attributes that adhere to standards, conventions or regulations in force and similar rules relating to data quality in a specific context of use
Confidentiality	Inherent and system-dependent	The degree to which data has attributes that ensure that it is only accessible and interpretable by authorized users in a specific context of use
Efficiency	Inherent and system dependent	The degree to which data has attributes that can be processed and provide the expected levels of performance by using the appropriate amounts and types of resources in a specific context of use
Precision	Inherent and system-dependent	The degree to which data has attributes that are exact or that provide discrimination in a specific context of use
Traceability	Inherent and system-dependent	The degree to which data has attributes that provide an audit trail of access to the data and of any changes made to the data in a specific context of use
Understandability	Inherent and system-dependent	The degree to which data has attributes that enable it to be read and interpreted by users, and are expressed in appropriate languages, symbols and units in a specific context of use
Availability	System-dependent	The degree to which data has attributes that enable it to be retrieved by authorized users and/or applications in a specific context of use
Portability	System-dependent	The degree to which data has attributes that enable it to be installed, replaced or moved from one system to another preserving the existing quality in a specific context of use
Recoverability	System-dependent	The degree to which data has attributes that enable it to maintain and preserve a specified level of operation and quality, even in the event of failure, in a specific context of use

4.3   Measurement Systems Represented as Data-Flow Architecture

In this section we introduce the concept of a measurement system as it is described in the applied ISO/IEC standards (ISO/IEC 15939:2007, Vocabulary in Metrology—VIM, [oWM93]), which is the context of this book. In particular, we focus on one perspective—data flow—from the raw data to indicators. We need this view during the reasoning and calculation of information reliability.

4.3.1   ISO/IEC Standards

In is important to observe how the information flows in a typical measurement system, which is illustrated in Fig. 4.1. The information is provided by (or collected from, depending on the information) people, projects (through databases, like defects tracking systems), and products (through databases or dedicated tools) in forms of various kinds of data. This data is stored in source files, e.g. database files or text files, or directly as raw data in MS-Excel or alike. The difference between source files and raw data is that source files usually contain much more data than is required while the raw data files contain the information relevant for the measurement systems.

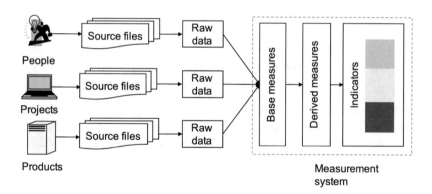

Fig. 4.1 Information flow in measurement systems

The raw data is used to calculate the base measures, which are then used to calculate derived measures (Fig. 4.2). Derived and base measures are eventually used to calculate indicators.

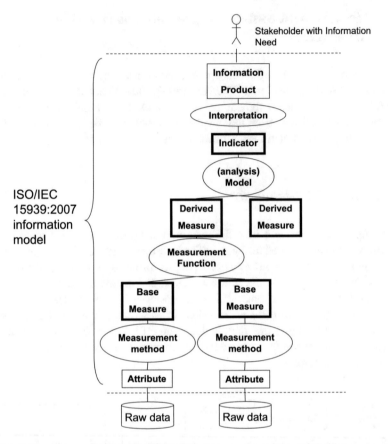

Fig. 4.2 Information model from ISO/IEC 15939, data sources and the stakeholder

The ovals in Fig. 4.2 are transitions of the metric data, while the rectangles are the components of metric data—different forms of measures and an indicator.

A measurement system is a set of measurement instruments assembled in order to measure a quantity of a specified type. The measurement instruments are used to measure a specific entity, for example a program or a model, and collect a number of measures from one entity. The measurement system uses the values of measures from one or several measurement instruments and calculates indicators from them.

In order to provide basic characteristics of the spread of different applications of measurement systems where this approach has been applied, we provide a list of example measurement systems from our industrial partners, [SM09a]:

1. Measuring reliability of network products in operation for the manager of the product management organization; example metrics in this measurement system are:

   • Product downtime per month in minutes
   • Number of nodes in operation

2. Measuring project status and progress—for project managers who need to have daily updated information about such areas as requirements coverage in the project, test progress, costs, etc.; example metrics in this measurement system are:

   - Number of work packages finished during the current week
   - Number of work packages planned to be finished during the current week
   - Number of test cases executed during the current week
   - Cost of the project up till the current date

3. Measuring post-release defect inflow—for product managers who need to have weekly and monthly reports about the number of defects reported from products in the field; examples of metrics:

   - Number of defects reported from the field operation of a product during the last month
   - Number of nodes in operation last month
   - Number of nodes which reported defects

4. Summarizing status from several projects—for department managers who need to have an overview of the status of all projects conducted in the organization, e.g. number of projects with all indicators "green"

These measurement systems were instantiated for a number of projects and products. Each of these instances has a distinct individual as stakeholder (who has the role of project manager, product manager, etc.) who uses the measurement system regularly. Depending on the stakeholder, each measurement can be calibrated to his/her specific information needs.

Measures used in these measurement systems can be collected both automatically from databases or manually from persons when the data is not stored in databases (e.g. by asking the project manager how many designers are assigned to remove defects from the software in a particular week). The sources of information are defined in the metrics specification and the infrastructure specification for the particular measurement systems. As shown in the checklists in Chap. 2, a different approach needs to be used when using manual and automated measurement instruments.

4.3.2   The Need for Information Quality

The measurement systems can differ in their purpose, and the number of metrics can be rather large (in some cases over 1000 data points per indicator). Naturally, the more the data is processed, the more important is the question about its quality. Often, the managers (both line and project) need to control whether the information is:

- Up-to-date—the data presents the latest possible status of the measurand,
- Calculated without errors—there were no problems when calculating the indicators, and
- Within pre-defined limits (e.g. the number of designers in the project cannot be negative).

4.4 Information Quality

The AIMQ framework [LSKW02] provides a model of information quality which was used as the theoretical basis for the information quality model presented in this chapter. The AIMQ framework defines the following quality attributes of information:

1. Accessibility: the information is easily retrievable,
2. Appropriate amount: the information is of sufficient volume for our needs,
3. Believability: the information is believable (non-doubtful credibility),
4. Completeness: the information includes all necessary values,
5. Concise representation: the information is formatted compactly,
6. Consistent representation: the information is consistently presented in the same format,
7. Ease of operation: the information is easy to manipulate for our needs,
8. Free of error: the information is correct,
9. Interpretability: it is easy to interpret what this information means,
10. Objectivity: the information was objectively collected,
11. Relevancy: the information is useful for our work,
12. Reputation: this information has a good reputation of quality,
13. Security: the information is protected from unauthorized access,
14. Timeliness: the information is sufficiently current for our work, and
15. Understandability: the information is easy to comprehend

This is a very good list from the perspective of information. However, when designing a measurement system, we need to categorize these attributes in a similar way as ISO/IEC 25012—the internal and external quality. Therefore, we refine this list by identifying two kinds of information quality:

- External quality—how the information is *perceived by the stakeholder*—semiotics of information: Accessibility, Appropriate amount, Believability, Concise representation, Consistent representation, Ease of operation, Interpretability, Objectivity, Relevancy, Reputation, Understandability. It is very similar to the concept of system-dependent data quality.

- Internal quality—how the information is obtained and composed from components—*internals of measurement systems*: Timeliness, Free of error, Completeness, Security. This is close to the concept of the intrinsic data quality.

Figure 4.3 illustrates the difference. The dotted line in the middle of the figure is a conceptual border between the internal and external information quality. The icon of the stakeholder indicates which parameters are important for the stakeholder and which ones are important for the metrics team.

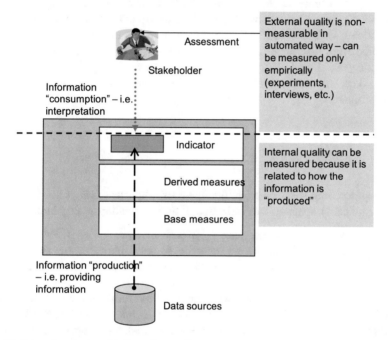

Fig. 4.3 Internal and external information quality

The external information quality defines the quality of the "design" of the information, e.g. whether a given measure measures what it is supposed to measure. Methods used for empirical measure validation are used to assess the external information quality, e.g. case studies or experiments with measures and indicators. The questions of the external information quality are handled when building the measurement systems—choosing measures and indicators.

The internal information quality defines whether the information is properly calculated from the component and whether it is up-to-date, complete and secure. This internal information quality can be checked during the run-time operation of measurement systems. The internal information quality describes what the stakeholders often consider as reliability of the information. Not all internal information quality can be measured in an automated way—e.g. we cannot automatically check whether designers reported defects correctly in defect databases—we can only check whether the database was updated, but not whether all known defects are reported.

At this point we can more precisely define the notion of reliability of information. Information reliability is the part of information quality which assures the end user (stakeholder) that the information is up-to-date and correctly calculated from the sources—and therefore refers to the internal working of measurement systems.

The reason for choosing AIMQ over other existing frameworks (e.g. [KSW02]) is the fact that it was relatively easy to operationalize the definitions of attributes into a set of executable checks. Using this framework also provided us with the possibility to assess how many of the information quality attributes can be checked automatically. We decided to define one information quality indicator, which is calculated from a series of checks of attributes of information quality. From our experience, we found that one is enough, because it signals problems to the stakeholders, and it indicates that the metric team needs to investigate the root cause of the problem.

4.4.1   Fundamentals

Before proceeding we need to outline the most important design decisions which have significant impact on the realization of the information quality indicators:

- We assess the information quality for each indicator using a dedicated information quality indicator. This means that for each indicator, the stakeholder is provided with an additional indicator showing whether he/she can rely on the data.
- We distinguish only between two states of the information quality indicator— reliable and unreliable. Even through different atomic checks (i.e. checking each stage of the data flow in the measurement systems), the information provided to the stakeholder is either correct or not.
- We provide additional information about each atomic check to the maintenance staff of measurement systems. This is done to ensure that the troubleshooting of problems is efficient and effective.

In practice the stakeholder is only informed about the main status in order not to overwhelm him or her with unnecessary information.

4.4.2   Assessing Information Quality: Realization

This section describes the solution to the need for checking the information quality in three parts: checking elements of data flow, technical realization of the checks, and communicating the results.

4.4.2.1 Checking Elements of Data Flow

In order to assess the quality of the information, we perform several atomic checks of each component and transition in the ISO/IEC information model and the underlying data, as is shown in Fig. 4.4.

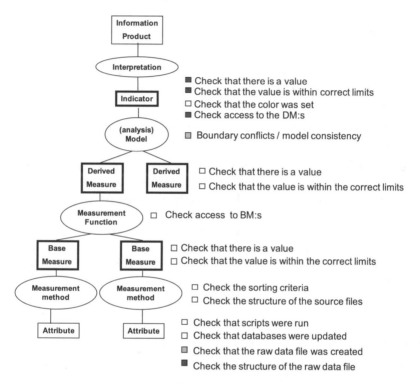

Fig. 4.4 Visualization of information quality checks on the information model

Entities and Attributes For each measured entity and its attributes we check:

- that the raw data file has been created: we need to know whether the underlying data files are updated, and
- that the structure of the raw data files is correct: we need to ensure that the data in the raw data files is correct, e.g. that the query from a database resulted in a text file with the correct structure.

The main goal of the first check is to make sure that the data provided for the calculations in measurement systems has been updated. The main goal of the second check is to verify that the structure of the raw data files is the same as assumed (when designing the measurement system). These checks provide the possibility for the stakeholder to be notified that the data is out-of-date (e.g. it might be the case that all calculations were correct, but the data is from the day before) or incorrect.

The first check measures the timeliness quality attribute of the information. The second check contributes to measuring the free-of-error quality attribute.

Measurement Method For each measurement method we check:

- that the structure of the source files is the same as assumed when designing the measurement system, that the files are in the correct locations, and are up-to-date, and
- that the criteria used to sort the data in the raw data files is correct—e.g. the data is for the projects which are supposed to be measured.

Both checks contribute to measuring the free-of-error information quality attribute and the first check also contributes to measuring the timeliness of the information.

Base and Derived Measures For each base measure and for each derived measure we check:

- that there is a value: we need to know that executing the measurement method (executing the measurement instrument) resulted in assigning a value to the base measure. In other words we check whether the measurement has been performed, and
- that the value is in correct limits: we need to know whether the result of the measurement is a correct value w.r.t. predefined criteria. As an example we could assume that the number of lines of code of a program has to be a non-negative number.

Both checks contribute to measuring the free-of-error quality attribute of the information.

Measurement Function For each measurement function we check:

- that the measurement function could access the values of base measures: we monitor whether the measurement function was provided with an input.

Analysis Model For each analysis model, we check that the decision criteria do not overlap, i.e. the analysis model is unambiguous. The same check also checks whether the criteria cover the whole set of allowed values for the indicator. These checks are important in order to ensure that the stakeholder does not experience ambiguity and non-determinism when calculating the indicator. The check contributes to measuring the free-of-error quality attributes.

We also check that the derived and base measures were accessible when calculating the value of the indicator. This check contributes to measuring the free-of-error attribute and the completeness attribute.

This check also contributes to measuring the free-of-error quality attribute. To some extent, it also measures the completeness of the information since the inability of accessing one or more base measures results in the information which is incomplete.

Indicator For each indicator we check that:

- the derived and base measures used in the formula could be accessed: we need to know whether the formula is provided with input values,
- there is a value for the indicators (i.e. that the formula provided a value): we need to check whether the value for the indicator has been produced by the formula,
- the value is within correct limits: before defining the indicator the stakeholder provides us with the information about the possible values of the indicators (limits). These values are used in decision criteria in the analysis model. We need to check whether the indicator has values outside of these limits, and
- the decision criteria were applied for the indicators: we need to check that the analysis model was applied correctly.

These checks measure the completeness of the information and the free-of-error attribute.

Stakeholder Information Quality Finally, it is important to bear in mind that the information quality in our method is dedicated to two purposes. The first purpose is to provide the stakeholders with the information whether they can rely on the information or not. The other is providing the maintenance staff with the possibility to quickly troubleshoot potential problems with information quality. In order to satisfy the first requirement, after each atomic check, we provide the summary of the information quality to the stakeholder. In our case, this summary is also atomic:

- the information can be trusted when all atomic checks were OK (i.e. no problems with information quality), and
- the information cannot be trusted when at least one of the checks was not OK (i.e. there were problems with information quality).

The stakeholder is not required to know the details of the checking of the information quality, and therefore it is the designers and maintenance staff who have to correct the causes of problems. The maintenance staff gets the information about the stakeholder's information quality via e-mail every time the measurement system has been updated (and the information quality checked).

4.4.2.2 Technical Realization

The technical realization of the information quality checks is an additional measurement system (we refer to it as the IQ measurement system). The IQ measurement system contains measurement instruments which implement the checks described so far in this section. The overview is presented in Fig. 4.5.

The figure presents the IQ measurement system built on top of the main measurement system. The main information quality indicator for the stakeholder is presented at the top. Checking the information quality is done after updating

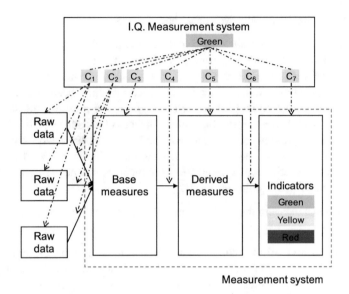

Fig. 4.5 Technical realization of IQ measurements

the main measurement system. The IQ measurement system is designed for the maintenance staff since it contains all information about checks (C1–C7) and their result. The visualization of the information quality is done in the IQ measurement system. Furthermore, the stakeholder information quality indicator is exported to the main measurement system, and to an MS PowerPoint presentation for the maintenance staff, who need to see all problems, in case there are any.

The data flow is presented in Fig. 4.6. The data flow includes four elements—the measurement system which is monitored for information quality, the log file which is used to log the steps of the data flow, the information quality measurement system and the visualization of the information quality checks.

The flow starts when the measurement system logs all steps of the calculations of the indicators to the log file (step 1). The log file contains the information about the success or failure of each step in the calculation of the indicator. The information quality measurement system uses this data from the log file to calculate the information quality (steps 3 and 4), and colors the information quality indicators in the visualization (step 5). In the final step, the IQ measurement system colors the stakeholder information quality indicator in the monitored measurement system.

The specification of each of the checks is done using the framework for measurement systems described in [SMN08]. The results of the evaluation of information quality are presented to the stakeholder. The evaluation of this approach is presented in [SM09b].

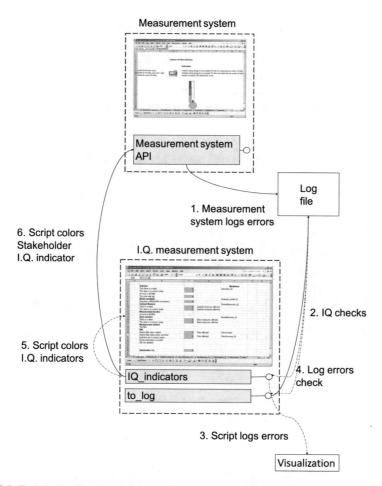

Fig. 4.6 Technical realization of IQ measurements—a data flow

4.4.2.3 Communicating the Results

Figure 4.4 shows the visualization of the checks for information reliability using the information model of the ISO/IEC 15939 standard. The dark boxes visualize all the checks which are performed and were described in Sect. 4.4.2.1.

Each of the checks is colored red (when there is a problem with that check) or green (when there is no problem).

The information quality indicator is placed next to the main indicators, for example as presented in Fig. 4.7. The figure presents a screenshot of a measurement system which satisfies the information need of a quality manager: *How many known and unresolved defects exist in project X?*[1] The figure shows an example of a simplified measurement system based on the framework and described in [SMN08]. The indicator and the information quality indicator are also provided to the stakeholder using MS Windows Vista gadgets. In real measurement systems, there are several (up to 20) indicators per measurement system, which makes controlling the information quality a rather complex task where automation is necessary.

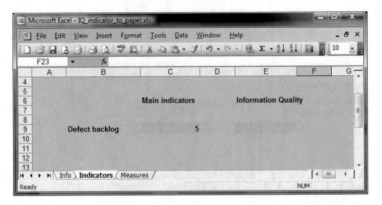

Fig. 4.7 Presentation of information quality indicator for the stakeholder

Another example of the visualization is the indicator in the MS Windows Sidebar gadget, presented as a green "IQ" box (left-hand side of the figure) or a red dot (right-hand side of the figure) in Fig. 4.8.

 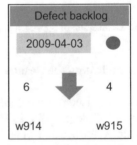

Fig. 4.8 Presentation of information quality indicator for the stakeholder in MS Sidebar gadget

---

[1]The number of defects presented in this example is fictitious.

Assessing the information quality is important because it is used during the run time of the measurement flow. Since the measurement flow is executed often (e.g. daily or hourly), controlling the information quality prevents decisions based on incorrect data. However, it should also be complemented with the assessment of the quality of the design of the measurement program. This assessment is done during the design of the measurement program.

4.5   Completeness and Predictiveness of Measurement Programs

Completeness and predictiveness of measurement programs is the degree to which the measurement program fulfills the information needs of the organization and how far ahead it provides the ability to predict status of the indicators.

4.5.1   Fundamentals

One of the risks is the fact that indicators for single stakeholders can lead to sub-optimizations of the whole system, since each stakeholder monitors only parts of processes—e.g. optimizing efficiency of the development part of a Lean software development program and "forgetting" to monitor test progress, which may lead to decreased efficiency of the complete program or deteriorated quality of the products. To illustrate this, let us consider an example of an indicator for monitoring the quality of a software product—an indicator that shows the number of defects discovered during in-house testing of a software product. If the number of defects discovered is too high, then the indicator warns about problems with quality. When the number of defects decreases, the indicator shows that the quality of the product is good enough. However, we can observe that for the whole product development project this indicator might lead to sub-optimizations, since the number of defects depends among other factors on the test progress. So, we could also reason that developing two indicators—one for controlling quality and one for controlling test progress—provides a more complete picture of the situation. Furthermore, we can reason that a decrease in the pace of testing (decreased test progress) is a warning signal of potential problems with quality—as it could also be the case that it is the delays in integration that might cause big-bang integration problems and thus decrease of quality.

The concept of predictiveness of measurement systems in our research has been adopted from the predictiveness of information in time-series analysis [PPB08]. The notion of completeness of information is adopted from the AIMQ framework [LSKW02].

4.5.1.1 Workflow Modelling

In our work we model workflows based on process models used in software
development projects. The method places the stakeholder downstream and all
related activities upstream as illustrated by Fig. 4.9. By doing this:

- we limit the number of activities/states that have to be described,
- we limit the number of metrics and indicators used,
- we organize the dependencies of listed activities, and
- we quantify listed activities timewise.

Figure 4.9 outlines how a process model, a workflow model and stakeholders'
information needs relate to each other. The process model at the top of the figure
denotes the prescribed software development process, used in the project with
activities which should be followed. The as-is workflow describes how the process
is instantiated in the particular project, which means that it includes activities that
are fully automated, and includes actual lengths of activities. Each stakeholder
in the project (Stakeholder 1 and Stakeholder 2) has a distinct role and distinct
information needs and therefore they have distinct needs for the monitoring of
different activities.

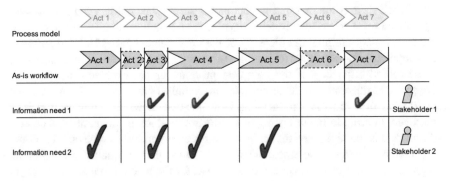

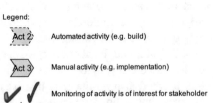

Fig. 4.9 Workflow modelling to capture completeness of the measurement flow

4.5.1.2 Completeness

The AIMQ framework defines completeness of information as information possessing the necessary values. The definition in the AIMQ framework is general although its roots are in one of the existing definitions of information quality. The deficiencies addressed by information completeness are related to incomplete representation of the real-world entities with metrics. This means that in the context of the study presented in this paper the completeness of a measurement system is the possibility to monitor all activities relevant for one information need in a process (workflow).

As an example let us consider the toy workflow presented in Fig. 4.10 with three activities in release planning—i.e. Requirements elicitation, Requirements prioritization and Product release planning. The stakeholder for that workflow is the release manager who is responsible for releasing the product with the right features and the right quality. That particular stakeholder is interested in two of the three activities—denoted with a tick under the activities.

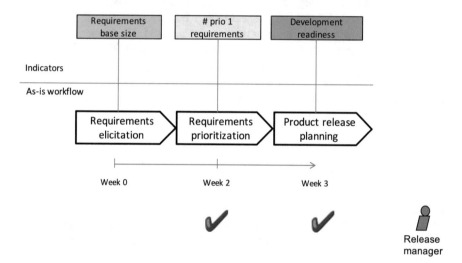

Fig. 4.10 Mapping workflow elements to indicators

Each of these three activities is linked to one indicator—"Requirements base size," "number of priority 1 requirements" and "Development readiness" with the status of the indicators—green, yellow and red respectively. If the stakeholder considers the workflow model to be complete, then the measurement system with the three indicators provides the stakeholder with the complete "picture" of the workflow according to the stakeholder's definition of completeness. The "picture" is complete since the indicators are defined according to ISO/IEC 15939 and the standard requires proper construction of metrics.

4.5.1.3 Predictiveness

Predictiveness is defined as the ability to foretell an event based on observation, experience or scientific event (Merriam-Webster dictionary). This definition is refined using the AIMQ framework's notion of timeliness, i.e. whether the information is sufficiently current for the stakeholder's work. This means that predictiveness of information is the ability of the information (i.e. the indicators in Fig. 4.10) to warn stakeholders of potential events, rather than show that the events already happened.

In the context of the study presented here—monitoring of processes—the predictiveness of measurement systems is the possibility of the indicators of a given measurement system to warn stakeholders downstream about potentially incoming problems. Since we model the workflow from the perspective of product development, we focus on the stakeholders that are downstream, and not upstream.

Figure 4.10 also contains a timeline (in the middle of the figure). The timeline shows how much time elapses between different activities. Using the timeline it could be deduced that the predictiveness of this measurement system is 3 weeks, since this workflow is executed in under a 3 week period. However, the ability of each indicator to issue warnings about problems for the stakeholders downstream is shorter, since the status (color) of the indicator may change during the process—for example the change from green to red of the "Requirements base" size indicator might happen a day before the requirements elicitation is finalized (i.e. 2 weeks and 1 day before the end of the workflow).

4.5.2 Assessing Completeness

In short, the main principles of our method are: (1) to create a process model of the existing workflow, (2) link appropriate and necessary measures to activities in this process, (3) link the time scale to the process and calculate the completeness of information provided by the measurement systems. The method results in

- time frame for how long in advance the indicators warn about/predict problems, and
- percent of completeness of measurement systems w.r.t. monitoring of activities.

We present the three parts of our method together with an illustrative example.

Step 1 Develop de facto process descriptions of the workflow. This measurement system should address the following information need—*What do you need to know in order to warn the stakeholder in the subsequent phase about coming problems?* Therefore the model should contain all activities that are relevant for this information need. The description should be in the form of a model, for example a model presented in Fig. 4.11 (which uses a UML-like notation). The model should show the de facto ways of working in the workflow and should be at the abstraction level of activities, not tasks. The flow depends on the stakeholder, and the process description covers only the aspects that are important from the perspective of the information need of the stakeholder. This means that the workflows are not prescriptive (as process models) but descriptive.

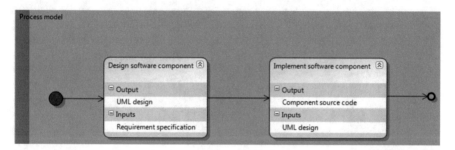

Fig. 4.11 Process model—an example

The figure shows two activities in an example process description—design software component and implement software component. This is how the stakeholders describe their contribution to the overall company product development, although there might be a number of smaller tasks which are part of these activities.

Step 2 Design measurement systems and link them to activities in the workflow. After describing the process the measurement system for monitoring the workflow is designed. This measurement system should address the following information need—*what do you need to know in order to warn the stakeholder in the subsequent phase about coming problems?* We propose using a method developed in one of our previous research projects, which uses the ISO/IEC 15939 information model as the basis for the specification of the measurement system. An example of this link between process model and metrics specification is presented in Fig. 4.12.

The figure shows the design of the measurement system for monitoring the workflow for this process. The measurement system monitors one of the two activities through three measures—number of requirements planned and number of requirements included in the design. It also contains one indicator—design process progress. The reason for having just this indicator is that the indicator warns the stakeholders downstream about the status of this activity and about the potential problems.

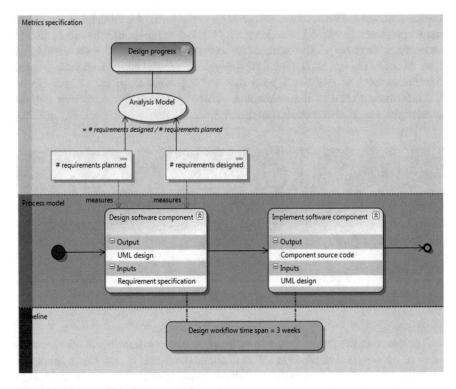

Fig. 4.12 Measures linked to process elements

Step 3 Add a timeline for the workflow and assess how often each stakeholder (e.g. a team leader) has to prevent the problem that he/she is warned about. When the measurement system is designed in the model, a timeline is added to show the time frame between activities in the process. The resulting model shows how *predictive* the measurement system is. It shows that the early warning in the first available measure can warn about potential problems later on in the process. By adding the timeline, we can reason about how far away into the future we can have an impact.

4.5.2.1   Calculating Predictiveness

Predictiveness is calculated by measuring the time between the first monitored activity and the last monitored activity in the workflow; in our example it is between the activities Design software component and Implement software component.

The predictiveness of the measurement system decreases over time as the time passes as the work moves towards the end of the workflow. This is also expected from the empirical point of view as the prediction horizon decreases—in the extreme case, at the end of the workflow, there is nothing to predict and therefore the predictiveness of the measurement system is 0. In the example presented in Fig. 4.10

the predictiveness is 3 weeks as the timeline between the first monitored activity (Design software component) and the last monitored activity (Implement software component) is 3 weeks.

4.5.2.2   Calculating Completeness

The natural complement to the assessment of the predictiveness of the measurement systems in this context is the assessment of completeness of the measurement system. In order to perform this assessment we use formula 4.2.

$$\text{Accuracy} = \frac{\text{number of activities with measures and indicators}}{\text{number of activities}} \qquad (4.2)$$

The number of activities with measures or indicators in this context means that we count also activities which have only measures (i.e. base or derived measures). This is dictated by the fact that sometimes it is not possible to set static decision criteria (in the analysis model) to develop an indicator, but a derived or base measure still holds important information about the status of the measured activity. The measurement system which provides measures or indicators for all activities in the monitored process is 100% complete. That number of indicators is given by the number of activities defined by the Info Need of the stakeholder that is downstream. That is why the number of activities and related measures vary given the stakeholder. In the example presented in Fig. 4.10 the information is 50% complete as only one of the two activities is monitored—Develop software component.

4.5.3   Completeness of Measurements in the Program

One of the important categories of the completeness of measurements in the measurement program is the ability to support analysis of data both in the short term (e.g. one software improvement initiative) and the long term (e.g. over a period of time including multiple changes of software processes/products). Therefore the measurement program should support using metrics in a wide range of areas—e.g. processes, products, businesses.

These metrics should also be **used** and not only **collected**, which leads to spreading the status information and analysis results in the company. The set of metrics used are organized into five sub-categories—business metrics, product metrics, design metrics, organizational performance metrics, and project metrics.

Business The business metrics quantify such aspects of company operations as customer strategies, value measurements, financial performance, product delivery efficiency and defects in products. This area of measurement is related to how well the company monitors its operations and has quantified strategies related to the metrics and indicators.

Product The business area quantifies the operation of the company and its business performance, but has to be complemented with the perspective of product performance. This area quantifies how good the product is, what the potential is (e.g. product feature backlog) or how ready the product is for being released.

Design Design measures are different from the product measures as they capture the internal quality of software [JKC04]. Robust measurement programs must distinguish between these two in order to provide a more complete coverage of the measured areas.

Organizational Performance Measuring organizational performance should be part of every mature, long-term measurement program. The measurement program should support the organization in measuring how good it is and how well it develops. This is important for the long-term evolution of the organization.

Project A robust measurement program includes measures and indicators for project managers for the monitoring of project progress. This category is one of the most mature fields of measuring and in the table we only give examples related to new trends in software engineering which contain modern metrics—e.g. metrics for Lean software development enterprises.

4.6 Assessing the Measurement Program's Organization

Assessing the quality of the data addresses the challenge of how we know that the content of the measurement program is correct and fulfills the requirements set by the standards. We complement this assessment with the assessment of the completeness of the measurement system, addressing the challenge of capturing the complete picture of the measured entity. Finally, the information quality provides us with the possibility to check the quality of the measures during the operation of the measurement system.

What remains, however, is the ability to assess the organization of the measurement program and its breadth—i.e. which measurement areas we capture. In this section we look into this problem; we provide the possibility to check whether the measurement program fulfills the needs and standards as well as whether it is supported by a standardized measurement organization. Fulfilling the criteria presented in this section allows the company to build a robust measurement program that can withstand organizational changes and adapt to them, not erode with them.

To do this we use parts of the robustness measurement program model, as defined in [SM16]. A robust measurement program is a program that continues to operate, despite changes in the information needs, stakeholders, measurement structure, and measurement support organization.

The measurement robustness model in [SM16] is built up by seven categories; see Table 4.2. These categories capture the most important dimensions of measurement programs, as discussed in Chap. 3.

Table 4.2   List of categories for assessment of measurement programs

Category	What to assess
Metrics organization[a]	Assess how metrics collection, analysis and visualization are done, and by whom
Metrics infrastructure	Assess how the measurement program is realized technology-wise
Metrics used	Assess which measures are used in the company or organization
Decision support	Assess how measures are used in decision processes in the company or organization
Organizational metrics maturity	Assess how the organization, as a whole, works with measures
Collaboration with academia	Assess the status of research-oriented activities at the organization
External collaboration	Assess the state of collaboration with other companies

[a]The category "Metrics organization" refers the metrics team. It covers all aspects, e.g. a formal metrics team, a virtual metrics team, or employees working with measuring, independently from each other, in the same company or organization

Each of the above dimensions is described by a set of checks, which we present in the subsequent tables. They are formatted as checklists, to enable easy use of them. The tables are adapted from [SM16].

4.6.1   How to Use the Tables/Checklists

The tables are formatted so that one can use them "as is," and they can e.g. be copied into an MS Excel worksheet and filled in during the assessment. Once filled in, we can summarize and visualize the results using radar plots.

The answers to the checks are important thing, but the most important is the discussion around each of the checks. For example, if the answer to a question is "no," then one should follow up the question by asking: "Why not?" Asking this question allows us to identify weaknesses that need to be addressed. It can also allow us to understand whether the check makes sense for the assessed organization, as some of the checks are not applicable to all contexts.

In the same manner, if the answer to a question is "I do not know," then one should follow-up the question by asking: "Who may know the answer?" This next-step question provides us with the possibility to make a map of all roles and persons involved in the design, maintenance and operation of the measurement program in the assessed company.

By following up on these two questions, the person that assesses the measurement program has the opportunity to get a better understanding (if the answer was "no"), or can continue his/her questions with another person (if the answer was "I don't know").

4.6.2 Who Should Assess the Measurement Program?

The tables/checklists should be used primarily by the quality manager of the company or organization, and the measurement sponsor.

The metrics team should use these checklists, (a) when designing and deploying the measurement program for the first time, and (b) after changes that may affect the performance of the measurement program, e.g. changes of the technical solution of the measurement infrastructure, measurement systems, and information products; major organizational changes; and changes in the customer scope.

4.6.3 Who Should Be Assessed?

There are mainly two "roles" that should be assessed: the metrics team and stakeholders. We need both roles as it is important to assess the suppliers of the measurement systems and their customers, as both roles have a different part to play. The stakeholders spread the information throughout the organization and the metrics team captures the organization's potential to measure various aspects of the enterprise.

One cannot assess all stakeholders of course, but it is important to capture the most important characteristics of stakeholders common to the assessed organization. Which stakeholder to assess depends on the focus of the assessment.

The purpose of assessing the metrics team is not to police it, but rather to support the team in its everyday work. For example, we can follow up all "no" answers with questions like, "How can we help you, to turn the "no" into a "yes"?"

Table 4.3 relates to the ways of working of the metrics team.

Table 4.4 assesses the measurement infrastructure. The questions are limited to just a few, but important ones. The rationale is that if just one question is answered with "no," then there exists a potentially big problem in the measurement program (since an ill-functioning infrastructure "spills over" to the whole program).

Table 4.5 assesses the aspect of the usefulness of the measures that have been deployed in the company or organization. For instance, one thing that is important to avoid is building up "graveyards" of measures, which is the rationale of the first question.

Table 4.6 assesses the support of the decision process. Its purpose is to capture the usefulness of the measures in the decision process.

Using the checks in Table 4.7 gives a clear indication as to how mature a company or organization is with regard to measuring. Less mature companies and organizations are bound to have one or more "no's." This can be used in a positive way, to help them decide what to improve, and with what priority.

Table 4.3 Assessing the metrics team

ID	Question	Yes/No/I don't know
1	Is there a metrics organization (e.g. team)?	
2	Does the organization have sufficient resources?	
3	Is there a metrics organization that maintains existing measures?	
4	Do measures support the organization (excluding the metrics team) with competence?	
5	Does the metrics organization give presentations, seminars and/or courses?	
6	Does the metrics organization have good knowledge of the company's or organization's products?	
7	Is it well defined and transparent, how the metrics organization prioritizes its assignments?	
8	Can the metrics organization handle emergencies?	
9	Does a strategy plan exist?	
10	Does a metrics champion exist?	
11	Does a measurement sponsor exist?	
12	Does a measurement analyst exist?	
13	Does a measurement designer exist?	
14	Does a measurement librarian exist?	
15	Does a metrics team leader exist?	
16	Is there a document describing how the metrics organization works?	
17	Is there a contingency plan?	
18	Does a statement of compliance towards ISO/IEC/IEE 15939 exist?	
19	Does a statement of compliance towards ISO/IEC 12207 exist?	
20	Does a statement of compliance towards IEE Std 1061 exist?	
21	Does a statement of compliance towards ISO/IEC 250xx family exist?	

Collaboration with academia provides many useful advantages, e.g., academia has a deep/extensive knowledge in many measuring-related areas, and a vast network with the software industry. Academia can thus help companies and organizations significantly to become better in measuring,

Table 4.4 Assessing the measurement infrastructure

ID	Question	Yes/No/I don't know
1	Does a structure exist that contains all/the most important measures?	
2	Is the infrastructure secure?	
3	Is the infrastructure built up, so that is supports automation?	
4	Do all measurement systems include information quality?	
5	Does the infrastructure support/enable dissemination of information products?	
6	Do naming of rules for folders and files exist?	

Table 4.5 Assessing the measures used

ID	Question	Yes/No/I don't know
1	Are all deployed measures used?	
2	Are all measures updated with specified frequency?	
3	Can all deployed measures be easily accessed?	
4	Can all information needs be realized?	

Table 4.6 Assessing the decision support

ID	Question	Yes/No/I don't know
1	It is clear/transparent who is interested in the metrics data?	
2	Are meanings/interpretations of measures defined?	
3	Are measures used for analyses of problems/root causes?	
4	Are measures and indicators used to formulate decisions?	
5	Are measures and indicators used to monitor implementation of decisions?	
6	Is it clear which measures and indicators, are used for technical and managerial areas respectively?	

Networking is a key element for the successful operation of the metrics team.[2] Networking should take place both internally, within the company, and externally with other companies. Exchanging successes, and failures and overcoming impediments between companies significantly improves the performance of metrics teams (Tables 4.8 and 4.9).

---

[2]This checklist is applicable to both the metrics team and the measuring parts outside the metrics team, e.g. stakeholders and measurement sponsor.

Table 4.7 Assessing the organization's measurement maturity

ID	Question	Yes/No/I don't know
1	Is there a prioritized list of defects per product?	
2	Is there a list over the most complex software modules?	
3	Are measures and indicators collected/calculated using documents and repeatable algorithms?	
4	Are measures and indicators collected/calculated manually?	
5	Are measures and indicators collected/calculated automatically?	
6	Are measures and indicators visualized with decision criteria?	
7	Are measures and indicators accompanied with information quality/reliability evaluation?	
8	Are measures and indicators available in standard tools (e.g. Eclipse, MS Excel), used and understood in the organization?	

Table 4.8 Assessing collaboration with academia

ID	Question	Yes/No/I don't know
1	Does the metrics organization have collaboration with academia?	
2	Does the metrics organization execute measure research projects?	
3	Does the metrics organization publish papers?	
4	Does the metrics organization have students on site?	
5	Does the metrics organization supervise bachelor/master theses?	

Table 4.9 Assessing collaboration with other companies

ID	Question	Yes/No/I don't know
1	Does the metrics organization have collaboration with other units of the company?	
2	Does the metrics organization have collaboration with other companies?	

4.7 Summary

The quality of a measurement program is a multi-facet entity. In this chapter, we looked at three different facets—assessing the quality of information in measurement systems, assessing the completeness of the measurement program and assessing the robustness of the measurement program.

The work presented in this chapter is based on our experiences with assessing the quality of measurement programs in industry. We have done these evaluations at over ten companies and we observed a large correlation between the longevity of measurement programs and the outcomes of our evaluations. In particular, we observed the need for professional support organizations and runtime information quality checking.

In the next chapter, we overview the most interesting tools used in contemporary measurement programs.

4.8   Further Reading

The basis for our research is one of the available frameworks for assessing information quality—AIMQ [LSKW02]. The framework contains both the attributes of information quality, and the methods for measuring it, and has been successfully applied in industry in the area of data warehousing. In our research we take the method one step further and develop a method for automatic and run-time checking of information quality in a narrowed field: measurement systems. The existing evaluation of the AIMQ framework is focused on all attributes in the framework, whereas in this paper we focus on a deeper understanding and automation of a subset of these attributes. There exist several alternative (to AIMQ) frameworks for assessing information quality, which we also investigated, for example Kahn et al. [KSW02], Meyen and Willshire [MW97], Goodhue [GT95], and Serrano et al. [SCT+04]. We decided to adopt the AIMQ framework since it covers such aspects important in our work as the timeliness of information. The possibility of automating some of the crucial components of the information was the main factor which made us adopt the AIMQ framework.

Assessing information quality is usually done using a category-based evaluation system [PS05] and is usually done by humans. An example of such a framework is the semiotic information quality assessment framework [PS05]. The framework is based on theory of information, signs, interpretations and pragmatics, semiotics and semantics of information. For our purposes the framework was too theoretical in the sense that too many assumptions had to be made to operationalize this theory. However, we use one of the concepts from that theory "information reliability" and automate it, which is a further development of that concept since the existing evaluation system in [PS05] is manual and requires human intervention.

Caballero et al. [CVCP07] developed a data quality information model based on the ISO/IEC 15939 information model. Caballero et al.'s research aims to standardize the nomenclature in data information quality and provide an XML schema for generating data quality measurement plans. In contrast with Caballero et al.'s research for measurement plans, our approach is dedicated to measurement systems, is based on a different platform (MS Excel), has a narrower domain (measurement systems) and takes the information quality one step further: runtime, automatic assessment of a subset of information quality. Generation of a schema-like textual specification is possible in our method as it is based on the existing framework, which allows automatic generation of specifications of metrics (including information quality).

Berry et al. [BJA04] conducted an empirical evaluation of two information quality assessment frameworks: AIMQ and a custom one. The focus of that evaluation was on the use of these frameworks by external reviewers (human subjects) to assess the quality of information provided by measurement systems. The results showed that the AIMQ framework was easier to use and provided results useful for improving measurement processes. The results also contributed to our adopting the AIMQ framework in our research.

One of the crucial steps in the design of measurement systems and their quality assessment is the ability to model them in a structured way. In our work, we have used domain-specific modelling languages to design and auto-generate the structure of measurement systems [SM09c, MS09].

The information quality can be used to design self-healing measurement systems as presented in [SM14]. Self-healing can be used to automatically repair measurement systems and therefore save maintenance effort for the measurement designers.

The following work is particularly useful for the purpose of assessing the external data quality: [BBNR05, RK00, SFKM02, ZL06].

Details of all measures presented in this section can be found in our previous work [SM16].

References

[BBNR05] Pierfrancesco Bellini, Ivan Bruno, Paolo Nesi, and Davide Rogai. Comparing fault-proneness estimation models. In *Engineering of Complex Computer Systems, 2005. ICECCS 2005. Proceedings. 10th IEEE International Conference on*, pages 205–214. IEEE, 2005.

[BJA04] Michael Berry, Ross Jeffery, and Aybüke Aurum. Assessment of software measurement: An information quality study. In *Software Metrics, 2004. Proceedings. 10th International Symposium on*, pages 314–325. IEEE, 2004.

[CVCP07] Ismael Caballero, Eugenio Verbo, Coral Calero, and Mario Piattini. A data quality measurement information model based on ISO/IEC 15939. In *ICIQ*, pages 393–408. Cambridge, MA, 2007.

[DPKM97] S. De Panfilis, B. Kitchenham, and N. Morfuni. Experiences introducing a measurement program. *Information and Software Technology*, 39(11):745–754, 1997. TY - JOUR.

[GT95] Dale L Goodhue and Ronald L Thompson. Task-technology fit and individual performance. *MIS quarterly*, pages 213–236, 1995.

[IM00] Jakob Iversen and Lars Mathiassen. Lessons from implementing a software metrics program. In *System Sciences, 2000. Proceedings of the 33rd Annual Hawaii International Conference on*, pages 11–pp. IEEE, 2000.

[Int] International Standards Organization. *Software engineering – Software product Quality Requirements and Evaluation (SQuaRE) – Data quality model*. ISO/IEC.

[ISO07] ISO/IEC. *ISO/IEC 15939:2007 Systems and Software Engineering – Measurement Process*, 2007.

[JKC04] Ho-Won Jung, Seung-Gweon Kim, and Chang-Shin Chung. Measuring software product quality: A survey of iso/iec 9126. *IEEE software*, 21(5):88–92, 2004.

[Kil01] T. Kilpi. Implementing a software metrics program at Nokia. *IEEE Software*, 18(6):72–77, 2001.

[KL90] Barbara A Kitchenham and SJ Linkman. Design metrics in practice. *Information and Software Technology*, 32(4):304–310, 1990.

[KSW02] Beverly K Kahn, Diane M Strong, and Richard Y Wang. Information quality benchmarks: product and service performance. *Communications of the ACM*, 45(4):184–192, 2002.

[LSKW02] Yang W Lee, Diane M Strong, Beverly K Kahn, and Richard Y Wang. Aimq: a methodology for information quality assessment. *Information & management*, 40(2):133–146, 2002.

[MS09] Wilhelm Meding and Miroslaw Staron. The role of design and implementation models in establishing mature measurement programs. In *Nordic Workshop on Model Driven Engineering, Tampere, Finland, Tampere University of Technology*, pages 284–299. Citeseer, 2009.

[MW97] Donna Meyen and Mary Jane Willshire. A data quality engineering framework. In *IQ*, pages 95–116, 1997.

[OC07] International Standard Organization and International Electrotechnical Commission. Software and systems engineering, software measurement process. Technical report, ISO/IEC, 2007.

[oWM93] International Bureau of Weights and Measures. *International vocabulary of basic and general terms in metrology*. International Organization for Standardization, Geneva, Switzerland, 2nd edition, 1993.

[PPB08] Gabriela Prelipcean, Nicolae Popoviciu, and Mircea Boscoianu. The role of predictability of financial series in emerging market applications. In *Proceedings of the 9th WSEAS International Conference on Mathematics & Computers in Business and Economics (MCBE'80)*, pages 203–208, 2008.

[PS05] Rosanne Price and Graeme Shanks. A semiotic information quality framework: Development and comparative analysis. *Journal of Information Technology*, 20(2):88–102, 2005.

[RK00] David M Raffo and Marc I Kellner. Empirical analysis in software process simulation modeling. *Journal of Systems and Software*, 53(1):31–41, 2000.

[SCT⁺04] Manuel Serrano, Coral Calero, Juan Trujillo, Sergio Luján-Mora, and Mario Piattini. Empirical validation of metrics for conceptual models of data warehouses. In *International Conference on Advanced Information Systems Engineering*, pages 506–520. Springer, 2004.

[SFKM02] Erik Stensrud, Tron Foss, Barbara Kitchenham, and Ingunn Myrtveit. An empirical validation of the relationship between the magnitude of relative error and project size. In *Software Metrics, 2002. Proceedings. Eighth IEEE Symposium on*, pages 3–12. IEEE, 2002.

[SM09a] Miroslaw Staron and Wilhelm Meding. Ensuring reliability of information provided by measurement systems. In *Software Process and Product Measurement*, pages 1–16. Springer, 2009.

[SM09b] Miroslaw Staron and Wilhelm Meding. Ensuring reliability of information provided by measurement systems. In *Software Process and Product Measurement*, pages 1–16. Springer, 2009.

[SM09c] Miroslaw Staron and Wilhelm Meding. Using models to develop measurement systems: a method and its industrial use. In *Software Process and Product Measurement*, pages 212–226. Springer, 2009.

[SM14] Miroslaw Staron and Wilhelm Meding. Industrial self-healing measurement systems. In *Continuous Software Engineering*, pages 183–200. Springer, 2014.

[SM16] Miroslaw Staron and Wilhelm Meding. MeSRAM – A method for assessing robustness of measurement programs in large software development organizations and its industrial evaluation. *Journal of Systems and Software*, 113:76–100, 2016.

[SMN08] Miroslaw Staron, Wilhelm Meding, and Christer Nilsson. A framework for developing measurement systems and its industrial evaluation. *Information and Software Technology*, 51(4):721–737, 2008.

[UE05] M. Umarji and H. Emurian. Acceptance issues in metrics program implementation. In H. Emurian, editor, *11th IEEE International Symposium Software Metrics*, pages 10–17, 2005.

[ZL06] Yuming Zhou and Hareton Leung. Empirical analysis of object-oriented design metrics for predicting high and low severity faults. *IEEE Transactions on software engineering*, 32(10):771–789, 2006.

Chapter 5
Tooling in Measurement Programs

Abstract When developing and deploying the measurement program, we can use a variety of tools. Depending on the set-up of the program, these tools differ from monolithic all-in-one-tools to specialized one-measure tools (specialized measurement instruments). In this chapter we explore different types of software tools which are used to realize measurement programs. We start by discussing the difference between measurement tools and measurement instruments, then we continue by describing tools used in various steps of data processing. Finally, we conclude the chapter with a guide on how to select the right visualization of measures and indicators.

5.1 Introduction

Tooling—the moving target in the stable organisation or the stable point in the chaos theory of agile organizations—we can never tell for sure. What we can tell, however, is that without tooling there would be no measurement programs; databases, spreadsheets, statistical tools and dashboards—all of them have their tiny rabbit hole in the organization's forest. The ability to choose the right set of tools and use them in the right context is like co-existence of goals and means. On the one side, the tools support business processes, and on the other side, they limit what we can do with our businesses.

For the measurement program, tooling needs to be flexible and broad. The tooling should support the organization and the metric team. It should not add new burden, so when deciding upon adding a new tool, the metric team should also decide which of the old tools to remove.

In this chapter we focus on all kinds of tooling that, when properly integrated, enable quantitative, fact-based decision-making. All kinds of companies can benefit from these tools—large and small, agile and waterfall, automotive and web-shops. By reviewing the types of tools that we can buy, we can fulfill the needs of both the rich and the poor, the open-source fans and the IT departments' maintainers.

After describing the measurement programs and their qualities we continue by going into details of the tooling required to make a measurement program work.

© Springer International Publishing AG, part of Springer Nature 2018
M. Staron, W. Meding, *Software Development Measurement Programs*,
https://doi.org/10.1007/978-3-319-91836-5_5

We describe such types of tools (and exemplify them) as: measurement instruments for collecting the data, databases for storing the data, analytics for processing the measurement data and finally dashboards for visualization of the measurement data. We present hands-on technical solutions, describing pros and cons for each such solution. We discuss also which solutions should be in place, given e.g. the metrics maturity and size of the company.

Now, it's common in the vocabulary to talk about metric tools, measurement instruments and measurement systems, so let us start by discussing the difference between these concepts.

5.2   Measurement Tools and Instruments

The definitions of the notion of measurement systems, which we use in this book and in the measurement systems built at our partner companies, are taken from ISO/IEC 15939:2007 (Systems and Software Engineering—measurement processes, [ISO07, SMN08, SM09]) and ISO/IEC VIM (Vocabulary in Metrology, [oWM93]). The notion of a measurement system is somehow different from the usually used (in software engineering) notion of a metric tool. Figure 5.1 illustrates the fundamental difference between metric tools (at the bottom of the figure) and measurement systems (at the top). In the vocabulary of ISO/IEC VIM the measurement systems are a set of measuring instruments and metric tools, adapted to measure quantities of specified kinds.

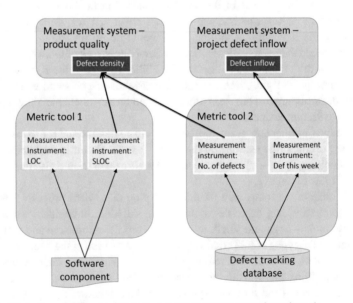

Fig. 5.1   Illustration of difference between measurement systems and metric tools

The metric tools, at the bottom of the figure are tools specializing in collecting metrics from one entity or source—e.g. a source code of a software component (collecting Lines of Code, Source Lines of Code, Non-commented LOC, complexity, etc.) or a defect tracking database.

The collected metrics are usually the base measures used in the measurement systems. The base measures are combined with other base measures, to become derived measures and indicators (when complemented with decision criteria). It is the indicators that are the information product of the measurement systems, and thus their main focus (in the figure the indicators are presented on a dark background in the measurement systems).

This distinction is important for our work as we do not generate or model information provided by metric tools, but we focus on measurement systems. This implication means that we import metrics (and their values in the runtime measurement systems) from various metric tools and do not define how these metrics are collected from the entities or data sources.

5.3 Measurement Instruments

Measurement instruments are used to quantify one specific property of one type of entity, as opposed to the measurement tools, which group a number of measurement instruments to quantify multiple properties of one type of entity. The term *measurement instrument* is used frequently in engineering disciplines in general; however, in software engineering, we are used a bit more to the term *measurement tool.*

Let us, therefore, focus on the measurement instruments in this section. We need to remember that the measurement instruments implement measurement methods, as described in Chap. 2. Therefore, when designing or selecting a measurement instrument for our purpose, we need to remember about:

- the type of measure which is the result of using the measurement instrument; the type affects which properties (non-functional requirements) the measurement instrument should fulfill, e.g. null-value.
- the documentation of the algorithm which is part of the specification quality measure element.

Once we articulate the correct requirements for the tools, we can start selecting from a plethora of available software programs that can perform the task at hand for us.

The measurement instruments can be proprietary software programs, which quantify one given property, but the majority of measurement instruments are available as open source software programs. A simple search for the phrases like "metric tool" on github.com reveals that there are plenty of these measurement instruments and measurement tools.

- LOC counters: 224 github repositories—LOC measurement is probably the simplest of quantification methods and probably the most overloaded; hence there are quite a few variants of this popular measurement instrument.
- Complexity calculators (counters): 37 github repositories—software complexity is another popular measures with many facets; in software engineering we have over 20 different measures of complexity which justify the number of programs in this category [ASS17].
- Static (code) analysis: 1234 github repositories—static code analysis is a popular subject in the software engineering community as it provides means to parse software code and quantify properties of blocks of code based on the grammar of the programming languages, as opposed to the solely structural properties of the text of the source code.
- Metric tool(s): 11,994 tools—as we indicated in the beginning of this section, this term characterizes all kinds of measurement tools and instruments; the large number of github entries for this term seems to support it.

It seems that open source software programs took over the market of software instruments; therefore, in this chapter, we focus on these instruments.

Table 5.1 provides the most basic set of criteria for selecting the right measurement instruments.

These criteria guide the selection, but they do not guarantee that the ideal tool exists. The measurement designers need to scan the market, and test the github or sourceforge open source repositories for the appropriate tools. From our experiences, it is important to choose a tool that is established and actively maintained; otherwise we risk either a tool lock-in or a quick death of the measurement initiative.

Sometimes, however, we compromise on the measurement instruments' perfect match to our needs, because we have a good-enough measurement instrument in the existing measurement tool. To limit the number of tools in the organization, and thus the effort to maintain them, we can use the best available instrument.

5.3.1   Examples of Measurement Instruments

An example of a widely used type of measurement instrument is a command line script measuring the number of physical lines of code in a program. A screenshot of this program ("wc"—word count) is presented in Fig. 5.2.

In Fig. 5.2, we can see two parts: the upper part where we list the program that is measured and the lower part where we apply the measurement instrument (line "wc -l hello.c") and obtain the result ("10 hello.c"). The measured entity (program hello.c) is shown in Fig. 5.3.

Another example is an open source software for the same purpose—measuring the number of physical lines of code—a program named "cloc" available at sourceforge.org. Figure 5.4 shows the results of applying cloc to the same program, in the same way as in Fig. 5.2.

Table 5.1   Criteria for selecting measurement instruments

Criterion	Rationale	Guidance
Flexibility of application	When we need to adjust the tool (e.g. recalibrate) before every use, then we should select tools that allow for manual manipulation of many parameters—configurable tools. Otherwise, we should find automated tools that ease the burden of tedious, repetitive execution of invariant measurement methods	Manual procedures (operations) vs. automated tools
Size of the problem	When the problem at hand is large and we are prone to making mistakes, we should choose automated tools. Choosing manual operations instead of automated measurement instruments increases the chances of making mistakes—thus reducing the measurement certainty	Manual vs. automated
Ease of integration	When we need to integrate the measurement instruments with the measurement systems, we need to control the execution of the measurement instruments from the measurement system. Therefore, GUI-based measurement instruments should be replaced by automated, command line interface (CLI) ones. The CLI-based instruments work well in the pipes-and-filters architectures of data flows [Sta17]	Automated GUI vs. automated CLI
Frequency of use	For one-off measurements, the best fit are the manual operations as they require almost no lead time. However, if we want to repeat our measurement procedure frequently, then we should aim for as much automation as possible. For infrequent, although repetitive measurements, we can go far with the automated, GUI-based tools; but if we have daily measurement tasks that require integration with other tools, we cannot use anything less than a full-grown automated tool with a command line interface	Manual vs. automated GUI vs. automated CLI
Size of the team/user base	If we use the tool only ourselves, then we can get by with an in-house script to automate our tasks. However, when the use base is a few persons, then we should turn towards open source tools which have an active support community behind them. We should also set aside ample time to support our colleagues in using the tools. When the user base is larger than one team, then we should definitely use commercial tools with full-blown support, otherwise we risk spending too much time solving tool problems rather than contributing to the company with data and facts	Commercial vs. open source vs. in-house
Long-term support	In the same spirit as the previous criterion, we should look for commercial and established open source instruments if the support for the tool is longer than one project; people move in the company, roles change, competence comes and goes and therefore we need to maintain the professional support level. The in-house tools have little overhead on the organization, but require support and maintenance which require core competence to remain in the team, a condition which can never be guaranteed to 100%	Commercial vs. open source vs. in-house

```
● ● ●                    📁 Chapter_5 — -bash — 80×14
[Miroslaws-MacBook-Air:chapter_5 Mirek$ cat hello.c
/* Hello World program
   for testing measurement instruments
*/

#include<stdio.h>

main()
{
    printf("Hello World");
[}Miroslaws-MacBook-Air:chapter_5 Mirek$ wc -l hello.c
      10 hello.c
Miroslaws-MacBook-Air:chapter_5 Mirek$ ▌
```

Fig. 5.2 Example of a simple measurement instrument—program for counting lines of code (wc -l)

```
● ● ●                    📄 hello.c — Chapter_5
 1    /* Hello World program
 2       for testing measurement instruments|
 3    */
 4
 5    #include<stdio.h>
 6
 7    main()
 8 ▼  {
 9        printf("Hello World");
10
11 ▲  }




Line:    2:39  │ C          ♢ │ Tab Size:  4 ∨ │ ⚙ ♢ │                    ♢ │ ●
```

Fig. 5.3 Measured entity, program hello.c

```
       1 text file.
       1 unique file.
       0 files ignored.

http://cloc.sourceforge.net v 1.64  T=0.01 s (89.7 files/s, 986.5 lines/s)
-------------------------------------------------------------------------------
Language                    files          blank        comment           code
-------------------------------------------------------------------------------
C                               1              3              3              5
-------------------------------------------------------------------------------
```

Fig. 5.4 Example of a simple measurement instrument—program for counting lines of code "cloc"

5.4 Measurement Tools

Measurement tools are dedicated to measuring a set of properties of one type of entity. They gather a family of measurement instruments under one roof. They are a convenient way of packaging available measurement instruments and, therefore, minimizing the need to maintain multiple tools that measure the same type of entity.

5.4.1 Source Monitor: A Simplistic Measurement Tool for Source Code

An example of a simple measurement tool is Source Monitor, which comprises of a number of measurement instruments for source code—McCabe code complexity and LOC counters. Figure 5.5 shows an example application of this measurement tool. The measured entity is the program hello.c, shown in Fig. 5.3.

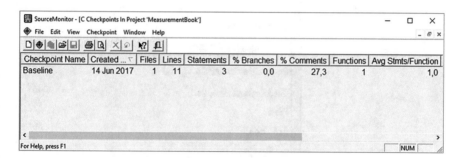

Fig. 5.5 Example of a simple measurement tool—Source Monitor

Compared to the measurement instruments like "wc -l," this measurement tool provides values of a number of base measures (e.g. LOC), and also calculates values of derived measures, such as average statements per function (AvgStmts/Function). As software engineers, we are used to working with measurement tools as they provide more value for the money. In contrast to the measurement instruments, once installed these tools give us more than just one measure.

5.4.2 Understand C++: An Integrated Measurement Tool and Static Analysis Tool

Source Monitor is a simple measurement tool, and these kinds of tools are rather common. However, modern software engineers often prefer tools that are more powerful than those that just collect simple base measures. In particular, contemporary software engineers look for tools that complement measuring of basic quantities with code analytics features. One of such tools is Understand C++ (https:// scitools.com). Understand C++ is a typical measurement tool which can provide a wide variety of measures—both the basic quantities like size and the advanced quantities from static analysis, such as number of uninitialized variables. Figure 5.6 presents a dialog box with a summary of measure values for a given program.

Fig. 5.6 Metric summary view in the understand tool

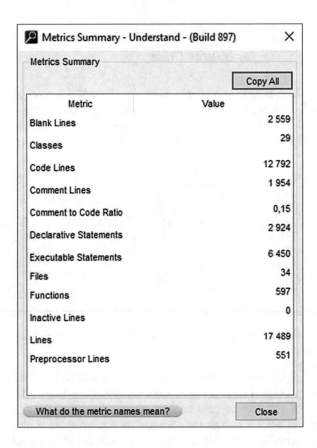

In the figure we can see that the number of measures is short, but once we dive a bit deeper into the tool we can explore a wider variety of measures, as shown in Fig. 5.7.

In the figure we can see a longer list of measures, and we can navigate over different granularity levels in the code to get different views. For example, we can navigate from the class to the package level and the tool re-calculates the measures, aggregates them and provides a different list of measures, specific to packages and not available for classes.

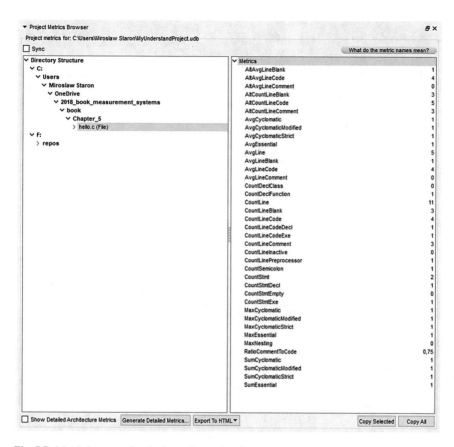

Fig. 5.7 Metric browser view in the understand tool

In addition to the measurement, tools like Understand C++ provide the ability to analyze the code and provide such information as dependencies in the code, which is shown in Fig. 5.8.

The dependency view represents the static analysis abilities of modern measurement tools. An example of a bit more advanced analysis is the ability to detect declarations of entities in the code, which is presented in Fig. 5.9.

Thanks to the declarations view, software engineers can explore the complexity and size of the code in a more semantic way—instead of just counting the code statements, they can explore how many different concepts (functions, variables) are declared and used in different code modules.

Yet another example is the ability to visualize two or more properties of code in a tree map, as shown in Fig. 5.10.

The tree map view provides the ability to explore dependencies between multiple measures and, therefore, the Understand tool can be seen as a basic visual analytics tool for software measures.

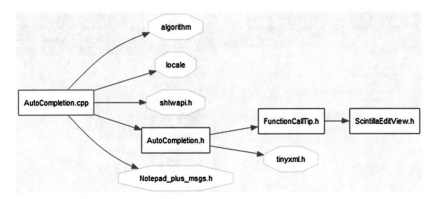

Fig. 5.8 Code dependency view in the understand tool

Fig. 5.9 Code declarations view in the understand tool

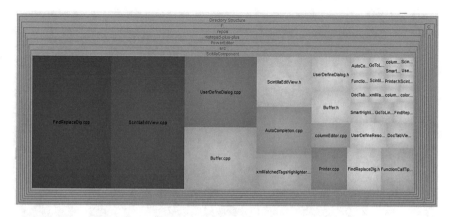

Fig. 5.10 Tree map view in the understand tool

5.4.3 SonarQube: An Integrated Measurement Analytics Tool

Understand C++ is a powerful tool, dedicated to collecting measurement data and exporting it to other systems. However, contemporary software engineers value tools which are even more powerful—integrate multiple source systems (e.g., source code editors and defect tracking database) and provide visualizations and diagrams in addition to the numbers. An example of such a modern, popular measurement tool is SonarQube (http://www.sonarqube.org). This measurement tool contains three major architectural components—data collection scripts (called scanners), measurement database and the visualization components.

The SonarQube tool has a set of measurement instruments defined for such measures as size (LOC), complexity (e.g. McCabe cyclomatic complexity), test coverage (e.g. decision coverage), and defects (e.g. number of defects). The list can also be extended with user-defined plug-ins with measurement instruments. What makes SonarQube so powerful, and popular on the market today, is the architecture of decoupling of the measurement instruments from the data collected. The measurement instruments are applied from a command-line interface or via plug-ins to build tools (e.g. Jenkins, Maven) and are non-invasive. The code is analyzed without the need to augment the code with special commands. Figure 5.11 shows a trace of using a scanner, which is a set of measurement instruments applied to the code of the project visualized in Fig. 5.12.

The scanners take care of all the practical aspects of the measurement method applied, such as:

1. time stamp: time stamp of when the measurement was done,
2. granularity: linking the measures to the measurands,
3. aggregation: aggregating measures to higher levels (e.g. complexity of functions aggregated to files),

```
C:\WINDOWS\system32\cmd.exe                                              —   □   ×

INFO: Java Test Files AST scan
INFO: 0 source files to be analyzed
INFO: Java Test Files AST scan (done) | time=0ms
INFO: Sensor JavaSquidSensor (done) | time=2563ms
INFO: 0/0 source files have been analyzed
INFO: Sensor SCM Sensor
INFO: SCM provider for this project is: git
INFO: 8 files to be analyzed
INFO: 8/8 files analyzed
INFO: Sensor SCM Sensor (done) | time=275ms
INFO: Sensor SurefireSensor
INFO: parsing F:\repos\vroom\target\surefire-reports
INFO: Sensor SurefireSensor (done) | time=1ms
INFO: Sensor JaCoCoSensor
INFO: JaCoCoSensor: JaCoCo report not found : F:\repos\vroom\target\jacoco.exec
INFO: Sensor JaCoCoSensor (done) | time=0ms
INFO: Sensor JaCoCoItSensor
INFO: JaCoCoItSensor: JaCoCo IT report not found: F:\repos\vroom\target\jacoco-it.exec
INFO: Sensor JaCoCoItSensor (done) | time=0ms
INFO: Sensor JaCoCoOverallSensor
INFO: Sensor JaCoCoOverallSensor (done) | time=0ms
INFO: Sensor XmlFileSensor
INFO: Sensor XmlFileSensor (done) | time=1ms
INFO: Sensor Zero Coverage Sensor
INFO: Sensor Zero Coverage Sensor (done) | time=12ms
INFO: Sensor Code Colorizer Sensor
INFO: Sensor Code Colorizer Sensor (done) | time=1ms
INFO: Sensor CPD Block Indexer
INFO: JavaCpdBlockIndexer is used for java
INFO: Sensor CPD Block Indexer (done) | time=37ms
INFO: Calculating CPD for 8 files
INFO: CPD calculation finished
INFO: Analysis report generated in 131ms, dir size=137 KB
INFO: Analysis reports compressed in 26ms, zip size=49 KB
INFO: Analysis report uploaded in 187ms
INFO: ANALYSIS SUCCESSFUL, you can browse http://localhost:9000/dashboard/index/VRoom
INFO: Note that you will be able to access the updated dashboard once the server has processed the submitted analysis re
port
INFO: More about the report processing at http://localhost:9000/api/ce/task?id=AVygQW-oY9qGtjWwuxvo
INFO: Task total time: 4.481 s
INFO: ------------------------------------------------------------------------
INFO: EXECUTION SUCCESS
INFO: ------------------------------------------------------------------------
INFO: Total time: 5.420s
INFO: Final Memory: 53M/584M
INFO: ------------------------------------------------------------------------
```

Fig. 5.11 Example of applying the SonarQube scanner

4. indexing: indexing the right measure to the right project, the right entity, etc., and
5. change management: identifying new and removed entities, measurands and measures.

The result of applying these measurement instruments is stored in the database, which is decoupled from the visualization component. The decoupling allows the measurement designers to use different database engines depending on the set-up of the measurement program, on the need for scalability, security, safety and access control.

The database has a link to the visualization component, which allows to navigate through projects, measures, and granularity. The visualizations can be customized so all stakeholders can have a view which satisfies their specific information needs. Figure 5.12 presents a detailed view of one of the projects. This dashboard contains three elements—the list of projects, a tree map with the size and complexity of a selected project and a bar chart with the complexity.

The detailed view can be customized with multiple widgets and visualizations; however, the main strength of the tools, such as SonarQube, is the ability to combine measures and define thresholds. The combinations of measures can be done either by combining the widgets on the same page or combining the values by adding thresholds. Figure 5.13 presents the dashboard in SonarQube for projects in an example set-up, customized to show the complexity of classes.

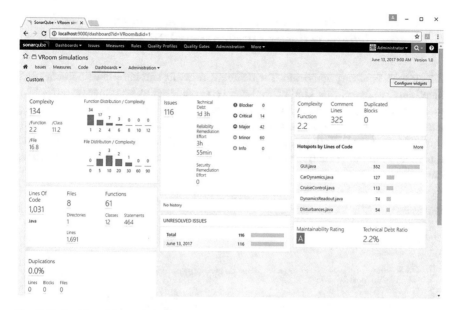

Fig. 5.12 Dashboard for a selected project

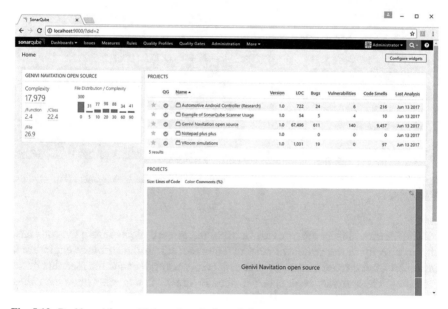

Fig. 5.13 Dashboard for multiple projects in SonarQube

5.4.4 Eclipse Metric Tool: A Measurement Tool Integrated in the Eclipse Software Development IDE

SonarQube is a very good tool for different roles in software development organizations. However, this kind of tool can be considered to be rather reactive. This means that the product code has to be developed, checked into the code repository and then measured. Contemporary software engineers often prefer tools that provide immediate feedback during code development, directly in the software development tools. An example of such a measurement tool is the Metrics plug-in for the Eclipse environment (Fig. 5.14).

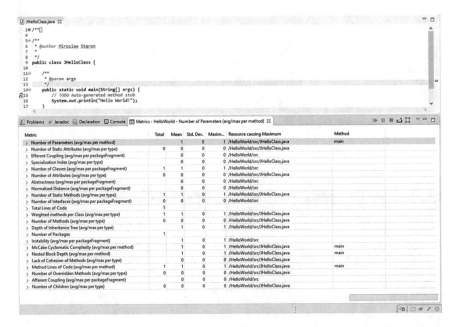

Fig. 5.14 Example of a measurement tool integrated with the software development IDE—Eclipse Metric plug-in

The Metrics plug-in tool provides a list of measures collected from the code base shown directly in the window above it. The feedback to the software engineers is immediate, but it requires that the software engineers understand the meaning of the measures. The software engineers also need to know when to react upon the values (e.g. what value of complexity should trigger their refactoring actions). The Metric plug-in contains also simple visualizations of dependencies, as shown in Fig. 5.15.

Software engineers appreciate the ability to browse their code and the measures at the same time. This co-existence of two views—the code and the measures—shortens the time needed to react upon the value of the measure. This, in con-

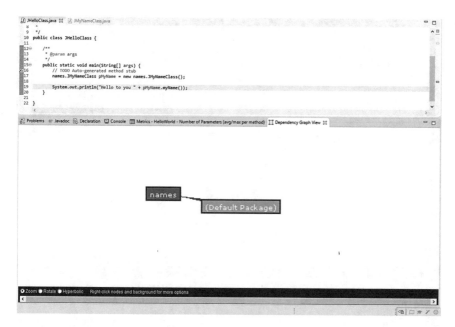

Fig. 5.15 Example of a visualization in an integrated measurement tool

sequence, leads to higher quality of the code and higher quality of the software product.

5.4.5   Microsoft Visual Studio Profiling Tools: Collecting Dynamic Runtime Measures

So far we have presented tools used for collecting data from static properties. However, many software engineers are interested in the performance of their applications, i.e., external quality properties of their products. These software engineers use measurement tools called profilers. Profilers augment the binary code and collect data from the usage of the functions, methods and procedures during their execution. Figure 5.16 shows an example of Microsoft Visual Studio Profiler, which is embedded in the software development IDE, just like the Eclipse Metric Tool.

In Fig. 5.16, we can see the runtime measures of CPU performance in the main screen, and the static code measures (like complexity) in the lower part of the screen.

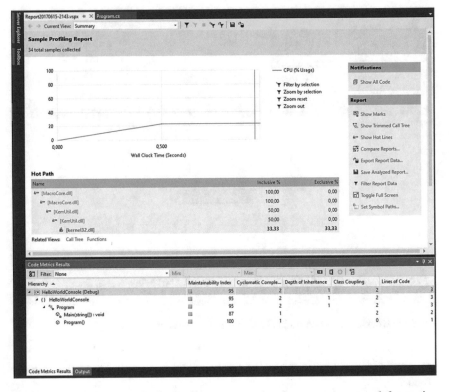

Fig. 5.16 Microsoft Visual Studio Profiler—an example of a measurement tool for runtime properties

5.4.6   Measurement Instruments and Measurement Tools Are Only the Beginning

Measurement instruments and measurement tools are often only the foundations of modern measurement programs. They are very important and without them no measurement program would exist. However, these tools are specialized for the purpose of data collection; thus they need to be complemented with the tools that package the data into information products used in modern measurement programs.

Therefore, let us explore the other types of tools needed for successful measurement program implementation, deployment and sustainable maintenance.

5.5   Tools from the Perspective of a Data Flow

The distinction between the metric tools and measurement instruments provides one classification of tools used in measurement programs. However, both the metric tools and the measurement instruments are first in the chain of tools used. We can organize this tool chain based on the stages of processing data, as presented in [Sta] and in Fig. 5.17.

The front end is naturally the part which is the most visible one, but it is far from being the most important one. Depending on the type of the measurement program, the set-up of the front end can differ significantly. For the measurement programs targeted at reporting, the front end needs to be interactive and support easy-to-use data input (e.g. reporting of time) whereas the visualization part is of less importance. We get back to the types of measurement programs and their visualizations in the next section.

The back-end layer consists of all the components which support the visualization—data sources, files storing the metrics/indicators, scripts making predictions and similar components. These components are necessary to store the data acquired from source systems, allowing us to analyze the data and prepare for its visualization.

The data acquisition layer is a set of scripts and programs used to collect the data from source systems. It could be metrics tools, measurement instruments, static analysis tools, scripts for mining data repositories and similar components. The responsibility of this layer is to harvest the data from the source systems (e.g. a source code repository) and place that data in the form of metric values in the storage of the back end of the dashboard.

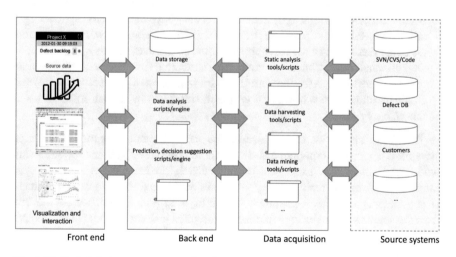

Fig. 5.17   Tool chain in a measurement data flow

Finally, the components which are "outside" of the measurement program, but are crucial for it (hence delineated using the dashed line), are the source systems. These systems are part of the normal operations of the company from which data can be acquired. Examples of such systems are source code repositories, defect databases, or integration engines (e.g. Jenkins).

5.6   Source Systems and Databases

The measurement instruments and the measurement tools quantify properties into numbers, which is great as long as the information to quantify is available in an electronic form. This means that the measurement instruments can access a specific electronic resource, execute the measurement algorithm and provide the number to the measurement stakeholder.

Example tools used in contemporary companies, which integrate easily with the measurement instruments and measurement tools:

- Software build tools, which are tools for automatically building software binaries from source code; Jenkins (http://jenkins.io) is an example of these tools.
- Requirement tools, which are tools for structured management of software requirements and variants; IBM Rational Reqpro and IBM Rational Doors (http://www-03.ibm.com/software/products/en/ratidoor) are two examples of such tools.
- SW development tools, which are tools for organizing the process of programming, building, debugging and testing of software; Eclipse (http://www.eclipse.org) and MS Visual Studio (http://www.visualstudio.com) are the two most popular software environments in this category.
- SW repositories, which are tools for organizing collaborative software development activities, in particular parallel programming and integration of source code; Git (https://git-scm.com/), SVN (https://subversion.apache.org/), and IBM Rational ClearCase (http://www-03.ibm.com/software/products/en/clearcase) are some of the most popular tools on the market today.
- Defect databases, which are tools for structured management of problem reports in software; Atlassian Jira (https://www.atlassian.com/software/jira) and BugZilla (https://www.bugzilla.org/) are the most common open source tools in this category.

The above categories of tools cover the most common categories of source systems. They can be complemented with more proprietary systems for collecting field data from product usage, customer feedback, financial status and employee satisfaction. The main feature of any source system is the ability to access the data in an automated, programmatic manner. This ability is important when we use the data from the source systems as input to the measurement instruments (and measurement tools).

5.6.1   Software Build Tools: Jenkins

Jenkins is one of the most popular software integration tools on the market today. It is a tool that allows us to automate all kinds of tasks related to software builds. Thanks to its modular architecture, it can be extended to build software in any programming language and integrate with static analysis tools, measurement tools, measurement instruments, testing tools and reporting dashboards. Its scheduling capabilities allow the designers to build software periodically and event-based, when a new source code commit is done.

Figure 5.18 shows an example of the main dashboard for the tool. This dashboard contains a list of two projects built using our set-up of Jenkins. The cloudy icon next to each of the projects shows a graphical representation of the status of our latest builds—in this case, one of two builds failed and therefore the status is "unstable" or cloudy.

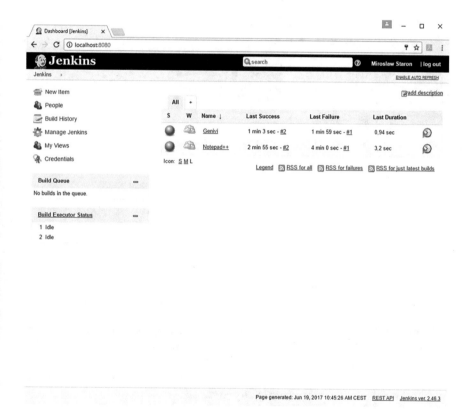

Fig. 5.18 A web interface of Jenkins continuous integration tool

The dashboard provides the overview, but the most interesting information for software designers is found in the detailed view of each project. An example of such a detailed view is shown in Fig. 5.19.

The information about the project is important and crucial for the configuration managers, but it is too verbose to use as input data for measurement for the measurement designers. Therefore, we can use a dedicated format for the output data from the integration, a JSON string. Using the JSON string provides the

Fig. 5.19 Status report of one project from Jenkins

possibility to access the information automatically and to process it by measurement instruments and measurement tools. Figure 5.20 shows an example of a JSON string for all projects. The address field in the browser, in Fig. 5.20, shows that this information is available by accessing a specific URL—in our case it is http://localhost:8080/job/Genivi/api/json?pretty=true.

Jenkins provides the possibility to access its internal database in JSON, XML and HTML formats. This variability provides the measurement designers with the flexibility of integrating Jenkins with multiple measurement systems. The challenge, however, is indexing information across different systems.

5.6.2   Requirement Tools: IBM Rational Doors

Jenkins is a very popular software tool for building software products—triggering updates from the code repositories, controlling compilers and linkers, as well as triggering various measurement instruments and tools. However, modern measurement

```
{
    "_class" : "hudson.model.FreeStyleProject",
    "actions" : [
        {
        },
        {
        },
        {
            "_class" : "com.cloudbees.plugins.credentials.ViewCredentialsAction"
        }
    ],
    "description" : "",
    "displayName" : "Genivi",
    "displayNameOrNull" : null,
    "fullDisplayName" : "Genivi",
    "fullName" : "Genivi",
    "name" : "Genivi",
    "url" : "http://localhost:8080/job/Genivi/",
    "buildable" : true,
    "builds" : [
        {
            "_class" : "hudson.model.FreeStyleBuild",
            "number" : 2,
            "url" : "http://localhost:8080/job/Genivi/2/"
        },
        {
            "_class" : "hudson.model.FreeStyleBuild",
            "number" : 1,
            "url" : "http://localhost:8080/job/Genivi/1/"
        }
    ],
    "color" : "blue",
    "firstBuild" : {
        "_class" : "hudson.model.FreeStyleBuild",
        "number" : 1,
        "url" : "http://localhost:8080/job/Genivi/1/"
    },
    "healthReport" : [
        {
            "description" : "Build stability: 1 out of the last 2 builds failed.",
            "iconClassName" : "icon-health-40to59",
            "iconUrl" : "health-40to59.png",
            "score" : 50
        }
    ],
    "inQueue" : false,
    "keepDependencies" : false,
    "lastBuild" : {
        "_class" : "hudson.model.FreeStyleBuild",
        "number" : 2,
```

Fig. 5.20 Status report of all projects from Jenkins as a JSON string

programs are focused on collecting the data from the software products themselves. One of the tools with the product data is a requirement management database. The database stores and version-controls requirements of software products. Its primary role is to organize requirements into releases, link them to specific product subsystems and link them to the test cases. IBM Rational Doors is one of the modern requirement management tools, shown in Fig. 5.21.

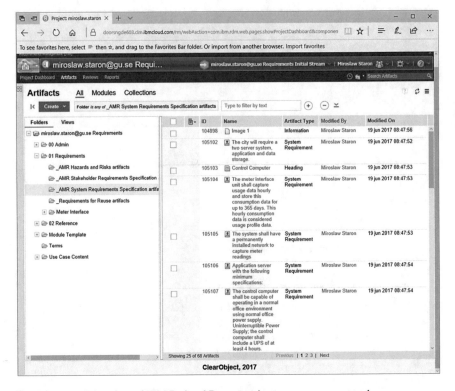

Fig. 5.21 A web interface of IBM Rational Doors requirement management tool

Requirement management tools provide a good way of working with requirements for business analysts, and they provide possibilities to extract data about these requirements for the measurement designers. The measurement designers are often interested in such data about the requirements as the status of a requirement, the status of the development of the requirement, the status of the testing of each requirement or the status of all requirements per subsystem, per component or for the entire product.

5.6.3 Software Repositories

Another example of a modern product development tool, used in the design of measurement programs, is the source code repository. The source code repositories are databases of all versions of the source code of the software product. These databases are specialized towards the most common tasks performed by software designers—parallel development of source code, merging different versions of the same code base, resolving conflicts cause by parallel development of the same source code module and baselining the software for release.

An example of an open source set-up of the Git repository is the github.com website, which hosts software development projects for the open source community. An example visual representation is shown in Fig. 5.22. The visual interface is important for the overview of the source code and its status. However, the main advantage of the source code repositories, from the perspective of the measurement designers', is the ability to use a command line interface to access the information.

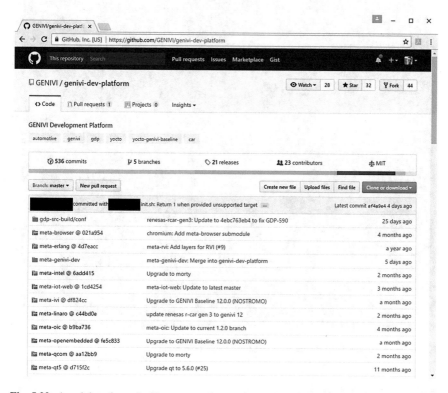

Fig. 5.22 A web interface of a Git source code repository—http://github.com

The command line interface provides the possibility to integrate with other software tools in the pipes-and-filters architectural style [Sta17]. This integration can be done either using a command line interface or using modern web techniques such as JSON queries. A screenshot of a Git command for printing out the information about committers and files is presented in Fig. 5.23.

Figure 5.23 shows the revision history of all files in the repository shown in Fig. 5.22. Such a full revision history is useful when designing measures for the progress of the development of software. The wide variety of formatting options provides an almost unlimited number of ways to get information out of a Git source code repository. It is also one of the reasons for why it is so popular in contemporary companies.

Fig. 5.23 An example of command line interface to a Git repository

5.6.4 Defect Databases

The last type of tool described in this book is the defect management database, also known as the defect database. The defect databases contain the information about all known defects, failures, faults and errors in the product. They are filled with this information by testers, designers and customer support engineers. The defect information is useful, primarily, for software designers, who need to fix the known defects. Secondarily, the information is also very important for the project managers and quality managers who can estimate the time needed to finalize the product. The information about the known defects are often used together with the test progress, the requirements implementation progress and the code volume information. Together, these data sources provide the necessary data to understand the quality of the product under development.

An example of a commonly used tool for defect management is the Bugzilla open source tool, presented in Fig. 5.24. The figure shows the web interface to the defect database, which is similar to the web interface of a requirement management tool.

ID	Product	Comp	Assignee ▲	Status ▲	Resolution	Summary	Changed
1372448	Toolkit	Add-ons Manager	aswan	UNCO	---	No new installation notification for sideload add-ons on <appid> directory	Wed 12:01
415529	Bugzilla	Documentation	documentation	UNCO	---	Successfull installation of bugzilla 3.0.2 on w/ lighttpd	2015-05-29
1072066	Bugzilla	Documentation	documentation	UNCO	---	installation guide is incorrect/incomplete for PostgreSQL	2015-04-09
1196879	Bugzilla	Documentation	documentation	UNCO	---	Installation instructions about running a2ensite require renaming bugzilla.conf file	2015-08-20
1271907	Bugzilla	Documentation	documentation	UNCO	---	Docs about installing full perl dependents missing "."	2017-05-20
815749	Air Mozilla	Krad Radio	drichards	UNCO	---	[krad] change build system to install client-library (.so) and headers for it	2012-11-28
368620	Core	Security	dveditz	UNCO	---	Installing a signed XPI with OCSP enabled causes "internal failure" error	2010-08-17
1187655	Bugzilla	Bugzilla-General	general	UNCO	---	Install instructions on Debian for Bugzilla 5 inaccurate	2017-07-25
1345926	Bugzilla	Bugzilla-General	general	UNCO	---	Provide a more informative error message when cpanm is not installed	2017-03-20
557555	Testopia	General	gregaryh	UNCO	---	determine which version of testopia i have installed (from cvs)	2010-04-06
632135	Testopia	General	gregaryh	UNCO	---	Testopia installation fails	2015-09-01
685205	Testopia	Environments	gregaryh	UNCO	---	"Menu.html" replaced by "menu.html" when installing in Windows	2013-12-05
1186616	Firefox OS	General	hobinjk	UNCO	---	B2G Installer Addon: Fix workflow issues	2015-07-27
1186620	Firefox OS	General	hobinjk	UNCO	---	B2G Installer Addon: Improve handling of Fastboot mode	2015-11-06
1285793	Firefox OS	B2gInstaller	l.hoerler	UNCO	---	add Fairphone 2 update for B2G-installer	2016-08-24
469734	Bugzilla	Installation & Upgra	installation	UNCO	---	Process .po files from templates to allow multiple $terms	2008-12-25
625781	Bugzilla	Installation & Upgra	installation	UNCO	---	Sending email with SMTP Auth fails due to missing Auth::SASL dependencies	2017-05-16
629975	Bugzilla	Installation & Upgra	installation	UNCO	---	mkdir from checksetup.pl fails due to missing data directory	2014-07-09
702935	Bugzilla	Installation & Upgra	installation	UNCO	---	[Oracle] checksetup.pl fails with ORA-01722	2011-11-16
862070	Bugzilla	Installation & Upgra	installation	UNCO	---	PG schema upgrade failed with single PG DB and multiple bugzilla SCHEMAS from bugzilla-4.0.11 to 4.2.7	2013-12-21
987598	Bugzilla	Installation & Upgra	installation	UNCO	---	An error (errno: 150) is thrown by MySQL when updating bugs_activity.comment_id column type (upgrading BZ from 4.2.1 to the 4.4.2)	2015-09-23
1082538	Bugzilla	Installation & Upgra	installation	UNCO	---	Do not delete old compiled templates till checksetup.pl compiled the new ones	2014-10-14
1222722	Bugzilla	Installation & Upgra	installation	UNCO	---	_missing_apache_modules in Bugzilla::Install::Requirements.pm does not quote path to httpd resulting in not checking for missing modules	2015-11-07
1336450	Bugzilla	Installation & Upgra	installation	UNCO	---	Bugzilla fresh installation fails: Cannot add or update a child row	2017-02-21
830032	SeaMonkey	Installer	installer	UNCO	---	updater: UAC doorhanger tells "publisher is unknown for updater.exe"	2015-08-13
1215786	SeaMonkey	Installer	installer	UNCO	---	Installation into existing empty user defined folder fails with error message	2016-01-01
1330221	SeaMonkey	Installer	installer	UNCO	---	layers.offmainthreadcomposition.enabled in not upgraded from seamonkey 2.40 to seamonkey 2.46	2017-01-10
935669	Tech Evangelism	Add-ons	jorge	UNCO	---	Addon removal triggered by another addon installation	2013-11-10
595466	Penelope	Installer	mdudziak	UNCO	---	Default email program name "Eudora" conflicts with classic "Eudora"	2013-01-04

Fig. 5.24   An example of defect database—Bugzilla at http://bugzilla.mozilla.org

In Fig. 5.24 we can see a list of defects reported for one product and their status. The tabular form of the report, together with the filtering functions, provides a good starting point to see problems to be fixed in the product before the final release.

The real advantage of the defect management tools, however, is the ability to export the information about defects in a format that can be used in the measurement program. Similarly to the build tools like Jenkins, the modern defect management tools provide the ability to export the data using JSON. Figure 5.25 shows the JSON string with the whole information about one defect in the database.

The information, presented in Fig. 5.25, includes the information about the failure, which was caused by the defect, and the history of what has been done in order to diagnose the cause of the failure (i.e. finding the defect) in order to fix the defect. It is common to set up the defect management databases to follow established standards in describing defects, such as Orthogonal Defect Classification [BA06] or Lightweight Defect Classification (LiDEC) [MST12].

Fig. 5.25 An example of result from using the REST API to get JSON string for a single defect report—Bugzilla at http://bugzilla.mozilla.org

For the designers of measurement systems, however, the most interesting information is the status of all defects for a particular product. This information can also
be extracted using the JSON string. The REST API allows us to export data about
all defects for one product as one long JSON string, which is shown in Fig. 5.26.

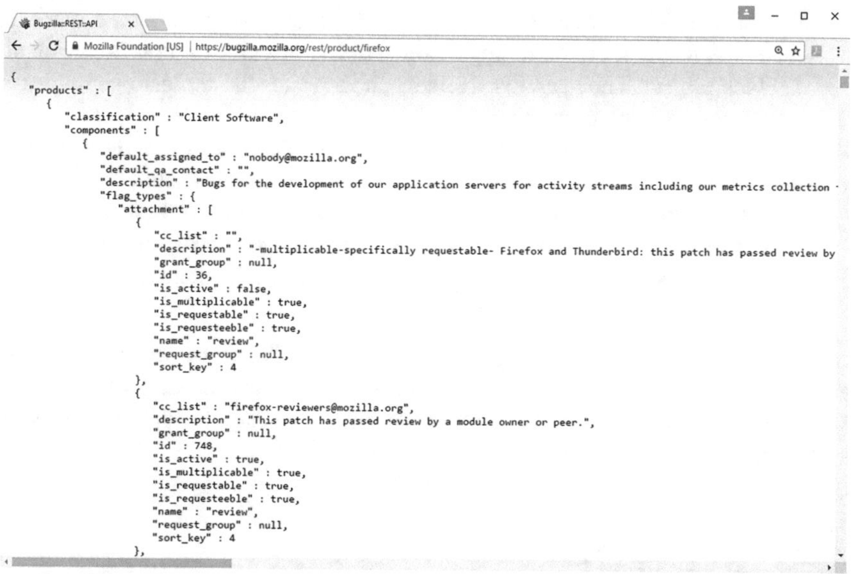

Fig. 5.26 An example of result from using the REST API to get JSON string for defects from the
same product—Bugzilla at http://bugzilla.mozilla.org

The JSON string with all defects, shown in Fig. 5.26, can be parsed to create
statistics of all found, open, and closed defects. It can also be parsed using natural
language techniques to find dependencies between defects and find the underlying
root causes [RAN07].

5.7   Data Aquisition

Data acquisition tools are a synonym for the measurement tools and measurement
instruments, which we have already described.

The important part of the acquisition of the measurement data is the ability to
store it in a flexible way. The data can be stored in the form of comma separated
files or MS Excel files or as part of measurement databases (as prescribed by the
ISO/IEC 15939 standard).

From our experiences, we could see that the databases for measurement data can be structured in two different ways:

1. Purpose-specific: each table in the database is defined based on the definition of the measure. In such a database, a measure for logical LOC would have one table for one product, another table for another product and another table for physical LOC for the first product, and so on. The main advantage of such a database structure is its ability to quickly get orientation of which measures are available for which project. The main disadvantage, however, is the explosion of tables as the measurement program grows.
2. Generic: tables in the database are organized into definitions and measurement data. In such a database, a measure for logical LOC would be stored in the same table as that for the physical LOC; each data point would have a reference to which measure is collected (a link to the definition). The main advantage is the simplicity of the structure and its flexibility. However, the main disadvantage is the large size of the table with the measurement data.

We recommend the second approach to structuring the measurement databases, as it provides a uniform way of treating all measurement data and supports a uniform way of controlling information quality (as described in Chap. 3). Figure 5.27 shows a schema for such a flexible database structure.

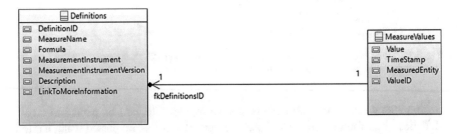

Fig. 5.27 Database schema for the generic measurement database

Figure 5.27 shows two tables—one with the definitions of measures (on the left-hand side of the figure) and one with the measurement data (on the right-hand side of the figure). These two tables are related using a foreign key, fkDefinitionID, which links each measurement data point to a specific measure. The link to the measurand is the attribute MeasuredEntity in the measurement data table.

Using such a flexible database schema provides a good, uniform guide to the next step in data processing—back end and statistical tools.

5.8   Back End and Statistical Tools

Once the data is acquired from the source systems and stored in databases or files, it needs to be processed to calculate derived measures, indicators and statistics. The results of these calculations need to be visualized. In modern measurement programs, the measurement designers use statistical tools for these purposes.

One of the most widely used statistical tools of today is R (www.r-project.org), shown in Fig. 5.28. R is an open source tool for statistical analyses of all kinds of data. At the time of writing of this book, it is a de facto standard as it is supported by a large community of developers, who constantly extend the tool with new packages.

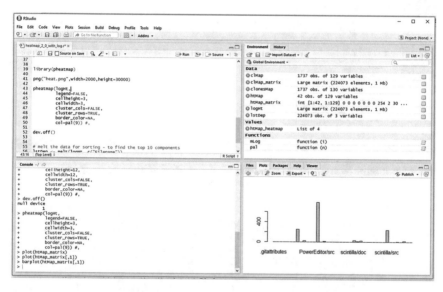

Fig. 5.28 Screenshot of RStudio

The strength of the tool is in the fact that it can be used in a user interface mode and in a command line mode. For the design of the measurement program, the measurement designers can use the user interface to develop analyses and once the analyses are finished, the measurement designers can deploy these analyses as R scripts.

Figure 5.29 presents such a script in the R Studio design environment. The script reads the revision history of Notepad++ (line 11), formats it (lines 14–24) and visualizes it as a heatmap (lines 33–40) [FSHL13, SHF+13].

The data used for the visualization is shown in Fig. 5.30. The data is in the form of a table with names of source code modules as rows and dates as columns. The numbers in the cells are the number of times each source code module was changed during the week starting with the date in the column heading.

```
 1  # define a function to create a logarithm of the revisions
 2▾ mLog <- function(i){
 3    if (is.na(i)) return (0)
 4▾   else    {
 5      if (i > 0) return (log(i))
 6      else return (0)
 7    } }
 8  |
 9  # read in the source file as the matrix
10  # the check.names line takes care of the x before the date
11  clonesMap<-read.csv("F:/repos/heat_powereditor_week.csv", head=TRUE, sep=";", check.names=FALSE)
12
13  # names of rows are the file names
14  row.names(clMap) <- clMap[,1]
15
16  # delete the module name from the data set, the previous line
17  # made it part of the row name instead
18  clMap[,1] <- NULL
19
20  # convert the data to matrix
21  clMap_matrix <- data.matrix(clMap)
22
23  # apply the logarithmic scale to emphasize smaller changes
24  logHt <- apply(clMap_matrix, 1:2, mLog)
25
26  # prepare the palette with scale from grey to red
27  pal <- colorRampPalette(c("white", "red"))
28
29  # read the library with the pheatmap function
30  library(pheatmap)
31
32  # draw the heatmap
33  pheatmap(logHt,
34           legend=FALSE,
35           cellheight=9,
36           cellwidth=9,
37           cluster_cols=FALSE,
38           cluster_rows=TRUE,
39           border_color=NA,
40           col=pal(9))
41
8:1    (Top Level) ≑                                                                              R Script ≑
```

Fig. 5.29 R script example—a script to visualize the revision history of Notepad++

	2017-01-01	2017-01-08	2017-01-15	2017-01-22	2017-01-29	2017-02-05	2017-02-12	2017-02-19	2017-02-26	2017-03-05	2017-03-12	2017-03-19	2017-03-26	2017-04-02
/PowerEditor/bin	2	0	0	2	0	0	0	2	0	0	2	0	0	0
/PowerEditor/gcc	0	0	0	0	0	0	0	0	0	0	0	0	0	0
/PowerEditor/installer	8	0	6	28	0	10	26	16	8	16	4	0	6	0
/PowerEditor/license.txt	0	0	0	0	0	0	0	0	0	0	0	0	0	0
/PowerEditor/misc	0	0	0	0	0	0	0	0	0	0	0	0	0	0
/PowerEditor/scintilla.original.forUpdating	0	0	0	0	0	0	0	0	0	0	0	0	0	0
/PowerEditor/src	34	10	34	88	6	32	42	44	62	18	24	34	30	0
/PowerEditor/Test	0	0	0	0	0	0	0	0	2	0	0	0	0	0
/PowerEditor/visual.net	2	2	4	4	0	0	0	0	0	0	4	0	0	0

Fig. 5.30 Revision history of Notepad++

The tabular presentation is taken directly from the measurement instrument that parses the Git log file history, but it is not very readable on its own. The visualization of this data as a heatmap shows which of the source code modules are more commonly changed than others, which is shown in Fig. 5.31.

The heatmap is clustered so that the components which are changed often are grouped together in the top of the diagram. We can directly see the advantage of using a diagram instead of the tabular presentation of the data. The results can be saved as a file (both the tabular and graphical).

Once the measurement designer is satisfied with the analysis, he/she can save it as an R Script and use it from the command line interface by using the program

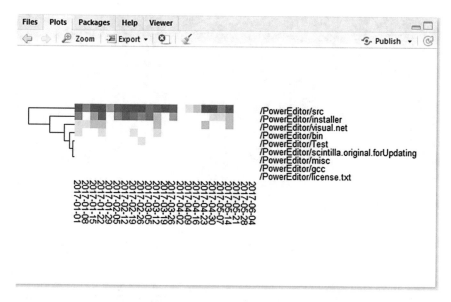

Fig. 5.31 Revision history of Notepad++ visualized as a heatmap

RScript.exe. Once again, using the command line interface allows the measurement designers to use R as part of a data flow pipes-and-filters architecture.

5.9 Front End and Business Intelligence

Business intelligence tools can be very simple and very advanced, depending on their purpose. We start our description of the business intelligence tools with a very simple, dedicated tool for drill-down into software commits. One example of a simple analytics framework is the CommitGuru tool, shown in Fig. 5.32.

The CommitGuru tool provides a dedicated set of built-in measurement instruments for analyzing software builds at the level of the entire product, and its subsystems, components and files.

A fully-fledged business intelligence tool is QlikView as shown in Fig. 5.33. The example shows two diagrams on the right-hand side of the figure and several filtering possibilities on the left-hand side of the figure.

A more useful view is the ability to visualize data exported from source code repositories, as shown in Fig. 5.34.

At first glance, the tool does not differ much from standard visualization tools like MS Excel. However, the strength of this tool lies in its ability to filter, process and visualize the data. Figure 5.35 shows the option for dimensioning the data in the diagram.

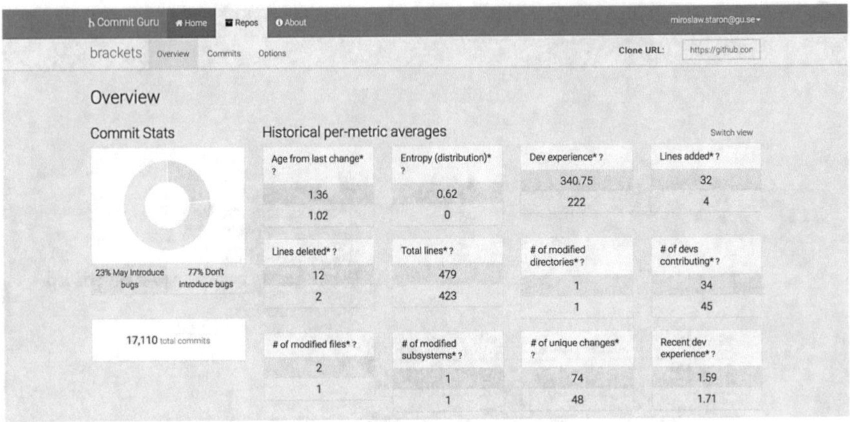

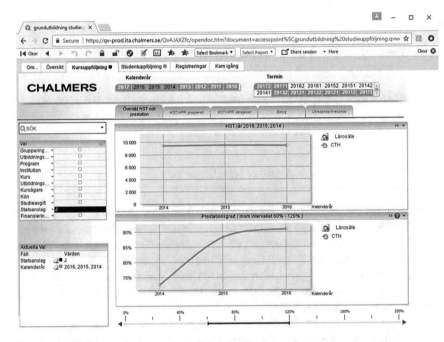

Fig. 5.32 CommitGuru—an example of a dedicated software repository analytics tool

Fig. 5.33 QlikView—an example of a business intelligence tool

These dimensions allow the measurement designers to visualize the right aspects of the underlying data, which complements the large number of built-in views of business intelligence tools. An example of such a complement is the transformation of the data, done directly in the tool. Figure 5.36 shows a dialog box specifying the transformation on the right-hand side, where the actual transformation is the code

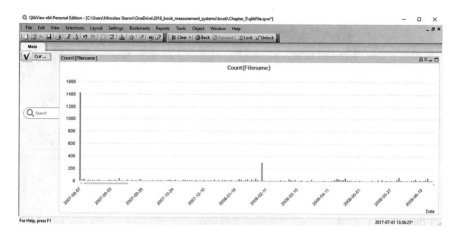

Fig. 5.34 QlikView—an example of a business intelligence tool visualizing the number of revisions per file; data from the github repository of Notepad++

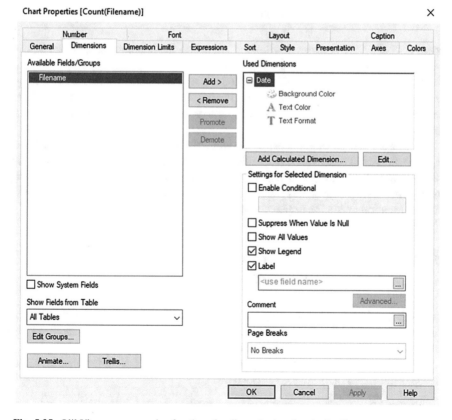

Fig. 5.35 QlikView—an example of options for dimensioning data in the diagram

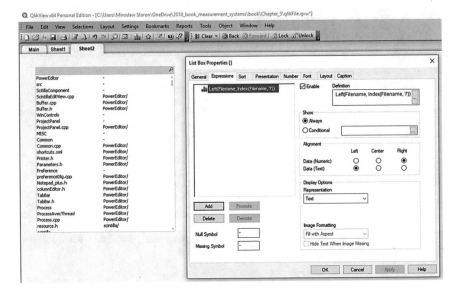

Fig. 5.36 QlikView—an example of data transformation

snippet "Left(...)," and the new field is shown on the left-hand side of the figure, showing the main folder for each filename.

The transformations, available in modern business analysis tools, are a good complement to the measurement instruments. When drilling-down into the data, stakeholders can define new fields without the need to alter the measurement instruments and their code.

Business intelligence tools provide a wide variety of instruments and options to work with data. These business intelligence tools are dedicated for data scientists who want to find patterns in the data and to identify new knowledge. However, many measurement designers require a static set-up of the visualization, to spread the information inside the organization—a dashboard.

5.10   Front End: Dashboards—A Popular Way of Visualizing Indicators in Measurement Programs

A dashboard is defined as an easy-to-read real-time user interface, showing graphical presentation of the current status (snapshot) and historical trends of an organization's Key Performance Indicators to enable decisions.

Dashboards can be used for multiple purposes and their design, technology and scope differ based on these usage scenarios:

1. Information radiators—dashboards designed to spread information about the status to large audiences, often designed as information screens placed in central places for projects, teams, or groups.

2. Management dashboards—dashboards designed to provide information to the managers on the status of the project and the underlying parameters of the status, often designed as desktop reports with the possibility to drill down in the data.
3. Business intelligence dashboards—dashboards designed to support product managers in accessing, visualizing and analyzing the data related to product development and its surrounding market, often designed as a desktop application with a potential for web-based access to reports.
4. Hybrid dashboards—dashboards combining two or three of the above usage scenarios.

A typical dashboard contains three elements:

- Heading explaining the content of the dashboard and its purpose
- Diagram visualizing the metrics
- Short explanation of the status and information in the diagram

These three elements are necessary to help the readers to understand the information about the dashboard. As dashboards come in many different shapes and forms and address a wide variety of purposes, the readers must be guided to get the right knowledge from the information presented in the dashboard.

In designing the pages of the dashboard, the principles of cognitive perception abilities should be taken into account, such as:

1. Elements of the dashboard should be logically and conceptually related to each other
2. The number of elements in the dashboard (diagrams, text fields, explanations, buttons) should be no more than 7 (+2 if necessary), as this is the number of elements an average person can keep in the short-term memory.
3. The use of colors should be limited to the minimum and the colors should extrapolate the information in diagrams and the important information in the dashboard.

An example of a dashboard is presented in Fig. 5.43, which presents a set of metrics for architecture of a software product.

5.10.1   Examples of Charts Used in Dashboards

Visualizations, diagrams and charts are very popular in modern dashboards. Besides the standard charts like the bar chart, boxplot or histogram, we can use more advanced visualizations to make our dashboards visually more appealing.

An example of a diagram which is often used in visualizations is a scatter plot, as shown in Fig. 5.37. The diagram is used to explore dependencies between two variables. In Fig. 5.37, we visualize the dependency between the lines of code and number of methods of one version of Eclipse projects. The data set is available openly from http://bug.inf.usi.ch/index.php.

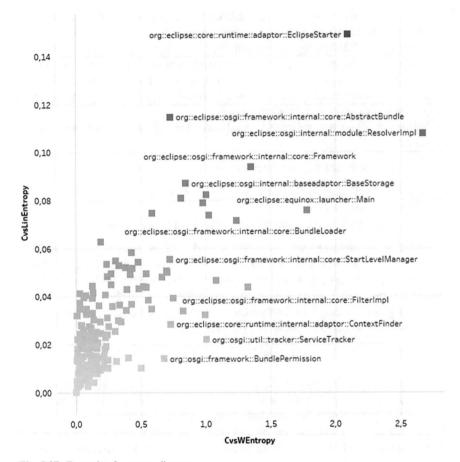

Fig. 5.37 Example of a scatter diagram

In the scatter plot we can see how two variables are dependent on one another. However, modern dashboards explore more than two variables, which means that we need to use more advanced types of scatter plots. For example, Fig. 5.38 presents the dependency between three variables.

Although 3D visualizations are interesting and provide the possibility to nicely interact by zooming in or rotating the diagrams along their axes, they cannot visualize dependencies between more than three variables. For that, we need another type of chart—correlogram. A correlogram consists of a number of scatter plots, which visualize dependencies between multiple variables pairwise. Figure 5.39 provides such a visualization.

Correlograms provide us with the possibility to capture collinearity between variables and therefore reduce the number of measures. It allows us also to observe deviations from the expected trend in collinearity.

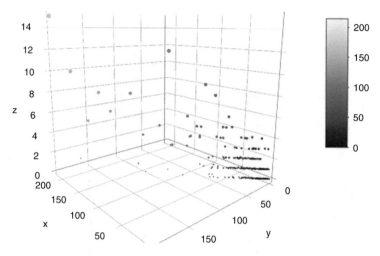

Fig. 5.38 Example of a 3D scatter plot

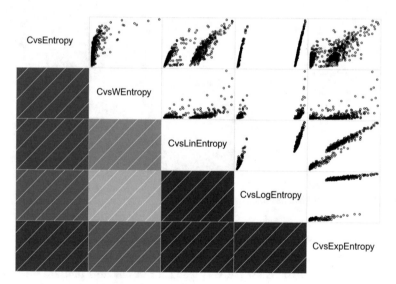

Fig. 5.39 Example of a correlogram

Now, many of the modern dashboards contain diagrams that show different types of size. Bubble charts are one of the examples of these diagrams. In Fig. 5.40, we present the visualization of the size of each Eclipse class used in the previous scatter plot.

The size of the bubble corresponds to the size of the class, which is one of several variants of the bubble chart. Other variants include the visualization of dependencies using the size or visualization of complexity. The varying color of each bubble is the number of methods (just like in our previous scatter plot). Bubble charts have

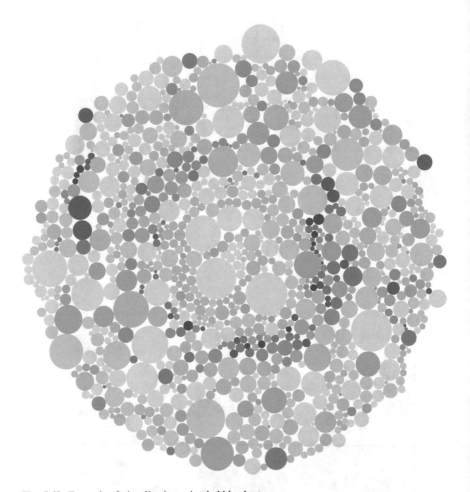

Fig. 5.40 Example of visualization using bubble charts

a tendency to draw attention to the largest bubbles with the most intensive color, which corresponds to the largest, most complex classes (in our example).

Charts like the bubble chart are very good for dashboards that are interactive. However, for the dashboards designed for hallways, lecture rooms or landscapes, bubble charts are not perfect. For such dashboards, interactive charts make little sense as the information needs to be much clearer and less interactive.

An example of a chart which is useful in this context is the KPI chart, which is shown in Fig. 5.41. The KPI chart presents a set of indicators, as specified according to ISO/IEC 15939, with the coloring and timeliness information (when the data was collected) [PSSM10a, Sta].

The KPI chart provides an overview, or a "temperature," of the measured entity. In Fig. 5.41, this is the temperature of a continuous integration flow [KSM+15,

Fig. 5.41 Example of a KPI chart from Tibco Spotfire tool

HF10]. The KPI chart is often combined with other types of charts to provide a more detailed and comprehensive view of the measured entity, as presented in Fig. 5.42.

Many of the modern visualizations intend to stimulate discussions about dependencies between elements of software construction. One of the charts used for the purpose is the circular chart, illustrated in Fig. 5.43. The example shows how components C1–C10 depend on one another, inspired by our experiences with visualization of architectural dependencies [SMHH13] and [Sta17].

Visualizing these dependencies provides architects with the possibility to reason about the quality of the system under construction. We can complement circular diagrams with dendrograms to show more details about the strength of the dependencies between components. Figure 5.44 presents a dendrogram showing the clusters of components from Eclipse.

Dendrograms come from statistics, where they are used to show clusters in data sets. However, they are used increasingly often in software development, having their renaissance. Many of the modern dashboards use treemaps to show clustering and showing three or four measures in the same diagram. Figure 5.45 presents such a treemap visualizing the size (size of the box) and complexity (color) of software components in the Eclipse project.

Treemaps are often effective for triggering technical discussions. They are also interesting for interactive dashboards as they can be hierarchical—i.e. clicking on one of the boxes opens up a new treemap with information about the subcomponents of the chosen component.

We finish the discussion about the visualizations with a diagram that is slightly different from the rest—a wordcloud. The diagram, exemplified by Fig. 5.46, shows the frequency of words used in a text. In the figure, we visualize the frequency of words in abstracts of some of the papers written by us. However, in practice, many companies use this to visualize the frequency of words used in requirements or defect descriptions.

Visualizing the frequency of words in defect descriptions triggers the discussion about the perception of "what is wrong in our system." It is a good way to present information in common, non-interactive dashboards in landscapes or information screen by the coffee rooms.

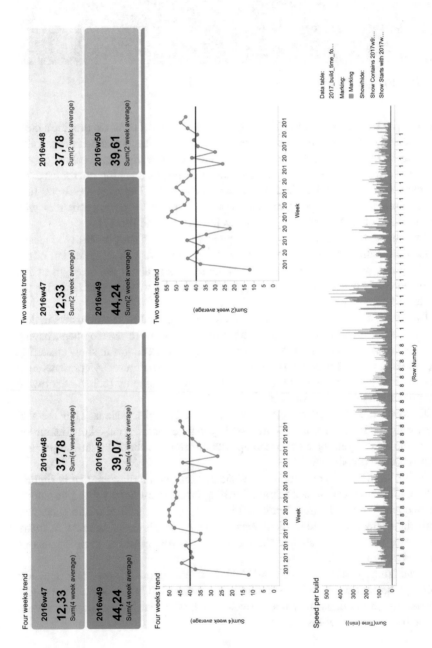

Fig. 5.42 Example of a KPI chart used in a dashboard

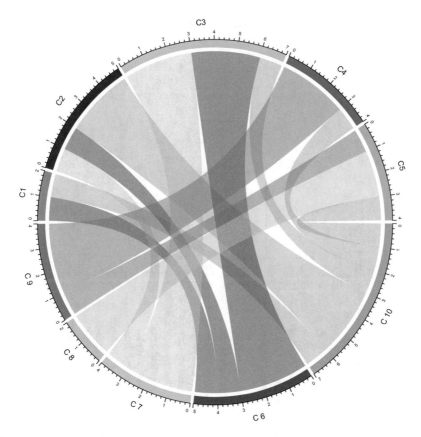

Fig. 5.43 Example of a circular diagram

5.11 Open Data Sources

Today, in addition to the source systems and statistical systems, we can access open data sources such as the PROMISE database at http://promise.site.uottawa. ca/SERepository. The database has started as a research initiative to provide data sets published at conferences to the scientific community. Today, the scientific community recognizes the importance of data from studies being openly available. This openness stimulates transparency and triangulation of data analyses. It also contributes to the prevention of breaking ethical principles of research.

Today, there is a growing number of open data sources, and below we can list some of them:

- Promise database, http://promise.site.uottawa.se/SERepository: contains data sets about external and internal quality of software products, e.g., number of defects, number of components.
- Lindholmen data set of open source UML models, http://oss.models-db.com/: contains data about the size and complexity of UML models, [HQC+16].

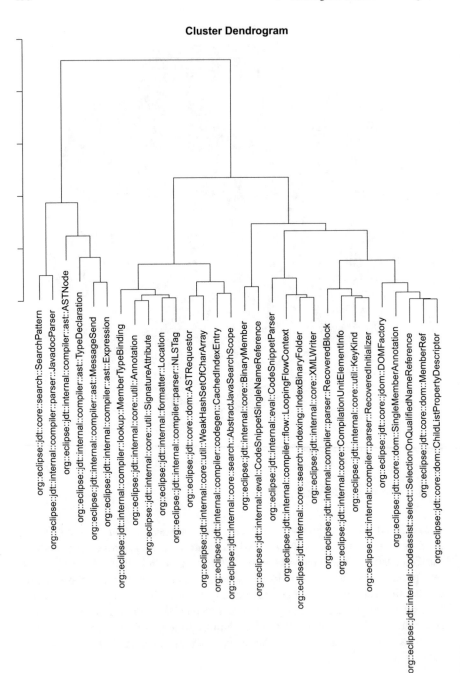

Fig. 5.44 Example of a dendrogram

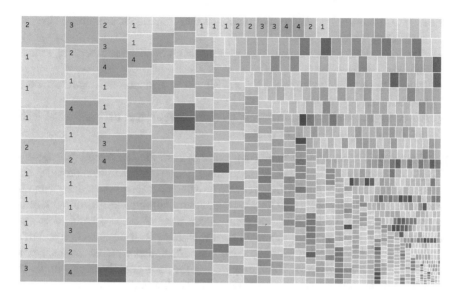

Fig. 5.45 Example of a treemap

Fig. 5.46 Example of a wordcloud

- ISBSG database, http://isbsg.org: contains data sets about functional size and project properties.
- Mandeley data, https://data.mendeley.com/: contains data sets used in articles published by Elsevier.
- OpenData.se, http://opendata.se: Swedish national data sets about software, weather, and city traffic.
- EU open data portal https://data.europa.eu/euodp/en/data/: EU data portal without limitations on the type of data sets.

The open data sets are important for the designers of the measurement programs. They can use these data sets to benchmark their organizations, projects and products. For example, the ISBSG data sets provide the measurement designers and stakeholders with the ability to access productivity and typical functional size of software similar to theirs. The stakeholders can use this data to build their own understanding about the organizational performance of their organization and thus make more informed decisions. The measurement designers can find more accurate thresholds for the indicators which they design for their organizations, simply by exploring which indicator values are common in similar organizations.

5.12   Summary

Tooling in software measurement is one of the cornerstones of success. In Chap. 3 we discussed its placement in the measurement program and in this chapter we overviewed some of the most interesting tools used in contemporary companies.

Software development has evolved from long-term projects and manual development to a field where automation and integration are of top importance. We integrate our tools to reduce the need for manual handover between activities. We integrate our products in order to increase the speed of software development. This integration is also an important trend in software measurement. Manual reporting belongs to the past and management demands insights by exploring the databases used in product development directly.

This chapter provides guidance on how to integrate systems for the purpose of measurement. It also showed how the measurement can be done without the need to manually report data, by showing how to extract the data from the source software development systems.

5.13   Further Reading

In our previous work we have created an online resource for the creators of the dashboards in software engineering [Sta16]. The movie complements the dashboard selection guide presented in this chapter with even more examples, focused specifically on automotive software engineering.

In this document we focused on dashboards for software development support. However, there exist a number of tutorials on how to construct a dashboard without the specific focus on software engineering, for example:

- Visualization aspects in software engineering, focused on graphics and the design of a dashboard [Tel14].
- Visualization of code repositories, focused on the information needs related to software repositories [VT07, TA08].
- Visualization of areas of interest in software architecture, focused on the information needs that software engineers have in their daily work [BT06].
- Designing and building great dashboards, focused on dashboard designs for different audience types [Smi15].
- Digital dashboards: Strategic and tactical, focused on the impact of the information provided by the dashboards [Kau17].
- Building dashboards that people love to use, focused on graphical design and layout of dashboards [Jui17].
- Examples of 24 web dashboards; provides a set of examples of dashboards for a variety of purposes [Lak13].
- How to build an effective dashboard, focused on the actionability of the dashboards [Wol17].
- Dashboard gallery: [Liq17].

Tornhill [Tor15] presents a very interesting work on visual analytics of source code. In his book, Tornhill describes how to use visualizations combined with mining techniques to discover risky areas of source code. He also describes how to understand their impact on the organizational performance and product quality.

Antinyan et al. [ASS17] studied the discrepancy between the software engineers' understanding of software complexity and the measures available for this property. The work of Antinyan et al. is interesting from the perspective of understanding how to improve industrial practices by using the right measures of software complexity in our measurement programs.

Telea [Tel14], in his book about visualization, included in-depth theoretical knowledge about the foundations of visualization of information. We recommend his work when building more advanced data visualization techniques and dashboards.

Bostock [BOH11], on the other hand, presented a great visualization framework based on JavaScript. This visualization framework provides its users with the ability to plot data directly from source systems (e.g. Atlassian Jira) or from the measurement databases. The alternatives to D3 include Google Charts framework [SMN12].

In our previous work, we studied the impact of different visualization techniques on the stakeholder's understanding of the data [PSSM10b, Sta]. The results showed that the simple visualizations are often the best, as they provide the stakeholders with a quick overview of the most important information. This quick overview supports the stakeholders in making decisions about their measured entities [Sta12, SMP12].

References

[ASS17] Vard Antinyan, Miroslaw Staron, and Anna Sandberg. Evaluating code complexity triggers, use of complexity measures and the influence of code complexity on maintenance time. *Empirical Software Engineering*, pages 1–31, 2017.

[BA06] Luigi Buglione and Alain Abran. Introducing root-cause analysis and orthogonal defect classification at lower CMMI maturity levels. *Proc. MENSURA*, page 29, 2006.

[BOH11] Michael Bostock, Vadim Ogievetsky, and Jeffrey Heer. D^3 data-driven documents. *IEEE transactions on visualization and computer graphics*, 17(12):2301–2309, 2011.

[BT06] Heorhiy Byelas and Alexandru Telea. Visualization of areas of interest in software architecture diagrams. In *Proceedings of the 2006 ACM symposium on Software visualization*, pages 105–114. ACM, 2006.

[FSHL13] Robert Feldt, Miroslaw Staron, Erika Hult, and Thomas Liljegren. Supporting software decision meetings: Heatmaps for visualising test and code measurements. In *Software Engineering and Advanced Applications (SEAA), 2013 39th EUROMICRO Conference on*, pages 62–69. IEEE, 2013.

[HF10] Jez Humble and David Farley. *Continuous Delivery: Reliable Software Releases through Build, Test, and Deployment Automation (Adobe Reader)*. Pearson Education, 2010.

[HQC⁺16] Regina Hebig, Truong Ho Quang, Michel RV Chaudron, Gregorio Robles, and Miguel Angel Fernandez. The quest for open source projects that use UML: Mining github. In *Proceedings of the ACM/IEEE 19th International Conference on Model Driven Engineering Languages and Systems*, pages 173–183. ACM, 2016.

[ISO07] ISO/IEC. *ISO/IEC 15939:2007 Systems and Software Engineering – Measurement Process*, 2007.

[Jui17] Juice, Inc. A guide to creating dashboards people love to use, 2017.

[Kau17] Avinash Kaushik. Digital dashboards: Strategic and tactical: Best practices, tips, examples, 2017.

[KSM⁺15] Eric Knauss, Miroslaw Staron, Wilhelm Meding, Ola Söder, Agneta Nilsson, and Magnus Castell. Supporting continuous integration by code-churn based test selection. In *Proceedings of the Second International Workshop on Rapid Continuous Software Engineering*, pages 19–25. IEEE Press, 2015.

[Lak13] Chris Lake. 24 beautifully-designed web dashboards that data geeks will love, 2013.

[Liq17] LiquidPlanner. Dashboard gallery, 2017.

[MST12] Niklas Mellegård, Miroslaw Staron, and Fredrik Törner. A light-weight software defect classification scheme for embedded automotive software and its initial evaluation. *Proceedings of the ISSRE 2012*, 2012.

[oWM93] International Bureau of Weights and Measures. *International vocabulary of basic and general terms in metrology*. International Organization for Standardization, Geneva, Switzerland, 2nd edition, 1993.

[PSSM10a] K. Pandazo, A. Shollo, M Staron, and W. Meding. Presenting Software Metrics Indicators: A Case Study. In *Proceedings of the 20th International Conference on Software Product and Process Measurement*, 2010.

[PSSM10b] Kosta Pandazo, Arisa Shollo, Miroslaw Staron, and Wilhelm Meding. Presenting software metrics indicators: A case study. In *Proceedings of the 20th International Conference on Software Product and Process Measurement (MENSURA)*, volume 20, 2010.

[RAN07] Per Runeson, Magnus Alexandersson, and Oskar Nyholm. Detection of duplicate defect reports using natural language processing. In *Proceedings of the 29th international conference on Software Engineering*, pages 499–510. IEEE Computer Society, 2007.

[SHF+13] Miroslaw Staron, Jorgen Hansson, Robert Feldt, Anders Henriksson, Wilhelm Meding, Sven Nilsson, and Christoffer Hoglund.   Measuring and visualizing code stability–a case study at three companies. In *Software Measurement and the 2013 Eighth International Conference on Software Process and Product Measurement (IWSM-MENSURA), 2013 Joint Conference of the 23rd International Workshop on*, pages 191–200. IEEE, 2013.

[SM09] Miroslaw Staron and Wilhelm Meding. Using models to develop measurement systems: A method and its industrial use. In *Software Process and Product Measurement*, volume 5891, pages 212–226. Springer Berlin/Heidelberg, 2009.

[SMHH13] Miroslaw Staron, Wilhelm Meding, Christoffer Hoglund, and Jorgen Hansson. Identifying implicit architectural dependencies using measures of source code change waves. In *Software Engineering and Advanced Applications (SEAA), 2013 39th EUROMICRO Conference on*, pages 325–332. IEEE, 2013.

[Smi15] Nick Smith. Designing and building great dashboards – 6 golden rules to successful dashboard design, 2015.

[SMN08] Miroslaw Staron, Wilhelm Meding, and Christer Nilsson. A framework for developing measurement systems and its industrial evaluation. *Information and Software Technology*, 51(4):721–737, 2008.

[SMN12] Yasutaka Sakamoto, Shinsuke Matsumoto, and Masahide Nakamura. Integrating service oriented MSR framework and Google Chart Tools for visualizing software evolution. In *Empirical Software Engineering in Practice (IWESEP), 2012 Fourth International Workshop on*, pages 35–39. IEEE, 2012.

[SMP12] Miroslaw Staron, Wilhelm Meding, and Klas Palm. Release readiness indicator for mature agile and lean software development projects. In *Agile Processes in Software Engineering and Extreme Programming*, pages 93–107. Springer, 2012.

[Sta] Miroslaw Staron. Dashboard development guide how to build sustainable and useful dashboards to support software development and maintenance.

[Sta12] Miroslaw Staron. Critical role of measures in decision processes: Managerial and technical measures in the context of large software development organizations. *Information and Software Technology*, 54(8):887–899, 2012.

[Sta16] Miroslaw Staron. Actionable dashboards, 2016.

[Sta17] Miroslaw Staron. *Automotive software architectures: An introduction*. Springer, 2017.

[TA08] Alexandru Telea and David Auber. Code flows: Visualizing structural evolution of source code. In *Computer Graphics Forum*, volume 27, pages 831–838. Wiley Online Library, 2008.

[Tel14] Alexandru C Telea. *Data visualization: Principles and practice*. CRC Press, 2014.

[Tor15] Adam Tornhill. *Your code as a crime scene*. Pragmatic Bookshelf, 2015.

[VT07] Lucian Voinea and Alexandru Telea. Visual data mining and analysis of software repositories. *Computers & Graphics*, 31(3):410–428, 2007.

[Wol17] Tamra Wolny. Build a visual dashboard in 10 steps, 2017.

Chapter 6
Examples of Measures in Measurement Systems

Abstract Never in history have we collected so much data as we have today; we have even coined an expression for this: "Big data." Never have we measured and analyzed data as much as we do today. Data is easy to collect and store. Statistical methods and tools, business intelligence (BI) tools, and machine learning, together with cheap data storage and processing, make this possible. Everybody (well, almost) claims to be an expert in measuring. What we see, though, are evidences to the contrary. Companies and organizations are drawn in data and measures, while at the same time, measures are incomplete, misused, or not trusted. If there is one question we have heard over and over again it is "What should we measure?" It is a question asked by everyone, regardless of title, role and position in the organization's hierarchy. In this chapter, we present a number of measures, how they "came to be," and how to develop and visualize them. We present also a structured way to categorize measures, into five measurement areas.

6.1 Introduction

Thanks to the technological advances in the last decade, access to data is today easy and fast. Companies and organizations have access to vast amounts of data, that span from customer feature usage, product performance and organizational efficiency, to CPU load and memory allocation. It seems a bit contradictory that on the one hand we have access to all this information, and on the other hand, the question that companies and organizations want (need) an answer to (the most), is "What should we measure?" In order to succeed with addressing this question, however, one needs to combine the automated data collection with smart analysis methods and smart usage of standards. The situation has become complicated as the process of measurement has gotten easy and therefore everyone can collect a lot of data, as many software development and management tools are automated. This leads to the perception that everyone perceives him-/herself as a measuring expert.

In this chapter we present a number of measures within different areas, as described in Sect. 6.3. We provide the background to these measures, and how they can be visualized, so that the reader can get a deeper understanding of each measure.

© Springer International Publishing AG, part of Springer Nature 2018
M. Staron, W. Meding, *Software Development Measurement Programs*,
https://doi.org/10.1007/978-3-319-91836-5_6

For some of the measures, we present also the measurement method behind them, so that the reader can replicate the method and recalibrate the measures for his/her company's or organization's specific context.

We also present how to categorize measures into measurement areas and sub-areas. Measures can be organized in a myriad of different ways, each one providing its own (unique) advantages and disadvantages. The measuring categorization presented here is based on our experience from frequent contacts with many software-intensive development companies and organizations, and their feedback that we have received over the years. We present also the rationale of some for the sub-measurement areas, including some examples of measures within these areas.

The overall purpose of this chapter is to elevate the measuring skills of companies and organizations by presenting real life measures, so that they, themselves, can answer the question "What should we measure?"

6.2   Examples of Measures in Measurement Programs

The examples presented in this chapter are taken from our experiences of working with over a dozen companies. They have been developed by software-intensive teams and organizations, to address their contemporary, specific needs.

For each measurement area we present the background of the measures, the measures themselves, and how they can be visualized. Some of the measures require an advanced approach to be developed. For these measures we present the method to do this, so that the reader can replicate the method at his/her own company or organization, and recalibrate the measures for his/her organization.

This section lists the following measures:

- release readiness, Sect. 6.2.1: quantifying the time that the organization needs to finalize their development cycle and deploy the product to their customers,
- forecasting defect backlog, Sect. 6.2.2: predicting the quality of the products in order to plan for development effort, needed to achieve a given quality goal,
- identifying and monitoring bottlenecks, Sect. 6.2.3: quantifying the throughput, queue and speed of software development,
- internal quality measures for software architects, Sect. 6.2.4: providing the insights into internal product quality and size for software architects,
- implicit architectural dependencies, Sect. 6.2.5: guiding software testing by predicting the components needed to be tested together,
- monitoring status of software development teams, Sect. 6.2.6: providing the means of communication of product development status for software teams, and
- customer defect inflow, Sect. 6.2.7: monitoring long-term trends in product quality and reliability.

We find these measures, and their corresponding areas, as valuable tools for software managers, architects and development teams. They help to speed up software development, reduce the probability of "surprises" and maximize value for the customers.

6.2.1 Release Readiness

6.2.1.1 Background

"When is our product under development ready for market availability?"

This is a question, an information need, that all software development companies and organizations want to know the answer to. It addresses the need to know how much time is left, before all development activities are successfully concluded, so that the product can be released to customers. Software development companies and organizations have, therefore, developed release-related checklists, to know if the product is ready for release. If the outcome during those assessments shows that the product is not ready for release, a new meeting is planned for.

In our experience, there is one main hindrance to the effective use of these checklists, and that is that organizations do not feel 100% confident that the checklists cover *all* necessary aspects. This has the effect, among other things, of there being a tendency to measure as much as possible close to the release assessments.

What we present here is *what* to measure, to address the information need for release readiness. More precisely, we provide two examples, A and B. Example A answers the information need "When will we be ready for release?", while example B addresses the information need "Are we ready to release the product?" Although both questions concern release readiness, the advantage with example A is that it is *pro-active*, since it provides the time that is left before the product can be released.

Example A uses just one formula for release readiness; example B presents a set of measures that *combined* address release readiness.

6.2.1.2 Release Readiness Measure: Example A

The formula for the release readiness indicator, which is based on [SMP12a, SMS10], is:

$$\text{Release readiness} = \frac{\text{Number of defects}}{\text{Defect removal rate} - (\text{Test execution rate} - \text{Test pass rate})} \tag{6.1}$$

where:

• Number of defects[1]: the number of open defects of the product.[2]

---

[1]The defects refer only to those found in the branch from which deliveries to the customers are made.

[2]Refers to the product that is under development, soon to be released to customers.

- Defect removal rate: the average number of removed defects,[3] during the last 4 weeks.[4,5]
- Test execution rate: the average number of test cases executed, during the last 4 weeks.
- Test pass rate[6]: the average number of test cases passed during the last 4 weeks.

Visualization: Example A

The best way to visualize this indicator is an MS Windows Gadget/MacOS Widget; see Fig. 6.1. This type of visualization/information product gives the stakeholder (who, in this case, is the project manager) the necessary information, in a simple and succinct way. As gadgets are located on the computers' desktops, one does not need to "search" for them—i.e. zero clicks to find the information!

In this example, the gadget shows that the project will be ready to release its product in 2 weeks' time.

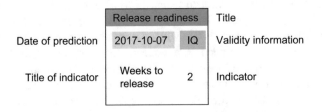

Fig. 6.1 MS Vista-like gadget, with predicted week of release

Though gadgets are not pre-installed after the MS Windows Vista version, add-ons can be downloaded from the web, e.g. http://www.intowindows.com/desktop-gadgets-for-windows-10/. Another option is to use an app for a mobile device.

6.2.1.3   Release Readiness Measure: Example B

In this example, we use a set of measures that address the following areas: requirements, tests and defects. The rationale behind including these three areas

---

[3]Refers to the number of defects (as defined in note 1) that were solved and closed during the last 4 weeks.

[4]Built into the formula is a period of time, defined to be sufficient to reason about the status of defects and testing.

[5]By choosing "week" as the time unit, the result of the formula is in *number of weeks*.

[6]In the formula, *all* requirements are traced to test cases, to verify that *all* requirements are implemented in the code.

is that before releasing a product, we need to know that all defined requirements are part of the product, and we need to know that all requirements have been implemented correctly in the product, and we need to know that there are no defects in the product (Table 6.1).

Table 6.1 Release readiness measures: example B

Measurement area	Measures	Expected value
Requirements	Number of defined requirements	Number of defined requirements
	Number of requirements tied to test cases	Number of defined requirements
Test	Total number of test cases	Total number of test cases
	Number of test cases planned	Total number of test cases
	Number of test cases executed	Total number of test cases
	Number of test cases passed	Total number of test cases
Defects	Number of defects	Zero

One could justly argue that there are more aspects than these three that need to be checked. However, on the other hand, it is impossible to measure everything; one can only focus on a limited number of measures, and from our experience, if you start with these measures you can come a long way.

Visualization: Example B

For the set of measures, we recommend using a worksheet in an MS Excel file. The worksheet can summarize the results, as in Fig. 6.2.

Fig. 6.2 Set of measures for release readiness, shown in a MS Excel worksheet

The measures were updated: 2015-08-23

Requirements	
Number of requirements defined	456
Number of requirements tied to test cases	399

Test	
Number of test cases	4,072
Number of test cases planned	3,176
Number of test cases executed	3,004
Number of test cases passed	2,475

Defects	
Number of open defects	16

If the company or organization has the technical competence and means, it is better to use the same set-up on a web-page, so that the information can be presented on monitors where the development organization sits. By doing so, the measures are always available to the measurement users.

6.2.2 Forecasting Defect Backlog

Historically, it was difficult to make accurate predictions about defect backlog, especially when the time frame was longer, e.g. a month or two. This is even more true today, as software development takes place in a dynamic environment. Lean and agile practices have shifted much of the mandate of the project management team (when using the waterfall, gate-based, software development models) to the development teams. Regardless, project managers, and their respective project management teams, still need to know when the product (that is under development) is free of errors, so that it can be delivered to customers.

6.2.2.1 Background

The measure presented here addresses the information need "How to forecast the level of defect backlog, in a simple and reliable way?"

Modern software development organizations focus more on trends, rather than on momentary values. This is the case with the defect backlog trend indicator, which we present here. The indicator is an arrow, as shown in Fig. 6.3. It shows if defects are going to increase or decrease in a week's time. The indicator is based on the study described in [SMS10].

The solution presented here provides two major benefits:

- The indicator is an arrow, which is a simple symbol, with an easy-to-understand interpretation.
- The formula is simple, and at the same time, accurate (Mean Magnitude of Relative Error, MMRE, of 16%).

6.2.2.2 Measures

The formula of the indicator's analysis model is:

$$db(i) = db(i-1) + \frac{db(i-1) + db(i-2) + db(i-3)}{3}$$
$$- \frac{do(i-1) + do(i-2) + do(i-3)}{3} \tag{6.2}$$

where:

- $db(x)$ is the defect backlog in week x (i.e. the number of non-fixed defects in week x)
- $di(x)$ is the defect inflow in week x (i.e. the number of defects discovered in week x)
- $do(x)$ is the defect outflow in week x (i.e. the number of defects fixed in week x)

The formula says that the defect backlog for the next week is the actual defect backlog of this week, plus the moving average of the defect inflow of the three last weeks, minus the moving average of the defect outflow of the three last weeks.

This means that:

- if $db(x) < db(x+1)$ then the arrow points up
- if $db(x) > db(x+1)$ then the arrow points down
- if $db(x) = db(x+1)$ then the arrow points to the right

In this example, which is quoted from [SMS10], the latency between making an attempt to fix a defect and its actual resolution, made the 3 week period an appropriate time frame window for the moving average. Also, the project used "1 week" as the prediction horizon. Other time frames may be used as well, but based on empirical experience we would not recommend a time frame longer than 2 weeks, because of the growing uncertainty and the need to predict new values based on already predicted ones (i.e., predictions over predictions).

6.2.2.3 Visualization

The indicator for forecasting defect backlog is an arrow. When it is pointing up, it means that the defect backlog will increase next week, and when it points down, it means that the defect backlog will decrease next week. When the indicator points to the right, it means that the defect backlog will remain the same. We recommend the use of an MS Windows Gadget, exemplified in Fig. 6.3.

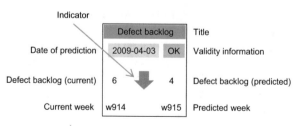

Fig. 6.3 MS Vista-like gadget, presenting the defect backlog indicator

The gadget lists, except for the indicator, additional information that is important for the stakeholder, i.e.:

- Title, i.e. the name of this specific gadget.
- Date of prediction, i.e. the date the gadget was last updated.

- Validity information, i.e. the information quality of the information presented. In this example it is "green," which means that the stakeholder can trust the information that is presented.
- Defect backlog (current), i.e. the number of non-fixed defects and the date the gadget was last updated (i.e. Date of prediction). In the formula, this variable corresponds to db(i-1); in this example it is "6."
- Defect backlog (predicted), i.e. the predicted value of the number of defects that are not fixed next week. In the formula, this variable corresponds to db(i); in this example it is "4."
- Current week, i.e. the week the value of "Date of prediction" belongs to.
- Predicted week, i.e. the week the value of "Defect backlog (predicted)" belongs to.

These two last dates can be replaced by just one date, with the same format as the "Date of prediction," showing the date of the "Defect backlog (predicted)" 7 days (i.e. 1 week) ahead. The organization that is using this indicator, [SMS10], uses the notion of "weeks" frequently in their information products. The organization finds it much easier/simpler to work with "weeks" than "dates," when there is no need for a granularity on a "day" basis.

The gadget allows one to focus on the task at hand, i.e. what the situation will look like the next week. The information presented is simple, unambiguous and succinct. The focus is set on the "near future," freeing one from "history baggage." Furthermore, since the indicator is integrated in the stakeholders' everyday work, there is no need for "green" and "red" thresholds.

Lastly, though gadgets are not pre-installed after the MS Vista version, add-ons can be downloaded from the web, e.g. http://www.intowindows.com/desktop-gadgets-for-windows-10/.

6.2.3   Identifying and Monitoring Bottlenecks

Efficiency is one of the main drivers in software development, and one of the main drivers behind the lean principles. Every software company and organization wants to have an efficient development, an efficient flow. Bottlenecks hinder efficient development of software, at the same time being difficult to identify and monitor.

This section focuses on *how* to identify bottlenecks and develop measurement systems to monitor them, i.e. the focus is on the *method* and not on the measures as such. The measures presented here serve to illustrate the method, since every company and organization has its own unique products, ways of working, and development environment. Following this method helps companies and organizations to identify, measure and monitor their own specific bottlenecks.

The method is built up by the following four steps:

1. identify the stakeholder and his/her/their information need,
2. identify the phases of the flow that is to be monitored,

3. define throughput and queue measures for each phase, and
4. visualize all measures in one information product.

The method and the measures presented here are from the research study presented in [SM11]. The terms that are used in this section are:

- Bottlenecks: a bottleneck is a phenomenon where the performance or capacity of an entire system (e.g. software project) is limited by a single or limited number of components or resources.
- Capacity: capacity is the total number of software features developed in one release.
- Flow: flow is the motion characteristic of elements or functionality under development (see also [Opp04]).
- Throughput: throughput is defined as the number of elements processed during a time period. The rationale behind this is that *throughput measures* notify the responsible stakeholder for the phase *after* the current one about potential problems with *overflow* of work in the current phase.
- Queue: queue is defined as the number of elements to be processed (to flow) through a specific phase or a software project. The rationale behind this is that queue measures notify the responsible stakeholder for the phase *before* the current one, about potential *shortage* of work in the current phase.

6.2.3.1 Measures

Step 1 out of 4: identify the stakeholder and his/her information need:

- Stakeholder: a project manager.
- Information need: "How to identify and monitor bottlenecks, in the software development process, from a release point of view?"

Step 2 out of 4: identify the phases of the flow that are to be monitored. The project manager defined the following phases of the software development process as most important:

- Development team: a development team is built up by designers, programmers, system engineers, function testers and object leaders. Each team is responsible for the complete development of one feature, and for delivering it to the main branch.
- Integration: when the teams are ready with their development, they deliver (i.e. they integrate) their code to the main branch. Two main principles drive integration activities: integration time slots should be used as effectively as possible, and the integration of features should be spread over the whole project, to avoid big-bang integration problems.
- Defect handling: this refers to the defects that are discovered during the function testing, in the teams, and during integration.

- System test: system test is the first phase where the source code is tested as a whole.
- Network integration test: this is the first phase where the whole product is tested in its target environment.

Step 3 out of 4: define throughput and queue measures, for each phase.
Table 6.2 groups all throughput and queue measures, for the five phases.

Table 6.2 Measures for throughput and queue, per phase

Phase	Throughput measures	Queue measures
Development team	Number of function test cases developed per week	Number of function test cases planned for the whole feature, but not yet developed
Integration	Number of features integrated per week	Number of features planned for integration up-to-date in the integration plan, but not yet integrated
Defect handling	Number of defects closed per week	Number of defects not closed
System test	Number of test cases executed per week	Number of test cases planned for execution up to a given week, but not executed
Network integration test	Number of test cases executed per week	Number of test cases planned for execution up to a given week, but not executed yet

6.2.3.2   Visualization

Step 4 out of 4: visualize all measures in one information product.

The above measures should be placed in one information product, and in sequence, as a flow; see Fig. 6.4. This set-up gives a good overview of all the measures, and acts as a common "dashboard" for the stakeholder/s, and all other project and line parties that are interested.

The measures are visualized as graphs, and not as numbers. Of course numbers can be part of the visualization, but trends give the chance to stakeholders to act proactively. For example, if a trend is negative over a longer period of time, they can take actions before the trend reaches levels that are below specified thresholds.

The X-axes are omitted, for simplistic reasons; they are all in "weeks." The five "blue" graphs show the throughput-related measures, and the "red" graphs show the queue-related measures.

The best way to visualize this information product is on a dashboard, presented on a monitor placed at the location of the development team.

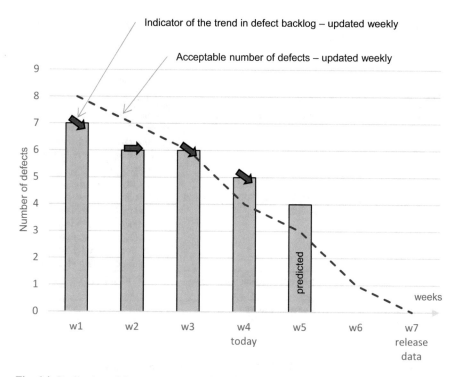

Fig. 6.4 Realization of the measurement system, for monitoring bottlenecks

6.2.4   *Internal Quality Measures for Software Architects*

Good software architecture is characterized, among other things, by high stability
and high modularity. Though many base measures are defined in the literature about
software architecture, e.g. [ISO16a, LTC03, SFGL07], there do not exist many high-
level measures [Sta17, MS10].

The purpose of this section is to provide software architects with a set of measures to enable easy monitoring of the main information needs. These information
needs can be internal quality, design stability or interface complexity. The measures
(indicators) are divided into three main measurement areas, [SM17, Sta17]:

- Architecture measures
- Design stability
- Technical debt/risk

6.2.4.1   Measurement Area: Architecture Measures

This area groups the product-related indicators that address the information need
about how to monitor basic properties of the architecture.

Four indicators are defined to capture the very basic properties of software architecture; see Table 6.3.

Table 6.3 Internal quality measure area for architects—architecture measures

Indicator	Formula	Rationale
Software architecture changes	Number of changes in the architecture, per time unit	To monitor and control changes over time, architects need to monitor trends in changes of the software architecture, at the highest level
Complexity	Average square deviation of actual fan-out, from the simplest structure	To manage module complexity, architects must understand the degree of coupling between components, to avoid coupling that can be cost-consuming and error-prone in the long-term evolution of the architecture
Internal interfaces	Number of internal interfaces	To control the degree of coupling on the interface level
External interfaces	Number of external interfaces	To have control of the external dependencies of the product

The measures, listed in Table 6.3, are visualized on a dashboard, presented on a monitor. We recommend that the measures are presented together with their indicators, since this connection gives an easy overview for the measurement users (Fig. 6.5).

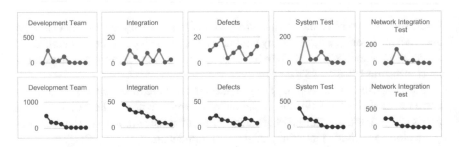

Fig. 6.5 Visualization of the measures in the architecture property area

6.2.4.2   Measurement Area: Design Stability

This area groups the process-related indicators that address the information need about how to ascertain controlled evolution of the architectural design.

Three indicators are defined, to address the need for software architectures to monitor the stability of a large code base; see Table 6.4.

Table 6.4 Internal quality measure area for architects—design stability

Indicator	Formula	Rationale
Code stability	Number of changes, per module, per time unit	To monitor the code maturity over time, architects need to see how much code has been changed over time, as it allows them to identify code areas where more testing is needed due to recent changes
Defects per modules	Number of defects per module, per time unit	To monitor the aging of the code, architects need to monitor the defect proneness per component per time
Interface stability	Number of changes to the interfaces, per time unit	To control the stability of the architecture over its interfaces

The best way to visualize these measures is to use heat maps. Figure 6.6 shows a simplified example of defects per module, [FSHL13, SHF$^+$13]. The X-axis is in weeks. It is easy to spot the "problematic" modules, just by looking at the heat map, i.e. modules 11 and 25.

The three measures are visualized in the same way, i.e. as heat maps (Fig. 6.7). Though they show different measures, they are organized in the same way, i.e.

- Y-axis is in weeks
- X-axis represents code modules or interfaces
- The intensity of the colors in the cells shows the intensity of the changes of the code modules or interfaces a given week

6.2.4.3 Measurement Area: Technical Debt/Risk

This area is related to the quality of the architecture, over a longer period of time.

Two indicators are defined, to address the need for software architectures to monitor the technical debt/risk of the architecture; see Table 6.5.

The visualization of the architectural dependencies shows the degree of coupling; see Fig. 6.8. Each area of the border of the circle represents a component, and the width of the "lines" shows the degree of the dependency between components.

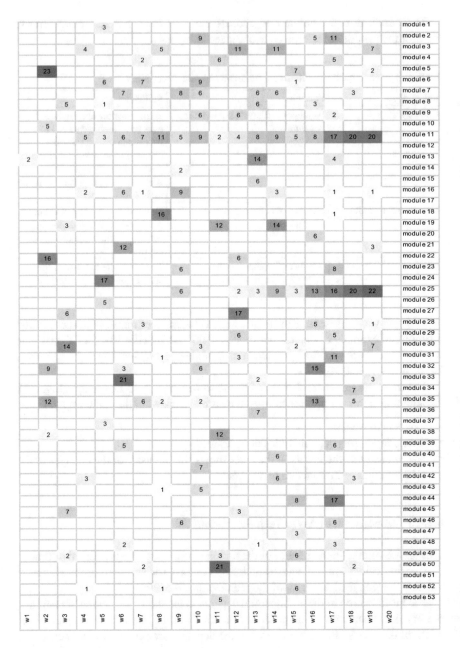

Fig. 6.6 Visualization of defects per module

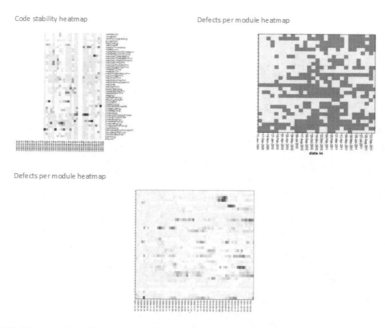

Fig. 6.7 Visualization of the measures in the architecture stability area

Table 6.5 Internal quality measure area for architects—technical debt/technical risk

Indicator	Formula	Rationale
Coupling	Number of explicit architectural dependencies	To have manageable design complexity, architects need to have an overview of the coupling between the components in the architecture[a]
Implicit architectural dependencies	Number of implicit architectural dependencies	To monitor where the code deviates from the architecture, architects need to observe that there are no additional dependencies introduced during the detailed design of the software[b]

[a]*Explicit architectural dependencies* are the links between components, which are introduced by the architects
[b]*Implicit architectural dependencies* are the links between components, which are part of the code, but not introduced in the architecture documentation diagrams, e.g. two features sharing the same code library

6.2.5 Implicit Architectural Dependencies

Today, software companies and organizations abide (fully or to some extent) by agile ways of working. As agile teams are self-organized, the architectural work

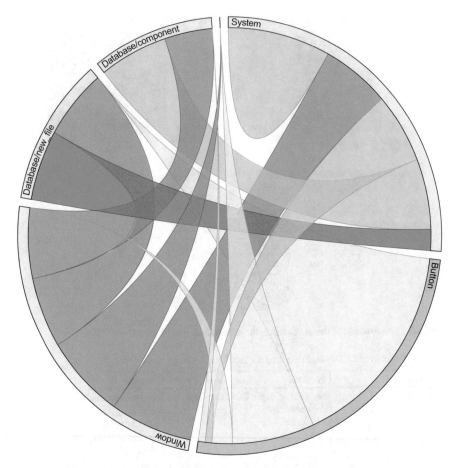

Fig. 6.8 Visualization of measures in the architecture technical debt/risk

is more distributed and harder to control centrally [Ric11] than before the agile
"era." The difficulties stem from the fact that agile software development teams
value independence and creativity, [SBB+09], whereas architecture development
requires stability, control transparency and pro-activity [PW92].

Simplified, we can assume that the architecture of a software product is built up
by components. There are rules defined, about how components can/should depend
on one another. Dependencies that are defined by architects, and implemented in the
code are called *explicit* dependencies.

The architecture of a software product changes over time. If changes are not
rigorously monitored and cared for, unintended dependencies may occur. Examples
of such dependencies can be component dependencies through common libraries or
protocols. E.g. two components implement protocols that are somehow dependent,
but these two components are not explicitly connected in the architecture model.

These types of dependencies are called *implicit*, and can lead to quality problems, and delays of software deliveries. Implicit dependencies are difficult to identify.

Thus, the purpose of this section is to provide the software architects with a method, and corresponding measures, to assess the validity of dependencies; it is based on [SMHH13].

6.2.5.1 Measures

The method to develop a formula is based on mining software repositories, to find situations where groups of components are updated within an arbitrary number of days, e.g. 1 week, [PW92]. The assumption is that the components which are often updated together (e.g. in the same week) depend usually upon one another.

To address this, we introduce the concept of source code change waves. A change wave is a chain of related changes of components in the source code, during a period of time, e.g. a week.

So, the strength of the dependency of two components is measured as the number of common change bursts (NoCB), and is defined as the number of bursts that contain both components.

Let us exemplify this with Figs. 6.9 and 6.10, [NB05]. The black dot represents architectural component A, and the white dot represents architectural component B.

In Fig. 6.9, component A is chosen as the starting point for the first burst; the white dots show the change event in another component (i.e. component B). In Fig. 6.10, component B is chosen as the starting point of the bursts.

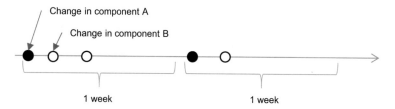

Fig. 6.9 Component change patterns, with bursts originating in component A

Figure 6.9 shows two change bursts originating in component A, of a length of 1 week each. The NoBC measure for pairs originating in component A is:

- NoCBA-B = 2: component B changes in both change bursts originating from component A

Figure 6.10 shows change bursts originating from component B. In the figure there are three bursts of size of 1 week that originate from component B.

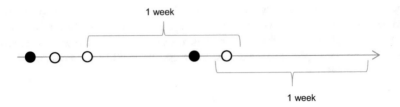

Fig. 6.10 Component change patterns, with bursts originating in component A

The NoBC measure for pairs originating in component B is:

- NoCBB-A = 2: component A changes in both change bursts originating from component B

To quantify the strength of dependency (SoD), we use the total number of bursts (NoB), as follows:

$$SoD = \frac{NoCB}{NoB} * 100\%$$

where:

- SoD: Strength of Dependency
- NoCB: Number of Common Change Bursts
- NoB: total Number of Bursts

This gives that, over a period of 1 week:

$$SoDA\text{-}B = \frac{NoCBA\text{-}B}{NoBA} * 100\% = \frac{2}{2} * 100\% = 100\%$$

$$SoDB\text{-}A = \frac{NoCBB\text{-}A}{NoBB} * 100\% = \frac{2}{3} * 100\% = 67\%$$

The results show that changes in component A may initiate changes in component B, but not the other way around (or, component B does not affect component A equally *strongly*).

6.2.5.2   Visualization

The results can be presented in a table; see Table 6.6. By using colors, as in a heatmap, it is easy to distinguish the pairs of components that should be considered first, i.e. the most color-intensive ones.

By examining the table, architects can identify dependencies that they can easily categorize into explicit and implicit. In these examples, the time interval is set to 1

Table 6.6 Strength of dependency, visualized in a table

	A	B
A		100%
B	67%	

week. This can of course be adjusted, to reflect the development ways of working of a company or organization. This example is a small one, with just two components. In real life, many more components are studied, which will of course result in a larger table!

6.2.6 *Monitoring Progress of Software Development Teams*

In modern software development companies and organizations, it is the teams that produce the detailed time plans for the development of the features. That has made it important for the teams to be equally good as project management teams in developing time plans and executing on them.

So, one of the greatest *administrative* information needs that software development teams have is how well they are progressing in their plans. This is also the purpose of this section, i.e. to provide a set of measures that will help the teams to show the status of their progress, in a simple, straightforward, and effective way.

We list four measures, which cover the progress of the team in total, i.e. how much work the team has left to conclude its task, the number of the defects that the team must handle, the progress of the testing, and (potential) unplanned activities.

The fourth measure is an important measure since it makes it evident how disturbances that are outside of the control of the team affects its progress. One typical such disturbance is when a team is ordered to help another team, without being given any extra time or resources to handle their ongoing assignment. The burn-up graph shows the rest of the project and the line why its burn-down graph does not follow planned execution.

This section is partially based on [Med17].

6.2.6.1 Measures

There are four measures, see Table 6.7, which should be part of every software developing team's information product.

Table 6.7 Monitoring progress of software development teams

Measurement area	Measure	Description/rationale
Burn-down	Number of estimated and remaining story points[a]	A burn-down graph shows how successful the team is on keeping its time plan
Defect backlog	Number of open defects	The measure shows how many defects the team has to solve before the end of the current sprint
Test progress	Number of passed function test cases over number of planned function test cases	The measure lists the total number of function test cases that the team has to successfully execute, before the end of the sprint. The reason for focusing on function tests is that the function test is usually the final test phase the team executes, before integrating their code into the whole product
Burn-up	Number of unplanned executed story points	A burn-up graph can be used by the team to show *unplanned* activities they have to do during a sprint. Such an example can be that they are ordered to help another development team

[a] A story is an atomic work package that can be executed during a sprint. A sprint is usually 2 or 3 weeks long. The team plans for a number of tasks during the sprint, and assigns a number of points to each task. When sum up, they give the total number of points for that sprint

6.2.6.2 Visualization

The measures in Table 6.7 are best presented together in the same information product, e.g. on a monitor, as presented in Fig. 6.11. This enables an overall view of the status of the team, both for the team itself, and for the rest of the project.

6.2.7 Customer Defect Inflow

Monitoring the product quality on the market is of the utmost importance. Unhappy customers are something every company and organization wants to avoid. There are of course many ways to monitor the quality of the product on the market. Every measure has its advantages and disadvantages. The goal, of course, is to have one measure that provides one with a variety of information, in the same graph.

The measure we present here measures the number of defects reported by customers, the so-called "customer defect inflow" measure.

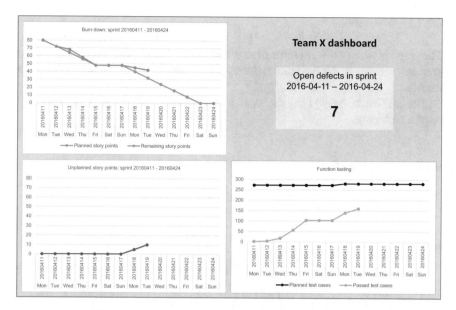

Fig. 6.11 Dashboard for a development team, with related measures

Measuring just the number of defects from customers does not give much. Using it as presented in Fig. 6.9 gives, though, a number of benefits.

There are two diagrams in Fig. 6.9. The bars show the number of defect inflows per month, and the lines show the accumulated number of defect inflows per year. Combining these two graphs says e.g. whether the product is getting better over the years, and if so, how much. The figure gives an easy, simple and powerful overview of the trend of the customer inflow.

Just by looking at the figure we can conclude that the number of defects reported over the years is decreasing. Is this decrease good enough though? Do improvements put in place show the desired result in the graph? These questions depend of course on, and can only be answered by, the responsible company or organization.

Another observation we can make is that during the summer months, more defects are reported. Why? This is something that should be investigated, since it may give insight as to the customer reporting patterns and/or the performance of the product during this specific period of the year.

The figure shows the customer defect inflow for one product. By considering the same figure for all products (both past and current) of the company or organization, useful conclusions can be drawn: "Are we getting better?", "Do all our products show the same behavior?"

6.2.7.1   Measures

The graph is based on the number of reported defects, by customers. The defects are grouped per month, for the bars, and they are accumulated per month and year, for the lines.

The data can be easily stored in a table, in MS Excel, and presented there as well, or on a web-page.

6.2.7.2   Visualization

Figure 6.12 shows the realization of customer defect inflow.

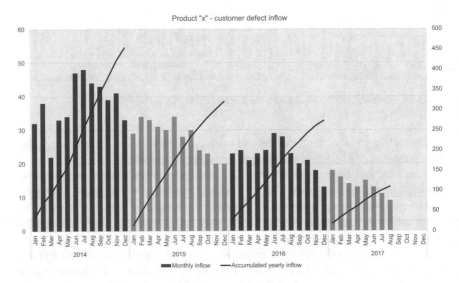

Fig. 6.12   Customer defect inflow, of the fictitious product "x"

The figure can include additional information, e.g. the bars can be split color-wise, into defect severity levels. Most companies and organizations define (at least) three levels of severity: 1, 2, 3, or A, B, C, and similar. One example of coloring could be to have severity 1 in "red," severity 2 in "orange," and severity 3 in "yellow."

6.3   Measurement Areas

One of the most frequently recurring questions in modern software development companies and organizations, is "What should we measure?" Companies and organizations need to know that their measures are both adequate and sufficient. The measures are adequate when we use the *appropriate* measures for what needs to be measured; sufficient is about using *all* measures that we need for our information needs.

Inability to assess whether the measures are adequate and sufficient leads to serious problems for companies and organizations, e.g. the organizations end up with too many measures, or do not trust the result of the measures.

In this section, we present guidelines on understanding what to measure in a specific context. We do this by providing a mind map over measurement areas, explaining the rationale behind the selected measurement sub-areas, and elaborating on what to consider when measuring.

We understand that the immediate question is "Why do you not list the exact measures we should use?" There are a number of reasons for that:

- It takes a few thick books to list "all" measures which exist in software engineering.
- The same question (information need) can be addressed with different measures, depending on e.g. the measuring maturity of those measuring, or the size of the parties measuring.
- Companies and organizations change their organizational structure, their ways of working, and the tools they use over time; the same information need must cope with every such change.
- As new technologies emerge (e.g. cloud and virtualization), new measures "emerge," complementing and/or replacing old measures.

This section is structured as follows:

- Section 6.3.1 presents a mind map of measurement areas and sub-areas.
- Section 6.3.2 goes through some measurement sub-areas, explaining their rationale, and presenting an example of a measure.

6.3.1 Measurement Areas: Mind Map

One of the main obstacles for developing a definitive list of measures is the uncertainty on how to categorize the measures. For example, measures can be categorized in many ways, e.g. per role (architect, tester, etc.), per development area (e.g. requirements, design, test, etc.), or per standard (ISO 25021, ISO 15939, etc.). They all provide pros and cons.

The list of measurement areas and sub-areas, which we present in this section, in Fig. 6.13, is the result of more than 4 years of cooperation between academia and software development companies. The measures are grouped into five main areas: project, design, organizational performance, product, and business. For each area, there is a list of sub-areas.

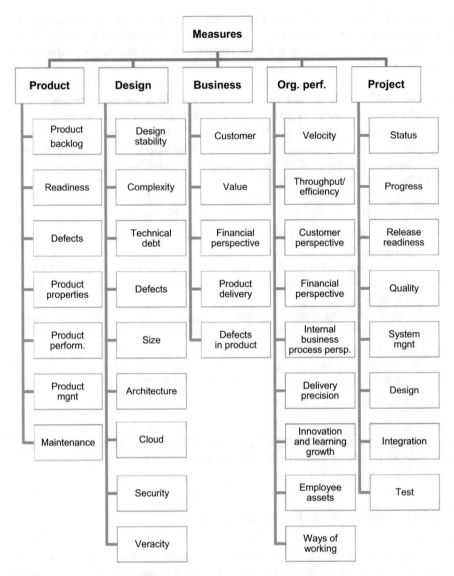

Fig. 6.13 Mind map of measurement areas and sub-areas

To address the question "What should we measure?", we can decide first to which area the question belongs. Many may think that is meaningless, it ought to be obvious to which area a question belongs! However, our experience shows otherwise.

For example, let us say that a product has *just* been released to the market. Defects reported on the product: where do they belong? Product, market or design?

We could argue that, since the product has *just* been released, the defects should be related to design; we can also argue that all defects found after the release date fall under the area product. So which perspective is right? It depends on what the strategy of the company or organization is, how design and maintenance organizations work, and whether they are close to each other, or totally separated?

Let us take another example; during the development of a product, the product management decides that the project has to address a technical debt, before the product is released. Who should take the cost, the product or the project management?

These two examples, and many more such similar ones, address another "challenge" with measuring, namely finding the right measurement area for each measure. This is also why we recommend that *before* you start defining measures, you should first define the measurement area, and then its sub-measurement area.

6.3.2 Measurement Sub-areas: Selected Details

This section lists some of the sub-measurement areas that are depicted in Fig. 6.10, by elaborating on their purpose and by giving some examples of measures.

6.3.2.1 Measurement Area: Product

The purpose of a project is to design and deliver a product according to a customer's specifications, in a given time and cost frame. Therefore, given this view, we go through the following sub-areas: status, progress, quality, system management, design, integration, and team.

Measurement Area: Project—Sub-area: Status

Every project, or more correctly, every project management team, should know the status of the project at any given time. They need to know it to answer the question *"Is everything according to the plan?"*

This is a tricky question; the challenge is, to what extent should this question be answered? Experience and best practices show that it is enough if the project management team focuses on a few main indicators, e.g. time, scope, quality and budget.

One example of a status-related measure is the delivered functionality this far, over the functionality that should have been delivered this far, in e.g. percent. Since functionality is what projects deliver, this measure is necessary for successful projects. Everything below "100%" can be considered a failure by customers, and therefore should be addressed accordingly. Another benefit of this measure is that it covers both time and scope!

Measurement Area: Project—Sub-area: Progress

In order to acquire a successful monitoring of the progress of the main activities of a project, effort must be put in planning different activities at the beginning of the project. The same is valid for the development teams. Regardless of whether the company or organization work is according to "old" (i.e. waterfall-like ways of working) or "new" (i.e. lean and agile ways of working) paradigms, good planning is of essence.

Plans must capture a number of aspects. For instance, if the progress is not according to the plan, then the project or the team is facing serious problems as deviations from time plans should always be alarming. If this is not the case, then the plan is not that important and can be omitted. Another aspect is that a plan should show a trend, i.e. it must be evident just by looking at the plan if the project or the team has made good progress.

Here are examples of measurement areas belonging to progress: overall time plan, workflow planning time, release readiness (as described in Sect. 6.2.1), progress within sprints, failure load, and duration [ISO16b].

Measurement Area: Project—Sub-area: Quality

The easiest way of measuring quality is to use a measure that relates to defects. Defects show problems that the project has to fix before the release date. One such simple, and well-known measure, is the defect backlog. The best way to visualize this is by showing both the status (e.g. in bars per week) and the trend of the defect backlog (as a line), in the same graph. The trend has to decrease, i.e. it has to come down to zero, the closer the project comes to the release date.

As a complement to this measure, one can forecast defect backlog, as we presented in Sect. 6.2.2, and/or monitor the actual defect inflow, related to its predicted values, as described in [SM10].

Fault slip through is used to see how well the organization is in capturing defects as early as possible. This is important, because the later a defect is identified, the more it costs to fix this defect, both because late test activities are more expensive than the early-ones, and because more design activities have been concluded, making it more effort-intensive to fix the defect. Fault slip through can (and should) be measured in all phases, from requirements review slippage, to the highest corresponding test phase for each company or organization.

Another measure is the number of faulty lines of code, [SM10], which also gives a quantitative measure of the quality of the code.

Measurement Area: Project—Sub-area: System Management

System management is the part of the organization that takes the high-level requirements, defined by the product management, and re-writes them in such a way that they can be understood and implemented by the development teams. Examples of measurement areas in system management are: requirements stability, change requests, and time required to determine product version.

One example of a system management measure is "number of change requests." A change request is a formal request, for a change of a defined requirement. Changes to already defined requirements show mainly two things: (1) how well defined the requirements were, to begin with, and (2) the effort that one or more development teams have to put to implement the change. Simply put, the more change requests, the more effort the teams have to put, the higher the risk of introducing errors in the code, the higher the risk of delays.

We do not provide any explicit number of how many change requests will cause problems to the project. This is up to each company or organization to define.

Measurement Area: Project—Sub-area: Design

Software design is about translating requirements into artifacts that can be used to program the requirements into the code. Therefore, design measures in this area relate more to planning and effort.

Some examples of design measurement areas are: number of high-level requirements, number of detailed requirements, number of requirements in test, number of change requests under review, number of approved change requests, number of change requests in test, number of story points.

One example for this area is the burn-down measure of story points. This measure shows how many story points a team has ticked off this far, related to the number of story points they should have ticked off this far. This is an excellent example of a simple, yet powerful measure that shows the progress of a development team in the design phase.

One best practice we have seen is to put burn-down measures for all development teams in one information product, e.g. a dashboard. The measure is simple for the teams to develop, and gives an easy/immediate overview of the progress of all the teams in the project.

Measurement Area: Project—Sub-area: Integration

Many of the modern software development companies have one main code branch per product; it is to this branch that teams deliver (integrate) their code, and from this branch that the company or organization delivers its product to its customers. There may be some variations to this, e.g. there may be one sub-branch for each product release, but regardless, activities around integration are considered today to be the very core of software development. Companies and organizations try to integrate code from the teams as often as possible, and at the same time keep it free of errors, so that they can deliver the code to the customers, as often as possible.

Some examples of measurement areas are: integration velocity, automated test coverage, number of commits, number of builds integrated per day, number of build failures per day, duration of build, cycle time, and throughput. Section 6.2.3 lists, among other things in Table 6.2, through put and queue measures. These measures are extremely important, as they relate to the efficiency of the integration process.

Measurement Area: Project—Sub-area: Team

Though the concept of team is far from new in software development, the way teams work today differs drastically compared to a few years ago. The agile paradigm has given modern software teams authority and autonomy to decide upon their time plans and budget.

Thus, it is important that the teams have a set of measures to use, to monitor their status and progress. Examples of such measurement areas are: team size, workload, multidisciplinary teams, percent of self-organizing teams, technology experimentation, team autonomy, rewards of success, obstacles, creativity, and people turnover. Section 6.2.6 lists a set of measures for the teams, to help them monitor their status.

6.3.2.2 Measurement Area: Design

By "design" we mean both the activities that relate to translating the requirements into artifacts that will enable the transition of text/models into code, and also the code as such. The design-related measures listed in the previous section relate to the planning, status and effort. This section relates in depth to the details of the design and coding disciplines.

In this section we discuss the following sub-areas: design stability, architecture and technical debt.

Measurement Area: Design—Sub-area: Design Stability

Design stability refers to both code and interface stability. Code stability means, among other things, that the code evolves under controlled forms. Interface stability is, among other things, a guarantee for explicit dependencies in the code. Examples of design stability measures are presented in Sect. 6.2.4.

Measurement Area: Design—Sub-area: Architecture

A good architecture is a prerequisite for a good design. Though companies and organizations put effort in developing and evolving architecture according to rules and best practices, measuring in architecture (in our experience) is not that common.

That is why we presented four simple/basic measures in Sect. 6.2.4, Table 6.3. This measurement set provides a good overview of the quality of the architecture, since it enables monitoring/control of changes, complexity, and internal/external dependencies.

Measurement Area: Design—Sub-area: Technical Debt

In our experience, if there is one measurement area that is (involuntary) neglected, it is technical debt. One main reason for this is the high pressure that is put on companies and organizations to deliver fast and frequently, leaving them little time to address technical debt in the code.

One simple way to measure technical debt is to focus on architectural dependencies, i.e. both explicit and implicit dependencies; see Sects. 6.2.5, 6.2.4, and Table 6.5. *Many* explicit dependencies, even if most of them are simple, can result into a complex code. Complex code leads to a number of difficulties, e.g. in finding errors and maintenance. Implicit dependencies are often very difficult to identify, and lead to effort-intensive activities to e.g. find errors, both during development and during maintenance. So, addressing just these two measurement sub-areas gives a high pay-back, since it is easy (easier) to develop and maintain a well-structured architecture/code.

6.3.2.3 Measurement Area: Organizational Performance

Organizational performance measures relate to how well an organization performs, how well ways of working are defined and followed up on. Important to emphasize here is that this area addresses the performance of companies and organizations, not the performance of individuals.

Some of the organizational performance-related measurement areas are: velocity, throughput, delivery precision, ways of working, operational quality, employee assets, and innovation. Since there is (often) an uncertainty of the difference between speed and velocity, we would like to elaborate a bit on these two notions.

Measurement Area: Organizational Performance—Sub-area: Speed

Speed is about how fast an artifact moves from one development phase/activity to another. An example of such measures can be the review speed of code—there, the code moves from submission to integration, passing the activity of code review. The speed is then the time from when the code is ready for review, until the review is done. The measure shows the average, minimum and maximum time, in days or hours, it takes for the company or organization to perform reviews.

Another example of speed is the time it takes for builds that have been delivered by the development teams on the main branch to be tested. The time can be measures in hours, showing the average time (waste) builds have to wait to be tested. This measure is comparable to the example presented in Sect. 6.2.3, Table 6.2, "Integration."

Speed measures should be a natural part of companies' and organizations' measurement sets, since they point out problem and/or improvement areas that relate to efficiency of ways of working.

Measurement Area: Organizational Performance—Sub-area: Velocity

Velocity is about how much is transferred from one place to another given a specific time frame. It is similar to the capacity that the organization has to produce and move artifacts (a) within the different development flow phases (e.g. average build time), and (b) among different development phases (e.g. average time it takes to develop a feature, from when the organization identified the need for such a feature, until it was released on the market).

Examples of velocity measures are, e.g. average number of builds that are integrated into the main branch per time unit (e.g. day or week), average time to develop and deliver features per time unit (e.g. week or month), and average time to fix defects (defect turnaround time) per time unit (e.g. hour or day). In addition to the measures using the central tendency statistics of average, it is beneficial to also measure median, maximum and minimum, to get a better understanding of the spread of the measurements.

Measurement Area: Organizational Performance—Sub-area: Innovation

The term "innovation" is often reserved for a specific group in companies and organizations and relates to the ability to bring in new products and services to companies' portfolios. The focus of this measurement sub-area is on the additional innovation activities, those activities that happen outside these dedicated innovation groups.

Additional innovation activities are not always given the appropriate focus, mostly due to the high pressure that companies and organizations have on delivering new products and new releases of existing products to the market. Our strong recommendation is to focus on this area, since innovation is a cornerstone for future products and solutions. Innovation is what helps companies and organizations to maintain and expand their position in the market.

In our experience, many organizations perceive it difficult to define good innovation measures. We have identified two main reasons for this. The first one is the difficulty of measuring the benefits that "good ideas" have (i.e. translate ideas into profit), and the second is the difficulty of following an idea, through the development process and out to the customers.

Our recommendation is to use measures that show that innovative activities take place; the focus should be on activities, not results. This is important, as experience shows that companies and organizations that have good innovation culture, thrive [Lal14].

Two very simple, yet powerful, measures are (a) number of hackathons organized by the company or organization, per year, and (b) time the employees spend on innovation (in percent, per year). These measures show both the willingness of the company or organization to provide the means to their employees to work with innovation outside their regular work description, and the motivation employees feel from participating in these activities.

6.3.2.4 Measurement Area: Product

The purpose of product-related measures is to not only monitor the performance of the product on the market, but also to e.g. ascertain that maintenance does not require unnecessary effort and cost, that there are no security issues, and that new product ideas (i.e. the product backlog) are developed and put on the market within reasonable time frames.

Some of the product measurement areas relate to product management, product backlog, readiness, product properties, flexibility, product performance, defects, maintenance, and security. In this section we discuss the following sub-areas: defects, maintenance and security [SMP12b, PW13].

Measurement Area: Product—Sub-area: Defects

Measuring the number of defects reported from customers is a measure that is found at every company and organization. The tricky part here is to choose those few measures that will give a good overview of the performance of the product, from the defect point of view [CD09].

Examples of such measures are the customer defect inflow [SM07, SM10]. This type of measure provides much information. Some parts are described in Sect. 6.2.7. The same type of graph can be used to show the defect inflow per defect severity, per market area, per customer "type," and per geographical area. When visualizing the defects inflow, it is important to think of attaching "many" attributes to the defects reported, to enable deeper analyses [PSSM10].

For instance, assume that many defects are reported to a specific market segment or a geographical area. It is then useful to have access to the precise revision of the code, to further investigate the quality properties of that particular code revision, and compare its performance in other market segments or geographical areas.

Measurement Area: Product—Sub-area: Maintenance

Maintenance-related measures are important, since they make it evident whether the product is easy to maintain, or not. By easy it is meant, among other, that it is easy for the maintenance organization to identify the source of reported errors, that the time to fix errors is limited, and that fixing errors does not result in introducing new ones.

Maintenance is a non-desired cost, and the less time companies and organizations have to put on maintenance, the higher their profits. Maintenance measures provide a clear picture about the degree of the quality of the maintainability of the product. Maintenance measures are also important so that the maintenance organization can present indisputable facts (i.e. give feedback) to the development organization if improvements are necessary for good, qualitative maintainability of the product.

The standard [ISO16a] presents several related maintainability measures, which we encourage the reader to study and implement.

Measurement Area: Product—Sub-area: Security

In our experience, security is an area that is of the utmost interest for companies and organizations, an area that receives (rightfully) high attention. Lack of security attention can have devastating results for the products and the companies/organizations that develop them.

Security thinking has to be integrated from the very beginning of the design of the software products. Regardless of how rigorous the testing of security is, before the release of the product to the market, it is imperative to continue to assess security throughout the lifetime of the product on the market.

Security covers many areas, e.g. standard [ISO16a] lists several areas, some of them being: confidentiality, integrity, accountability, and authenticity. We urge the reader to refer to this standard and study proposed measures thoroughly.

6.3.2.5   Measurement Area: Business

The business measurement area is the last of the five categories. The sub-categories can be grouped into two areas: the "financial" sub-areas and the "engineer" sub-areas. The "financial" sub-areas are Value, Financial perceptive, Cost, Risk and Customer; the "engineer" sub-areas are product delivery and defects in products.

The financial measures are very important to companies and organizations. Members of the metrics team may feel that they are out in "deep water," since these measures present several challenges. For instance, engineers are not that familiar with the "financial language," which may pose a challenge when talking to "financial" stakeholders. Another challenge that the metrics team must address is security; i.e. all financial and customer-related information should be considered sensitive, and be treated accordingly. This means that e.g. the information must be encrypted, and that the information must be limited to a predefined group of persons. Examples of measures in these sub-areas are:

- Value: business value delivered, use of functionality.
- Financial perspective: sales growth, return of investment, cash flow.

- Cost: revenue, appraisal cost, conversion rates.
- Risk: user risk index, producer risk index, business risk.
- Customer: market share, win rate, brand recognition.

In this section we present two measures: ISP, which is a measure in the Customer sub-area [SHF$^+$13, SMT$^+$], and "Time to Market," which is a measure in the Product delivery sub-area.

Measurement Area: Business—Sub-area: Customer

Though most of the business-related measures focus on "non-engineer" aspects, there are a few such measures, e.g. In service Performance (ISP). ISP-related measures focus on the performance of the product on the market. ISP is not one measure, but a set of measures that together provide a holistic view of the performance of the product. ISP measures are found in all software development companies and organizations [SHF$^+$13, SMT$^+$].

There are many different ISP measures, since ISP measures depend on the type of the product, e.g. availability is one such parameter; there are software products that are critical for the function and safety of the public, e.g. monitoring of power grids and traffic lights. These products have different ISP that e.g. games such as on mobile devices.

Examples of ISP measures can be planned and unplanned downtime. These measures are used, among others, by the telecommunication network providers.

Planned downtime refers to the time the telecommunication network-related product has be taken down for e.g. maintenance. It is measured in e.g. hours over a year. It is the yearly trend that is important here, i.e. that the planned downtime becomes lower and lower over the years. This is important, because during downtime, the product cannot be utilized by the customer.

Unplanned downtime is the time that the product does not function due to a malfunction (whatever the cause). Unplanned downtime can have severe impact on the customers (e.g. one cannot call 112, or 911), so the downtime should be "zero." This measure is used both by the telecommunication network providers and the telecommunication network users. Unplanned downtime is measured in minutes per year. The requirement today is that a telecommunication network should have at least "five nines" (99.999%) availability (also called "uptime"), or in other words, a telecommunication network can "fail" only 5.3 min a year.

Measurement Area: Business—Sub-area: Product Delivery

Today, more than ever, fast response to customer demands for product updates and new product features is of the utmost importance for the success/survival of software development companies. That is one of the reasons for the implementation and focus on e.g. lean and agile paradigms in companies and organizations: to remove all obstacles (impediments) that hinder the smooth and fast development of products, and to be able to cope with customer requirement changes (i.e. to be agile).

There are several measures related to how fast a company or organization is in delivering products to the market. By delivering products, we mean both new products and updates of products that are already in the market.

Examples of such measures are "time to market," "delivery speed," and "development time." These measures look at different phases of deliveries. "Delivery speed" focuses on the time it takes, from when the product is ready, to reach the customers; "development time" focuses on the time it takes to develop the product. "Time to market" is a well-known and frequently used measure, since this measure looks at the whole chain of delivery. The "clock" starts when a customer demand reaches the product management, and stops when the product reaches the customer. The measure is usually presented in number of days or weeks.

It is necessary though, to be able to split this measure into the phases that, together, build up the whole chain of delivery. This is important, so that each phase gets its own execution time frame (i.e. the maximum time it should take to complete the respective phase), so that appropriate actions can be taken for those phases that do not fulfill stated "time" requirements.

6.4   Summary

As software measurement has been researched since the 1950s, the number of measures available in research papers, tools and websites is enormous. It has been a trend that new technologies bring in new measures to show the effects of these new technologies.

In this chapter, we provided an overview of what kinds of measures exist in software engineering and which measures we encountered in our work with software development companies. In total, we have catalogued over 1000 and we still feel that this is just a fraction of all existing ones. Nevertheless, we see that our catalogue, or portfolio, of measures provides guidance for modern companies in addressing the question of what to measure.

The examples of measures provided in this chapter are intended to guide the measurement designers when addressing the question of what to measure. These examples show how we work with the definitions of measures, and can be complemented with the definitions of measures provided in Chap. 2.

In the next chapter, we review some of the new techniques for working with software measures—machine learning, big data and defining measurement reference etalons.

6.5 Further Reading

Although there exist many measures for similar properties, we can often observe that they are highly correlated. For instance, Schröder et al. [SBK⁺17] compared different measures of model size to observe multiple correlations. Similar finding has been done on the source code size measurement by Gil and Lalouche [GL17]. Therefore, we recommend exploring the work on using machine learning to prevent the explosion of measures and rather use flexible configurations to calibrate the existing measures [OSB⁺17, SDR17].

The measure of release readiness shown in this chapter has been evaluated in our previous study at one of our partner companies [SMP12b]. The details of the evaluation of this measure provide an understanding of how the company used it in practice—both to plan releases, and to monitor the agility of their software development.

Kitchenham [Kit10] conducted a systematic mapping study of software measures. The results, although almost a decade old, are still valid and show that the field has been evolving. It also shows how broad the field is.

The study of Abdellatief et al. [ASGJ13] is an example of a narrow study of measurement approaches in a sub-domain, similar to the study of Fotrousi et al. [FFFLG14].

McGarry [McG02] presented a number of measures, compatible with the ISO/IEC 15939 standard. We recommend this book for the measurement designers who would like to get a complementary view on software measurement.

References

[ASGJ13] Majdi Abdellatief, Abu Bakar Md Sultan, Abdul Azim Abdul Ghani, and Marzanah A Jabar. A mapping study to investigate component-based software system metrics. *Journal of systems and software*, 86(3):587–603, 2013.

[CD09] Cagatay Catal and Banu Diri. A systematic review of software fault prediction studies. *Expert systems with applications*, 36(4):7346–7354, 2009.

[FFFLG14] Farnaz Fotrousi, Samuel A Fricker, Markus Fiedler, and Franck Le-Gall. Kpis for software ecosystems: A systematic mapping study. In *International Conference of Software Business*, pages 194–211. Springer, 2014.

[FSHL13] Robert Feldt, Miroslaw Staron, Erika Hult, and Thomas Liljegren. Supporting software decision meetings: Heatmaps for visualising test and code measurements. In *Software Engineering and Advanced Applications (SEAA), 2013 39th EUROMICRO Conference on*, pages 62–69. IEEE, 2013.

[GL17] Yossi Gil and Gal Lalouche. On the correlation between size and metric validity. *Empirical Software Engineering*, 22(5):2585–2611, 2017.

[ISO16a] ISO/IEC. ISO/IEC 25023 - Systems and software engineering - Systems and software Quality Requirements and Evaluation (SQuaRE) - Measurement of system and software product quality. Technical report, International Standards Organization, 2016.

[ISO16b] ISO/IEC.   ISO/IEC 25023 - Systems and software engineering - Systems and software Quality Requirements and Evaluation (SQuaRE) - Measurement of system and software product quality. Technical report, International Standards Organization, 2016.

[Kit10] Barbara Kitchenham.   What's up with software metrics? – A preliminary mapping study. *Journal of systems and software*, 83(1):37–51, 2010.

[Lal14] Frederic Laloux.   *Reinventing organizations: A guide to creating organizations inspired by the next stage in human consciousness.* Nelson Parker, 2014.

[LTC03] Mikael Lindvall, Roseanne Tesoriero Tvedt, and Patricia Costa.   An empirically-based process for software architecture evaluation. *Empirical Software Engineering*, 8(1):83–108, 2003.

[McG02] John McGarry.   *Practical software measurement: objective information for decision makers.* Addison-Wesley Professional, 2002.

[Med17] Wilhelm Meding.   Effective monitoring of progress of agile software development teams, in modern software companies – an industrial case study. In *MENSURA*, pages 1–8. ACM, 2017.

[MS10] Niklas Mellegård and Miroslaw Staron.   Characterizing model usage in embedded software engineering: a case study. In *Proceedings of the Fourth European Conference on Software Architecture: Companion Volume*, pages 245–252. ACM, 2010.

[NB05] Nachiappan Nagappan and Thomas Ball.   Use of relative code churn measures to predict system defect density.   In *Software Engineering, 2005. ICSE 2005. Proceedings. 27th International Conference on*, pages 284–292. IEEE, 2005.

[Opp04] Bohdan W Oppenheim.   Lean product development flow. *Systems engineering*, 7(4), 2004.

[OSB+17] Miroslaw Ochodek, Miroslaw Staron, Dominik Bargowski, Wilhelm Meding, and Regina Hebig.   Using machine learning to design a flexible loc counter. In *Machine Learning Techniques for Software Quality Evaluation (MaLTeSQuE), IEEE Workshop on*, pages 14–20. IEEE, 2017.

[PSSM10] K. Pandazo, A. Shollo, M Staron, and W. Meding.   Presenting Software Metrics Indicators: A Case Study. In *Proceedings of the 20th International Conference on Software Product and Process Measurement*, 2010.

[PW92] Dewayne E Perry and Alexander L Wolf.   Foundations for the study of software architecture. *ACM SIGSOFT Software engineering notes*, 17(4):40–52, 1992.

[PW13] Daniel Port and Joel Wilf.   The value of certifying software release readiness: An exploratory study of certification for a critical system at JPL. In *Empirical Software Engineering and Measurement, 2013 ACM/IEEE International Symposium on*, pages 373–382. IEEE, 2013.

[Ric11] Eric Richardson.   What an agile architect can learn from a hurricane meteorologist. *IEEE software*, 28(6):9–12, 2011.

[SBB+09] Helen Sharp, Nathan Baddoo, Sarah Beecham, Tracy Hall, and Hugh Robinson. Models of motivation in software engineering. *Information and software technology*, 51(1):219–233, 2009.

[SBK+17] Jan Schroeder, Christian Berger, Alessia Knauss, Harri Preenja, Mohammad Ali, Miroslaw Staron, and Thomas Herpel. Comparison of model size predictors in practice. In *Proceedings of the 39th International Conference on Software Engineering Companion*, pages 186–188. IEEE Press, 2017.

[SDR17] Miroslaw Staron, Darko Durisic, and Rakesh Rana. Improving measurement certainty by using calibration to find systematic measurement error – A case of lines-of-code measure. In *Software Engineering: Challenges and Solutions*, pages 119–132. Springer, 2017.

[SFGL07] Cláudio Sant'Anna, Eduardo Figueiredo, Alessandro Garcia, and Carlos JP Lucena. Effective monitoring of progress of agile software development teams, in modern software companies – an industrial case study. In *European Conference on Software Architecture*, pages 207–224. Springer, 2007.

[SHF+13] Miroslaw Staron, Jorgen Hansson, Robert Feldt, Anders Henriksson, Wilhelm Meding, Sven Nilsson, and Christoffer Hoglund. Measuring and visualizing code stability–a case study at three companies. In *Software Measurement and the 2013 Eighth International Conference on Software Process and Product Measurement (IWSM-MENSURA), 2013 Joint Conference of the 23rd International Workshop on*, pages 191–200. IEEE, 2013.

[SM07] Miroslaw Staron and Wilhelm Meding. Predicting weekly defect inflow in large software projects based on project planning and test status. *Information and Software Technology*, page (available online), 2007.

[SM10] Miroslaw Staron and Wilhelm Meding. Defect inflow prediction in large software projects. *e-Informatica Software Engineering Journal*, 4(1):1–23, 2010.

[SM11] Miroslaw Staron and Wilhelm Meding. Monitoring bottlenecks in agile and lean software development projects – A method and its industrial use. *Product-Focused Software Process Improvement*, pages 3–16, 2011.

[SM17] Miroslaw Staron and Wilhelm Meding. A portfolio of internal quality metrics for software architects. In *International Conference on Software Quality*, pages 57–69. Springer, 2017.

[SMHH13] Miroslaw Staron, Wilhelm Meding, Christoffer Hoglund, and Jorgen Hansson. Identifying implicit architectural dependencies using measures of source code change waves. In *Software Engineering and Advanced Applications (SEAA), 2013 39th EUROMICRO Conference on*, pages 325–332. IEEE, 2013.

[SMP12a] Miroslaw Staron, Wilhelm Meding, and Klas Palm. Release readiness indicator for mature agile and lean software development projects. In *Agile Processes in Software Engineering and Extreme Programming*, pages 93–107. Springer, 2012.

[SMP12b] Miroslaw Staron, Wilhelm Meding, and Klas Palm. Release readiness indicator for mature agile and lean software development projects. In *Agile Processes in Software Engineering and Extreme Programming*, pages 93–107. Springer, 2012.

[SMS10] Miroslaw Staron, Wilhelm Meding, and Bo Söderqvist. A method for forecasting defect backlog in large streamline software development projects and its industrial evaluation. *Information and Software Technology*, 52(10):1069–1079, 2010.

[SMT+] Miroslaw Staron, Wilhelm Meding, Matthias Tichy, Jonas Bjurhede, Holger Giese, and Ola Söder. Industrial experiences from evolving measurement systems into self-healing systems for improved availability. *Software: Practice and Experience*.

[Sta17] Miroslaw Staron. *Automotive software architectures: An introduction*. Springer, 2017.

Chapter 7
New Techniques

Abstract Measurement, as a discipline, accompanied other software development activities from the beginning of the discipline. Since the beginning, new measurement theories, methods and tools have been developed to accompany the rapid development of the field of software engineering. Today, the main trends which shape the development of the discipline of measurement are (1) availability of large data sets, (2) availability of off-the-shelf machine learning tools, and (3) research in measurement reference etalons. In this chapter, we discuss these three trends, and describe the most prominent techniques useful for the discipline of measurement.

7.1 Introduction

The field of software measurement evolves, just as the entire discipline of software engineering evolves. In the early years of software measurement, the focus of the field was on using quantitative methods in decision making [Gil77]. Later on, the measurement experts understood the need for formalization of software measures and using applicable measurement theories [FP98, FB14]. However, in recent years we observed the increased focus on standardization and alignment with other disciplines [OC07, Abr10].

In this chapter, we look at the current trends in software engineering that influence the evolution of the field of software measurement. We explore the technologies related to Big data, machine learning and measurement reference etalons as we see that they have the potential to drive the evolution of the field.

The technologies related to Big data open up possibilities to store, process and use large quantities of measurement results—the data. This leads to the fact that we are closer to collecting enough measurement data to be able to develop standardized models for quantifying software development [Abr10]. Thanks to the open source technologies from Big data, we can now process data of different formats in real time, which allows us to build measurement systems for decision support in cars, planes and telecom nodes to the extent not possible before.

The popularization of machine learning, in addition, provides us with a set of off-the-shelf algorithms and tools to use when processing measurement results. Thanks

© Springer International Publishing AG, part of Springer Nature 2018
M. Staron, W. Meding, *Software Development Measurement Programs*,
https://doi.org/10.1007/978-3-319-91836-5_7

to the open source algorithms for classification, prediction and deep learning, we can use complex reasoning models. These models can now include such advanced parameters as uncertainty and probability. Thanks to open source tools, like Weka or R, almost any software engineer and software designer can use these algorithms. As many of these algorithms are open source, we can also use them in our products more often.

Finally, the theories from mature measurement disciplines in physics and in metrology, like the measurement standard etalons, provide us with the possibilities to standardize measurement processes. We can provide reference quantities and therefore reduce the ambiguity when using measurement instruments. We can also calibrate our measurement instruments and therefore we are able to compare results, obtained from different tools, with higher accuracy.

We conclude the chapter with a short overview of other technologies that have the potential of impacting the field of software measurement. We also describe our view on their potential impact.

7.2 Big Data

Big data is a term used to denote a set of methods, tools and techniques for manipulating large data sets (e.g. petabytes of information) with high speed and providing high value. Big data is important for our measurement for a number of reasons. First, the data is often in the form of measurement values and therefore measurement theories apply when we want to ensure the quality of the data. Second, the availability of big data sets opens up new possibilities for the measurement designers to define new measures, and to validate the existing measures on the available new data sets.

When discussing Big data, we can often characterize it by using the term five V's, which is coined to describe the five major characteristics of data:

1. Volume—the amount of data in the big data sets or streams often reaches terabytes, petabytes or even zetabytes. Typical data streams are internet data, mobile network data or the space observatory data.
2. Velocity—the speed of processing the data is very important and the new techniques for processing the data streams often use parallelization to achieve such velocity as can be used in safety-critical systems or real-time systems.
3. Value—the data stored in the big data sets possesses certain business value and the balance between the cost of storage and processing is lower than the business value of the data. We often hear about the data being the new oil of the modern information society.
4. Variety—the format, structure and meaning of the data in large data sets often vary and, therefore, the techniques used to process the data needs to be able to process different types of data.

5. Veracity—the data should be truthful in the data streams, meaning that all the processing of this data, and all decisions made based on the data, can only be correct if the data is true. In the presence of "lies," the value is much lower.

When describing these five V's we use open source technologies as reference, since these technologies, over time, become de facto references and standards in the area of Big data. In particular, we use the technologies from the Apache ecosystem, http://www.apache.org.

7.2.1 Volume and Velocity

The ability to handle large quantities of data, i.e. the ability to process large volumes of data, opens up the possibility to define more accurate and more universal measurement models. Once we have the technology to process terabytes of information, we have the possibility to run millions of online experiments [YMM$^+$17] to understand the behavior of our software and our customers. In these experiment systems, we are able to test different versions of software simultaneously and collect usage data, thus finding the optimal ways of developing the software or determining which software features are the most important for the users. Companies like Google use this kind of technology to optimize their products towards users' needs [LM15].

Technology that enables processing large data sets can be based on such open source products as:

1. Apache Hadoop—a general MapReduce()-based large data processing environment, used in such applications as Facebook [BGS$^+$11], and
2. Apache Spark—a general SQL-based large data processing engine, used more widely as it supports SQL [ZXW$^+$16].

These products are based on novel programming models, where parallelization of storage and processing is included in the programming frameworks and independently of the programming languages used. The ability to use distributed data sets, as if they were one data set, and order the data sets according to their properties (during the Reduce() operation), gives the measurement engineers the ability to run algorithms faster.

7.2.2 Value and Variety

The value of Big data was emphasized in 2014, in the article in Wired magazine about data being the new oil of our economy [Too14]. The value of data was recognized to be crucial for modern businesses, as without the right measurements and the right measurement data, modern enterprises are blind to the market needs.

Since the publication of the article, a number of initiatives have been started to share data at the national and international levels, e.g.:

1. European Union Open Data Portal, http://data.europa.eu/euodp/en/data/, where research and development projects can share data for others to replicate studies and to build more correct models.
2. International Software Benchmarking Standards Group (ISBSG), http://isbsg.org/, where software companies can donate measurements of their projects for comparison and benchmarking with other companies.
3. Swedish National Data Service (SND), https://snd.gu.se/en, where researchers can document and publish data sets for reuse and scrutiny of other researchers, and
4. PROMISE data repository, http://promise.site.uottawa.ca/SERepository/, where researchers can donate data sets for replications of studies and comparison.

Even companies like Audi have recognized the benefits from enabling others to use their software development data to replicate studies and to find new patterns in existing data [ASD+15].

For the field of software measurement, this means that we can be faster in developing universal models because we can cross-validate our models throughout different data sets, projects, or companies. This means that we can experiment with old techniques to improve them and be able to find new industry standards [FDGLDG14].

Using the technologies based on flexible data structures (e.g. CouchDB or Elasticsearch), which do not require a specific structure of the data, enables the measurement engineer to work with a variety of data. The variety means that the measurements can come from different entities and come from different measurement instruments; the measurements can also be of very different kinds (e.g. LOC and complexity). Thanks to the flexibility, and advanced mechanisms for replication, we can take advantage of processing a variety of data at high speeds.

7.2.3 Veracity

Historically, the notion of veracity is derived from the area of sociology and its major popularity lies in the area of criminology—the ability to detect whether a witness is veracious or not [LPM99, MV06]. In that particular context, the term veracity is used both in relation to actors (e.g. witnesses) and their statements (i.e. data) [CMB70]. The latter refers to judging the truthfulness of a statement and is in scope for our purposes as well.

In our context, we consider the definition of veracity as quoted by Krotofil [KLG15], who defines veracity as *the property that an assertion truthfully reflects the aspect it makes a statement about*. We can see a direct relation to the field of criminology and also see the challenges related to automated assessment of veracity in the context of software systems [SS16]. We can apply the same reasoning for contextualizing the concept of veracity of measurement. We need both the measurement method and the measurement result to be veracious. This means that we always need to consider the veracity of the measurement instruments as their ability to measure the true value. In this case, the automatic measurement instruments might not be better as there is a limit to what we can automate. Certain measurements require advanced techniques, which make assumptions and therefore can lead to low veracity data.

An example of a situation illustrating the use of the advanced techniques is when we want to measure graphical objects, such as the number of cars, based on images captured by a camera. In order to recognize shapes, the camera may need to apply heuristic algorithms; such algorithms usually have limitations on the weather conditions, light conditions or the shape of the cars. Therefore, the algorithms may not recognize all cars, which therefore leads to measurement data which is not veracious.

Other examples where we can violate the veracity of data are:

- limitations of our ability to measure the physical property in general (e.g. our limitations to measure time),
- non-adequate measurement of a physical property by a measurement instrument, because of the inappropriate design of the instrument,
- non-adequate measurement caused by a faulty measurement instrument during the operation,
- non-adequate measurement caused by an obstructed measurement instrument, and
- faulty data caused by a malicious agent's tampering with the measurement instrument's data

Naturally, there are differences in the countermeasures, preventing the malicious manipulation of measurement instruments or causing other unintentional problems. However, dealing with the non-veracious data does not differ—the system making a decision based on the data needs to ensure that its actions do not cause harm to the system and the environment it operates in.

From our experience, having true measurement results is very important for the reliability of information products. The data integrity checks and the runtime information quality assessment, described in Chap. 4, are prerequisites [SM09]. However, the trueness of the measurement is key, mentioned in the ISO VIM standard [oWM93]—the measurement result should truly reflect the measured entity and its parameters.

A comprehensive description of and discussion on veracity of data in general can be found in the book by Berti-Equille and Borge-Holthoefer [BEBH15]. Their discussion is directed mostly for assessing the information in general, not necessarily measurement. An example of such information is a statement about a fact that can be verified—"It is raining at the moment." The statement seems to be simple to verify—we can intuitively check whether it is raining or not. However, the calculation of the trueness of this statement can be more complex as in practice there are limitations related to the data collection and instrumentation (e.g. very sensitive measurement instruments can be triggered by a small amount of rain, unnoticeable to a human being), parametrization (e.g. small rain is not considered to be rain by the instruments, but can be considered to be rain by the human being) or timeliness (e.g. the statement was made yesterday about yesterday's weather but the information was not updated).

Therefore, in practice, we often consider trueness as a parameter with gradation and we talk about truth computation and reasoning.

7.3 Machine Learning

The availability of large data sets, and the technology to process this data, can be complemented with the availability of easy-to-use machine learning algorithms. In the last decade, the field of machine learning has evolved from being accessible mostly to statistical experts, to being accessible to almost everyone with basic knowledge in statistics. One major reason for that was the availability of easy-to-use open source tools implementing machine learning algorithms—e.g. Weka or R.

Figure 7.1 shows one of the most popular machine learning platforms used in research—Weka. The tool provides software engineers, and measurement designers, with the possibility to experiment with different algorithms. The tool can also generate Java code implementing these algorithms, to be used in measurement systems.

The availability of tools like Weka lets the measurement designers work with algorithms for clustering entities based on their measured properties, classify entities given a specific measurement goal and predict trends in data based on measurements. As the field of machine learning is growing rapidly, we only focus on these three in this chapter, leaving such techniques as reinforced learning, deep learning and knowledge discovery to dedicated literature about machine learning [Qui14, Lan13, Har12].

For measurement designers, machine learning algorithms are useful when making sense of the measurement results—providing interpretation to the measurement data.

7.3.1 Clustering

One of the application areas for machine learning is clustering. In measurement programs, the measurement designers are often faced with the problem of grouping elements based on a given characteristic or finding how many groups of entities are measured by a given data set. The measurement designers can use a number of

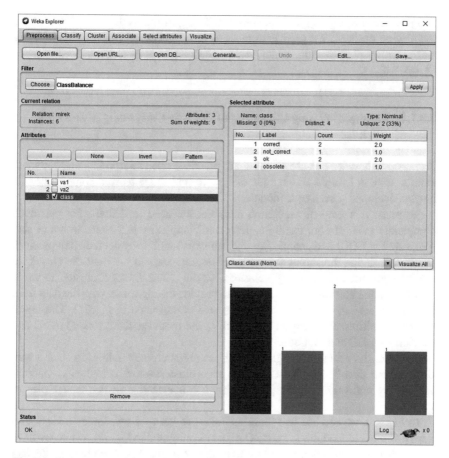

Fig. 7.1 Open source tool for machine learning—Weka

algorithms to address this challenge of how many clusters of entities exist in the
data set, e.g.:

1. k-Nearest Neighbour (kNN), which is a centroid-based algorithm dividing the
   data set into clusters based on finding centroids and the distance between data
   points and centroids.
2. Hierarchical clustering, which is a connectivity-based algorithm dividing the data
   set into clusters based on the similarity between individual data points and groups
   of data points.
3. Expectation-maximization algorithm, which is a distribution-based algorithm
   dividing the data set based on the probability that data points belong to the same
   distribution.
4. DBSCAN, which is a density-based algorithm dividing the data set based on
   identifying regions in the data set of varied density.

From our experience, one of the most useful algorithms is the kNN algorithm for identifying clusters. We used it in our previous studies because of its simplicity and intuitive visualization, which makes the results easy to explain in practice [ASM+14].

7.3.1.1   Example of Using Clustering to Find the Complexity of Software Modules

To illustrate how we can use clustering in practice, when interpreting measurement results, we can explore an example of how to find the perceived complexity of a newly developed source code module.

To make this kind of prediction possible, we need to define what perceived complexity mean. In our example, perceived complexity is a combination of size (measured in LOC) and complexity (measured in McCabe cyclomatic complexity). We do not define thresholds for these values, and instead we want the clustering (kNN) algorithm to find the right clusters. We only limit the set of clusters to three.

To teach the kNN algorithm we need to provide the algorithm with the data from the current system. In our example, this data is presented in Fig. 7.2. The figure shows nine different modules (1–9), each of the modules characterized using two measures—LOC and McCabe.

To make the example straightforward, we prepared the modules in such a way that we can clearly see that there are three clusters—low complexity, medium complexity and high complexity, which we can visualize in the scatter plot in Fig. 7.3.

In Fig. 7.3, we can see that these modules are grouped into three clusters. The newly developed modules are characterized as presented in Fig. 7.4, where we have three modules, also characterized by LOC and McCabe. When we look at the data about the newly developed modules, we can intuitively see that these three modules belong to three different clusters. Now, we can also use the kNN algorithm to classify them.

The script, which we use to make the clustering and find where the newly developed modules belong, is presented in Fig. 7.5.

Lines 1–10 prepare the data sets for analyses; the data files are read into the arrays in R, and the module names are removed from the data (lines 7–8), as we do not need them for the clustering algorithm.

Line 13 is where we execute the clustering algorithm, to find the three clusters in the data and name these clusters (line 16). The plot in Fig. 7.3 is plotted in line 22.

Finally, the actual classification of the newly developed modules to the three clusters is done in line 28. That is when the classification is bound to the data set and printed in line 32. The result of this algorithm is shown in Fig. 7.6, where we can see that the three modules are classified into three different clusters. The results of the execution of the algorithm provide us also with the statistics related to the actual clustering such as means of squares or distances to centroid. However, these are not needed in practice as they describe the quality of the clustering process.

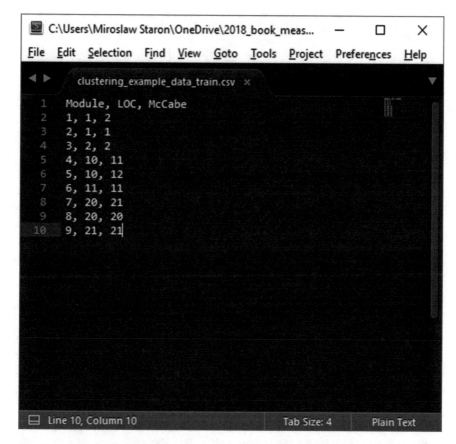

Fig. 7.2 A set of current modules

This simple example illustrates how we can use machine learning clustering to provide interpretation for the measurement results. When we use this machine learning algorithm over time, the predictions get better, and the burden on the stakeholders decreases. The stakeholder need not make manual assessments of the data, but the algorithm can use the previous assessments to derive the new ones. From our experience, this can be very useful when constructing analogy-based prediction models and analysis models.

7.3.2 Classification

Generally, the problem of classification is similar to the problem of clustering, with one significant difference. The classification problem is focused on which class a given new observation belongs to. The classes are derived from a training set.

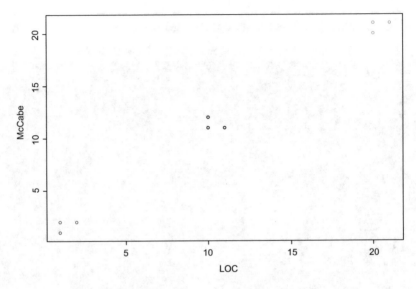

Fig. 7.3 A set of current modules visualized as a scatter plot; colors indicate clusters

In the example of clustering in Sect. 7.3.1, the last step, where we classified the newly developed module, is already touching upon the classification area in machine learning. However, the classification problems can be within a number of areas, e.g.:

1. binary or multiclass—depending on whether the classification results in assigning one of two classes (e.g. defect is easy or difficult to fix) or multiple ones (e.g. defect is very easy, moderately easy or difficult to fix), and
2. black-box or white-box—depending on whether we know the rules of how the classification is done (white-box) or not (black-box)

The current trend in machine learning is the focus on deep-learning algorithms with multiple layers of classification, clustering, prediction, etc. This focus has also driven the popularization of simpler techniques such as decision trees for classification.

Decision trees are useful in software measurement, in similar areas to the usage of clustering algorithms—to automatically provide interpretations of the measurement data. The difference between the clustering algorithms and the classification algorithms is that the clustering algorithms are unsupervised, while the classification algorithms are supervised. For the unsupervised algorithms, there are no right-wrong answers, and therefore for the clustering algorithms there is no such thing as a wrong cluster. For the supervised algorithms there is a right and a wrong answer, and therefore for the decision trees there are right classifications and wrong classifications.

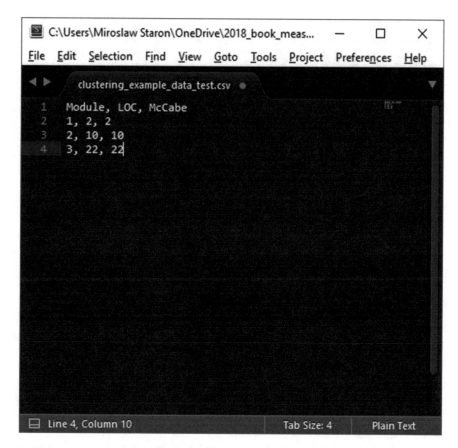

Fig. 7.4 A set of newly added modules

The most common and simple decision tree algorithms are:

1. classification tree, which predicts the class the entity belongs to, and
2. regression tree, which predicts a number, like the number of defects next week or the cost of a project,

7.3.2.1 Example of Classifying Defects Using Decision Trees in Weka

For this section, we can focus on the classification trees and their usage for solving a problem of classifying defects. Imagine we would like to find if we should prioritize a specific defect or not. Figure 7.7 shows this conceptually.

To exemplify how the classification works, we use a set of defects to train the decision tree on. We use the data set presented in Table 7.1.

```
 1    # read the data
 2    modulesData <- read.csv("clustering_example_data_train.csv", sep=",")
 3    newModulesData <- read.csv("clustering_example_data_test.csv", sep=",")
 4
 5    # removing the names of the modules
 6    # as they are not needed in the analyses
 7    modulesData[,1] <- NULL
 8    newModulesData[,1] <- NULL
 9
10    set.seed(1)
11
12    # Finding the clusters
13    fit <-kmeans(modulesData, 3)
14
15    # changing the names of clusters to the text
16    complexityLabels <- factor(fit$cluster, levels= c(1,2,3), labels=c("low", "high", "moderate"))
17
18    # binding the name of the cluster to the data row
19    clusteredModules <- cbind(modulesData,complexityLabels)
20
21    #visualizing the clusters with different colors
22    plot(LOC,McCabe, col=clusteredModules[,3])
23
24    # using the names of the clusters as complexity classes
25    complexityClasses <- clusteredModules[,3]
26
27    # finding the cluster where the new modules are classified
28    newModulesComplexityClass <- knn(modulesData, newModulesData, complexityClasses, k = 3)
29
30    newModulesComplexity <- cbind(newModulesData, newModulesComplexityClass)
31
32    print(newModulesComplexity)
33
```

Fig. 7.5 R script for clustering

In Weka, we use the J48 decision tree algorithm, which produces the classification tree as shown in Fig. 7.8. The classification tree has found that if the submitter is "john," then the majority of defects is "difficult," regardless of which phase they are found in. If the submitter is "mary," then the majority of defects is "easy." However, if the submitter is "tom," then the classification depends also on the phase where the defect was found.

Now, as we mentioned before, classification trees are a type of supervised learning, which means that we can test whether the classifications are good in practice. For this, we use the data set specified in Table 7.2.

If we examine the test set, we can see that there are defects which do not fall under the classification easily (i.e. we could expect some deviations between the classification and the test data). For example, defect with ID of 3 is such an example. After applying the classification tree to the test set, Weka produces the output visible in Fig. 7.9.

In the output from the classification we can see three parts: (1) summary, (2) accuracy by class, and (3) confusion matrix. The summary part summarizes the parameters of the classification, such as the number of accurately classified instances, Kappa statistics or mean absolute error. The first two lines, the number of classified instances, gives us a good overview of how good the algorithm is—in our case 10 defects were classified correctly and three were not.

The detailed accuracy section provides us with more details on which class was the most difficult to classify correctly. In our case, this was the class with the moderate defects as we did not have any moderate defect in the test set. The class that was classified best was the class of impossible defects. To find out more

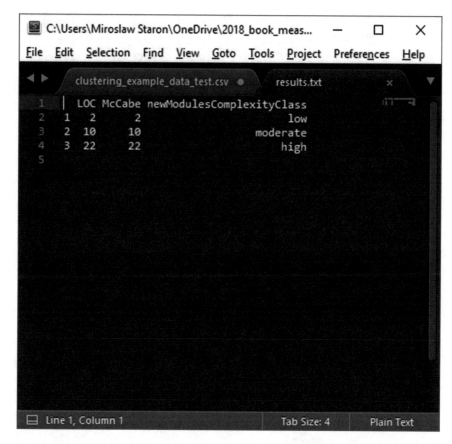

Fig. 7.6 Classification results

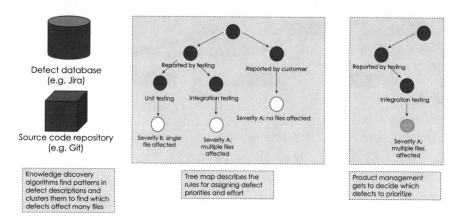

Fig. 7.7 A conceptual view on classifying defects using machine learning

Table 7.1 Existing defect
data—training set

ID	Submitter	Phase	Difficulty
d1	John	unit_test	Easy
2	Mary	unit_test	Moderate
3	John	component_test	Moderate
4	John	integration_test	Difficult
5	Mary	component_test	Moderate
6	Tom	customer	Impossible
7	Tom	integration_test	Impossible
8	Tom	unit_test	Difficult
9	Tom	unit_test	Difficult
10	Mary	unit_test	Easy
11	John	integration_test	Difficult
12	Tom	customer	Impossible
13	Mary	customer	Easy
14	John	customer	Easy
15	John	customer	Difficult
16	Mary	customer	Easy
17	Tom	integration_test	Impossible
18	Tom	integration_test	Impossible

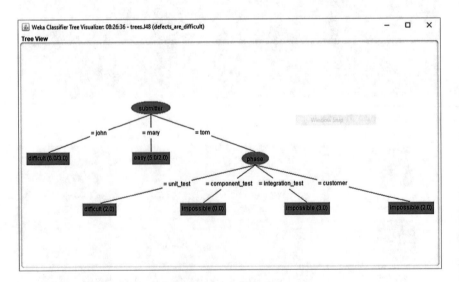

Fig. 7.8 Decision tree build by Weka's J48 algorithm

about how many cases were classified incorrectly and to which classes, we need to
examine the last section—the confusion matrix. The matrix shows how many cases
were classified to which class and where they should be classified.

Table 7.2 Existing defect
data—test set

ID	Submitter	Phase	Difficulty
1	John	integration_test	Difficult
2	Mary	unit_test	Moderate
3	John	component_test	Moderate
4	John	component_test	Difficult
5	Tom	component_test	Impossible
6	John	integration_test	Difficult
7	Mary	component_test	Easy
8	John	customer	Difficult
9	John	customer	Difficult
10	John	integration_test	Impossible
11	Tom	integration_test	Impossible
12	Tom	integration_test	Impossible
13	Mary	customer	Easy

```
=== Evaluation on test set ===

Time taken to test model on supplied test set: 0 seconds

=== Summary ===

Correctly Classified Instances        10            76.9231 %
Incorrectly Classified Instances       3            23.0769 %
Kappa statistic                        0.6638
Mean absolute error                    0.2315
Root mean squared error                0.3372
Relative absolute error               62.4618 %
Root relative squared error           78.4626 %
Total Number of Instances             13

=== Detailed Accuracy By Class ===

            TP Rate  FP Rate  Precision  Recall  F-Measure  MCC    ROC Area  PRC Area  Class
            1,000    0,091    0,667      1,000   0,800      0,778  0,955     0,667     easy
            0,000    0,000    0,000      0,000   0,000      0,000  0,727     0,267     moderate
            1,000    0,250    0,714      1,000   0,833      0,732  0,875     0,714     difficult
            0,750    0,000    1,000      0,750   0,857      0,822  0,875     0,827     impossible
Weighted Avg. 0,769   0,110    0,685      0,769   0,707      0,654  0,865     0,673

=== Confusion Matrix ===

 a b c d   <-- classified as
 2 0 0 0 | a = easy
 1 0 1 0 | b = moderate
 0 0 5 0 | c = difficult
 0 0 1 3 | d = impossible
```

Fig. 7.9 Results from applying the classification algorithm on the test data

7.3.3   *Other Machine Learning Applications in Software Measurement*

In addition to the application of clustering and classification algorithms, we have observed the use of predictions as one of the applications. However, the use of predictions in software measurement is an established field with its roots in statistics. In modern enterprises, however, the area of predictions is important as it is a part of modern software measurement programs. In particular, the modern software enterprises focus on reliable predictions for decision making rather than on "gut feeling." The stakeholders observe trends in their indicators, and use regression methods to predict the new values.

In addition to the prediction, classification and clustering methods, it is deep learning that is deemed to be the next "big thing" in the area of software measurement. Thanks to the ability of combining multiple techniques for different layers of the learning network we can obtain very accurate results when recognizing patterns in the measurement data.

7.4   Measurement Reference Etalons

One of the newest theoretical contributions to metrology in software engineering, is the concept of measurement reference etalons. This contribution is mentioned by Abran in his newest book on software measurement, "Software metrics and software metrology" [Abr10], and work together with his colleagues on the methodology for establishing measurement reference etalons [KA07b] and [KA07a].

In VIM, the measurement standard etalons are defined as "the realization of the definition of a given quantity, with stated quantity value and associated measurement uncertainty, used as a reference." In practice, the measurement standard etalons, also known as measurement reference etalons, are base quantities of value 1 which are used to calibrate the measurement instruments and the measurement systems. Conceptually, we could compare them to the measurement reference etalons from physics—a kilogram. Figure 7.10 presents the kilogram etalon as stored in the international standardization body in Paris.

As we can see in the figure, the etalon is stored under very controlled conditions in a double vacuum container. This controlled storage prevents the influence of external environment, e.g., temperature or light conditions. Having measurement reference etalons provides us with the possibility to calibrate the measurement instruments, wages in the case of kilogram.

The concept of the measurement standard etalon relates closely to the concept of calibration and uncertainty, and therefore is used frequently in the context of understanding of the measurement uncertainty and measurement error.

In software engineering, however, we do not have any established etalons. The first work in this area is by Abran [Abr10], who defined a data movement etalon in the context of the function point measurement. The definition of the data movement etalon is not as precise as the definition of the kilogram, but it provides a good uniform way of relating results of function point measurement to each other.

There are two ways of defining the measurement standard etalons—one is through the definition of the reference quantity and the other one is through the definition of the measurement method.

Fig. 7.10 A replica of the prototype of the kilogram at the Cité des Sciences et de l'Industrie, Paris, France. Author: Japs 88; licensed under the Creative Commons Attribution-Share Alike 3.0 Unported license

Using the reference quantity can be exemplified by the definition of the kilogram. The reference quantity is stored under controlled conditions and can be used to calibrate measurement instruments which are then used to measure other quantities of the same kind—i.e. mass.

Using the reference measurement method, however, is different. In physics we can exemplify this by the reference measurement method for meter (length). In 1795 it was defined as a length along the meridian—$\frac{1}{10,000,000}$ part of the quadrant along the meridian.[1] The associated absolute uncertainty was in the range of 500–100 μm. Depending on our ability to measure the meridian, the measurement uncertainty was rather large.

In 1799, the meter was defined using a reference length—a stickyard platinum bar stored just like the kilogram. The absolute uncertainty was reduced to 50–10 μm, but since the physical conditions of the environment of the platinum bar could slightly change (e.g. temperature, light), there was still some measurement uncertainty.

---

[1] Source: Wikipedia.

However, in 1960, the definition was changed to a certain number of wavelengths of a light emitted by a specific isotope, which led to a significant improvement of uncertainty to 4 nm.

Finally, in 1983, the definition was changed to be the length of the path travelled by light in a vacuum in $\frac{1}{299,792,458}$ s. Since this measurement method is independent of many physical conditions, the uncertainty was further reduced to 0.1 nm.

The example with meter illustrates the evolution of the measurement reference etalons and their associated measurement standard uncertainty. One of the practical observations is that over time, the reduction of uncertainty can lead to the increase in the complexity of the measurement method. The measurement of length using the time of the travel of light is rather simple, but it requires very advanced measurement instruments—for example to measure the time of $\frac{1}{299,792,458}$ s. This advanced measurement instruments mean that the ability to assess the measurement error of a given length requires advanced competence.

7.4.1 Measurement Reference Etalons in Software Engineering

Abran [Abr10] presents an example of the first measurement reference etalon used in the measurement of size of software in terms of COSMIC function points. The methodology presented in that book consists of seven steps (quoted below; for full reference please see the original publication):

1. Analysis and selection of textual description of candidate functional user requirements.
2. Identification and selection of quality criteria for the measurement process.
3. Quality improvement to the set of functional user requirements by transforming the set into the selected specification language.
4. Selection or design of an etalon template for presenting the measurement process and measurement results.
5. Initial measurement of requirements documented in the adopted specification notation by an experienced measurer to produce a draft of results in the designed etalon template.
6. Selection of a group of experts to review the initial measurement results.
7. Verification by the expert measurers.

The above methodology has an aspect important for a broad adoption of proposed etalons—consensus building among experts and measurers. The process is similar to the process of establishing measurement reference etalons by such organizations as the British Weights and Measures Office in the past or ISO/IEC in the present. The result of applying this methodology in the area of COSMIC function point is the data movement etalon, which provides a reference measure of inputs in the measurement of function points.

7.4.2   How to Define New Measurement Reference Etalons

Based on the definitions of the measurement reference etalons in physics and the description of the methodology for defining measurement reference etalons for function points, we can discuss how to define measurement reference etalons in general. Although it is important to have measurement reference etalons for the base quantities, the challenge in software engineering is that we do not have a list of base quantities. We use several proxies for various quantities—for example we use the lines of code or COSMIC function points as proxies of size or McCabe cyclomatic complexity as a proxy of complexity.

Therefore, what we advise, based on our experience, is to define reference etalons for the measures used in research and in practice in software engineering. When defining a new measure, we should include the definition of the measurement reference etalon. As we see it, there are two aspects for defining the etalons—a precise definition and the consensus among the experts and measurers.

The **precise definition** of the etalon has to include three elements—the definition of the measure, the definition of the reference quantity (or the reference measurement method) and the definition of the measurement uncertainty.

For the definition of the measure we can use the templates of Quality Measure Elements provided by the ISO/IEC 25000 standards and discussed in Chap. 2. We can also use mathematical formulas. The definition of the measure should also fulfill the properties relevant for the type of measure as discussed in Chap. 2, e.g. the null-value property of size measures.

For the definition of the reference quantity, we need to use either a reference definition of an atomic measurand, i.e. a measurand which results in the value of 0. We can also use the reference measurement method, i.e. a reference measurement instrument. If possible, we should provide both and we should also provide a set of examples of how to measure quantities larger than 1.

The definition of the uncertainty can be done based on statistical analyses of the dispersion of measurement (random error) and based on the model of the measurement instruments and the prescribed measurement procedure (systematic error).

The **consensus among the experts** has to include the same elements as pre-scribed by Abran—documentation of the measurement results and their evaluation. In practice, when defining new measures, this can only be done through empirical studies evaluating measures and through focus groups.

7.5   Other Trends

There are trends in contemporary software engineering which do not directly influence the area of software measurement, but have the potential of making software measurement different in future. Containers are one of such trends. The containers are a technology for packaging software components, together with the needed parts of operating systems' libraries, for use in other systems without the need to manually replicate the execution environment. The technology is similar to the technology of virtual operating systems and hypervisors, with the difference that it does not require a full virtual operating system, but allows the containers to run on a native operating system. Today, this technology is used for replicating software execution environments, but in the future it has the potential to secure the replication of the environment for the measurement instruments used in defining measurement reference etalons.

We have also observed the increased organizational diversity and dynamics. In the last decade we have observed trends in the organization of software development, such as outsourcing, agility, insourcing and using post-deployment experimentation, to better understand the customers. These trends in the organization of software development lead to a large diversity of the ways in which software is developed today—combining open-source with proprietary software, new supplier-client relationships [SMNS16] and customer-data driven development [Bos16]. The diversity of the software development models, combined with the fast pace of the software market, required new ways of handling measures as strategic value for software enterprises, e.g. by using the customer analytics to discover new business areas.

Technical debt [KNO12] is one of the new areas which provide a new umbrella over measurement of software quality. In short, the technical debt is a metaphor of how much bad quality is built into software products due to taking shortcuts. The novelty of this category of measures is that the metaphor of technical debt can be used to recalculate a number of measures of different types (e.g. complexity, LOC and number of defects) into a single measure of how much time is needed to reduce the problems related to the measures. For example, one can set thresholds saying that complexity over a certain limit should be counted as technical debt and that reducing it would cost a certain amount of person-hours. A number of research groups investigate specific types of technical debt [AMdM$^+$16], e.g. the one related to architecture [MBC14, MB15].

References

[Abr10]   Alain Abran. *Software metrics and software metrology.* John Wiley & Sons, 2010.

[AMdM$^+$16]   Nicolli SR Alves, Thiago S Mendes, Manoel G de Mendonça, Rodrigo O Spínola, Forrest Shull, and Carolyn Seaman. Identification and management of technical debt: A systematic mapping study. *Information and Software Technology,* 70:100–121, 2016.

[ASD$^+$15]   Harry Altinger, Sebastian Siegl, Dajsuren, Yanja, and Franz Wotawa. A novel industry grade dataset for fault prediction based on model-driven developed automotive embedded software. In *12th Working Conference on Mining Software Repositories (MSR).* MSR 2015, 2015.

[ASM⁺14] Vard Antinyan, Miroslaw Staron, Wilhelm Meding, Per Österström, Erik Wik-strom, Johan Wranker, Anders Henriksson, and Jörgen Hansson. Identifying risky areas of software code in agile/lean software development: An industrial experience report. In *Software Maintenance, Reengineering and Reverse Engineering (CSMR-WCRE), 2014 Software Evolution Week-IEEE Conference on*, pages 154–163. IEEE, 2014.

[BEBH15] Laure Berti-Equille and Javier Borge-Holthoefer. Veracity of data: From truth discovery computation algorithms to models of misinformation dynamics. *Synthesis Lectures on Data Management*, 7(3):1–155, 2015.

[BGS⁺11] Dhruba Borthakur, Jonathan Gray, Joydeep Sen Sarma, Kannan Muthukkaruppan, Nicolas Spiegelberg, Hairong Kuang, Karthik Ranganathan, Dmytro Molkov, Aravind Menon, Samuel Rash, et al. Apache Hadoop goes realtime at Facebook. In *Proceedings of the 2011 ACM SIGMOD International Conference on Management of data*, pages 1071–1080. ACM, 2011.

[Bos16] Jan Bosch. Speed, data, and ecosystems: The future of software engineering. *IEEE Software*, 33(1):82–88, 2016.

[CMB70] Peter W. Carey, Jacques Mehler, and Thomas G. Bever. Judging the veracity of ambiguous sentences. *Journal of Verbal Learning and Verbal Behavior*, 9(2):243–254, Apr 1970.

[FB14] Norman Fenton and James Bieman. *Software metrics: A rigorous and practical approach*. CRC Press, 2014.

[FDGLDG14] Marta Fernández-Diego and Fernando González-Ladrón-De-Guevara. Potential and limitations of the ISBSG dataset in enhancing software engineering research: A mapping review. *Information and Software Technology*, 56(6):527–544, 2014.

[FP98] Norman E Fenton and Shari Lawrence Pfleeger. *Software metrics: A rigorous and practical approach*. PWS Publishing Co., 1998.

[Gil77] Tom Gilb. *Software metrics*. Winthrop, 1977.

[Har12] Peter Harrington. *Machine learning in action*, volume 5. Manning Greenwich, CT, 2012.

[KA07a] Adel Khelifi and Alain Abran. Design steps for developing software measurement standard etalons for ISO 19761. In *WSEAS International Conference on COMPUTERS*, 2007.

[KA07b] Adel Khelifi and Alain Abran. Software measurement standard etalons: A design process. *International Journal of Computers*, 1, 2007.

[KLG15] Marina Krotofil, Jason Larsen, and Dieter Gollmann. The Process Matters. In *Proceedings of the 10th ACM Symposium on Information Computer and Communications Security – ASIA CCS*. Association for Computing Machinery (ACM), 2015.

[KNO12] Philippe Kruchten, Robert L Nord, and Ipek Ozkaya. Technical debt: From metaphor to theory and practice. *Ieee software*, 29(6):18–21, 2012.

[Lan13] Brett Lantz. *Machine learning with R*. Packt Publishing Ltd, 2013.

[LM15] Eveliina Lindgren and Jürgen Münch. Software development as an experiment system: A qualitative survey on the state of the practice. In *International Conference on Agile Software Development*, pages 117–128. Springer, 2015.

[LPM99] Timothy R. Levine, Hee Sun Park, and Steven A. McCornack. Accuracy in detecting truths and lies: Documenting the "veracity effect". *Communication Monographs*, 66(2):125–144, Jun 1999.

[MB15] Antonio Martini and Jan Bosch. The danger of architectural technical debt: Contagious debt and vicious circles. In *Software Architecture (WICSA), 2015 12th Working IEEE/IFIP Conference on*, pages 1–10. IEEE, 2015.

[MBC14] Antonio Martini, Jan Bosch, and Michel Chaudron. Architecture technical debt: Understanding causes and a qualitative model. In *Software Engineering and Advanced Applications (SEAA), 2014 40th EUROMICRO Conference on*, pages 85–92. IEEE, 2014.

[MV06]   Samantha Mann and Aldert Vrij. Police officers' judgements of veracity tenseness, cognitive load and attempted behavioural control in real-life police interviews. *Psychology, Crime & Law*, 12(3):307–319, Jun 2006.

[OC07]   International Standard Organization and International Electrotechnical Commission. Software and systems engineering, software measurement process. Technical report, ISO/IEC, 2007.

[oWM93] International Bureau of Weights and Measures. *International vocabulary of basic and general terms in metrology*. International Organization for Standardization, Geneva, Switzerland, 2nd edition, 1993.

[Qui14] J Ross Quinlan. *C4.5: programs for machine learning*. Elsevier, 2014.

[SM09]   Miroslaw Staron and Wilhelm Meding. Ensuring reliability of information provided by measurement systems. In *Software Process and Product Measurement*, pages 1–16. Springer, 2009.

[SMNS16] Miroslaw Staron, Wilhelm Meding, Kent Niesel, and Ola Söder. Evolution of the role of measurement systems in industrial decision support. In *Handbook of Research on Global Supply Chain Management*, pages 560–580. IGI Global, 2016.

[SS16]   Miroslaw Staron and Riccardo Scandariato. Data veracity in intelligent transportation systems: the slippery road warning scenario. In *Intelligent Vehicles Symposium*, 2016.

[Too14] Joris Toonders. Data is the new oil of the digital economy. *Wired. https://www.wired.com/insights/2014/07/data-new-oil-digital-economy/ (accessed 17 August 2017)*, 2014.

[YMM+17] Sezin Gizem Yaman, Myriam Munezero, Jürgen Münch, Fabian Fagerholm, Ossi Syd, Mika Aaltola, Christina Palmu, and Tomi Männistö. Introducing continuous experimentation in large software-intensive product and service organizations. *Journal of Systems and Software*, 2017.

[ZXW+16] Matei Zaharia, Reynold S Xin, Patrick Wendell, Tathagata Das, Michael Armbrust, Ankur Dave, Xiangrui Meng, Josh Rosen, Shivaram Venkataraman, Michael J Franklin, et al. Apache Spark: A unified engine for big data processing. *Communications of the ACM*, 59(11):56–65, 2016.

Chapter 8
Maintaining and Evolving Measurement Programs

Abstract There is a broad misconception about measurement programs as many believe that it is enough to set up measurement systems, and then you have (more or less) a measurement program in place. Or, that after hard work the established measurement program will live and thrive forever. This cannot be more far from the truth. The way in which measurement programs are introduced, maintained, and evolved in companies and organizations is of the utmost importance. Keywords like soft issues, involvement, respect, responsiveness, and evolution must be part of the everyday work with the measurement program. These are the topics we address in this chapter

8.1 Introduction

For the most part, maintenance is perceived to be boring and tiresome. Truth of the matter is that if focus and effort are put during the design phase, maintenance can be, if not the most exciting job that the software industry has to offer, at least, easy and time-efficient. That is why we start this chapter by talking about how to design measurement programs for sustainability, laying the cornerstones for easy and time-efficient maintenance. The section after that, i.e. Sect. 8.4, focuses on maintenance. It describes what the maintenance of measurement program is, and it provides hands-on checklists for some of the measurement roles of the measurement programs.

Every software development company and organization evolves its products and ways of working. This means that the measurement program must also evolve, to keep up with those changes. Section 8.5 describes what to think of so that the measurement program continues to "live and thrive," while adjusting to product and organizational changes.

Many assume that measuring is about handling data (information) in an effective and efficient way, and fail to understand that behind this data are people. An example of a soft issue in measuring is to measure performance, without pointing fingers at individuals.

© Springer International Publishing AG, part of Springer Nature 2018

M. Staron, W. Meding, *Software Development Measurement Programs*,

https://doi.org/10.1007/978-3-319-91836-5_8

8.2   Designing Measurement Programs for Sustainability

In Chap. 3, we presented how to design a measurement program. In this section we complement this discussion with addressing the challenge of how to design sustainable measurement programs. Designing for sustainability means that maintenance and evolution aspects are taken into consideration from the very beginning. Companies and organizations want to have measurement programs that are easy to maintain, and easy to adapt to changes, irrespective of if these changes are initiated by companies and organizations themselves, or by customers.

In this section we have put focus mostly on information products. The reason for this is that information products are what stakeholders and measurement users see and use in their everyday work. If stakeholders and measurement users have access to information products that address their information needs effectively, succinctly, and unambiguously, then the chances for the successful and long lasting use of the measurement program increases dramatically.

8.2.1   Designing Long Lasting Information Products

8.2.1.1   Comments About Indicators

Based on our experiences, the following aspects are important for the definition of indicators:

1. An indicator has always a stakeholder, an analysis model, and actions tied to the different areas of the analysis model. If one of those three is missing, then the measure is not an indicator (just a base or derived measure).
2. Never use an indicator to sum up the status of other indicators. Let us take the following example: a project uses four KPIs (Key Performance Indicators): cost, plan, quality, and scope. Let us say that cost is red and the other three are green (on a green, yellow, and red scale). What is then the total status? Red or yellow? Or do three greens triumph over one red, making the status green? The four indicators should be presented one by one!
3. It is common knowledge that companies and organizations should have few indicators. But how few are few? Our recommendation is that a company should have no more than eight indicators. A project, regardless of size, should have a maximum of five indicators. A development team should not have more than three or four indicators.

8.2.1.2   Evaluating Information Products After Deployment

Just because an information product has been designed and implemented does not mean that the work of the designer of the information product has finished.

Designers of information products should use the questions below, from time to time, to ascertain that information products still satisfy the information need of stakeholders. The questions are based on [PSSM10]:

1. On a scale of 1–5, how easy is it to overview the indicator?
2. On a scale of 1–5, how easy is it to interpret the results?
3. On a scale of 1–5, how easy is it to find the detailed value of the indicator?
4. On a scale of 1–5, how easy is it to understand the metaphors used in the information product?
5. On a scale of 1–5, how well does the information product fulfill the information need of the stakeholder?

8.2.1.3 Selecting the Correct Type of Information Product

To effectively trigger decisions, support evolutions and prevent problems, the way in which the measures are visualized and communicated must vary. In order to make this variation structured and organized, in this section we present a model that helps the stakeholders to decide upon the type of information product to use, depending on their information needs. Table 8.1 lists areas to consider (i.e. dimensions), the "range" of each dimension (i.e. is the data acquisition fully manual, fully automated, or somewhere in between), and a short explanation. This section is based on [SNM15], where we presented the model. The model has been used in over a dozen companies to drive their dashboard initiatives.

8.3 Selecting the Right Dashboard

The dashboard selection model consists of seven categories describing seven aspects of dashboards:

1. Type of dashboard—defining what kind of visualization is needed. Many dashboards are used as reports where the stakeholders input the data and require flexibility of the format—this alternative is named report—whereas some require a strictly pre-defined visualization with the same structure for every update—the alternative designated as dashboard. There are naturally a number of possibilities of combining the flexibility and the strict format, which is denoted by the scale between fully flexible and fully strict.
2. Data acquisition—defining how the data is input into the tool. In general the stakeholders/employees can enter the data into the tool—e.g. making an assessment—the alternative is named manual; or they can have the data be imported from other systems—this alternative is named automated. The previous selection of a dashboard for visualization quite often correlates to the selection of the automated data provisioning.

3. Stakeholders—defining the type of the stakeholder for the dashboard. The dashboards which are used as so-called information radiators often have an entire group as a stakeholder, for example a project team. However, many dashboards which are designed to support decisions often have an individual stakeholder who can represent a group.
4. Delivery—defining how the data is provided to the stakeholders. On the one hand the information can be delivered to a stakeholder in such forms as e-mails or MS Sidebar gadgets—this alternative is called delivered—or on the other hand it can be fetched, which requires the stakeholder to actively seek the information in the form of opening a dedicated link and searching for the information—which is denoted as fetched.
5. Update—defining how often the data is updated. One alternative is to update the data periodically, for example every night, with the advantage of the data being synchronized but with the disadvantage that it is not up-to-date. The other alternative is the continuous update, which has the opposite effect on timeliness and synchronization.
6. Aim—defining what kind of aim the dashboard should fulfill. One of the alternatives is to use the dashboard as an information radiator—to spread the information to a broad audience. The other option is to design the dashboard for a specific type of decision in mind, for example release readiness.
7. Data flow—defining how much processing of the data is done in the dashboard. One of the alternatives is to visualize the raw data, which means that no additional interpretation is done, and the other is to add the interpretations by applying analysis models and thus to visualize indicators.

Graphically the dashboard selection model can be presented as a set of "sliders" which allow us to prioritize between poles in these dimensions—as presented in Fig. 8.1.

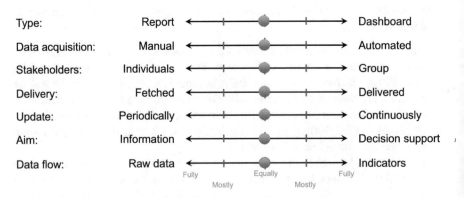

Fig. 8.1 Dashboard selection model

8.3.1 Examples

The dashboard selection model can be applied to a set of existing tools and classify them based on the dashboard model which they represent. For example, MS Excel can be used to visualize the data, but it primarily is dedicated to other purposes. If MS Excel is used to visualize measurement systems, and contains a dedicated visualization of indicators, its classification could be done as presented in Fig. 8.2. This example comes from our previous work on the frameworks for developing measurement systems [SMN08].

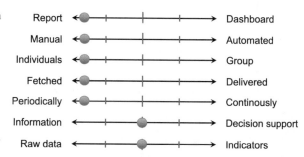

Fig. 8.2 Dashboard selection model—classification of MS Excel with indicators

An example of such a measurement system is shown in Fig. 8.3. The colored cells present the indicators and the measures, trends and raw data are available in other worksheets in the same workbook.

The evaluation of the MS Sidebar gadgets as a means of visualization of measures and indicators is classified as shown in Fig. 8.4. An example gadget from our previous works is also shown in Fig. 8.5

In such a gadget, the data is pre-processed in the form of indicators, fetched from core product development systems, widely spread, used both for radiation and for decision support [SMN08, SMP12a, SMH+13, SM09b].

Another example of a tool used for similar purposes is Tableau, which has been evaluated in our previous studies [PSSM10] and is presented in Fig. 8.6. The tool provides a number of pre-defined visualizations and analysis recipes, but is interactive and therefore not fully suited as an information radiator [Coc06]. However, it is important that the presentation is understandable [KS02, SKT05].

An example of a dashboard developed in Tableau is presented in Fig. 8.7.

Yet another example is a class of tools referred to as information radiators, i.e. dashboards dedicated to spreading the information to a broad audience. Their classification is presented in Fig. 8.8. These tools are designed with one purpose in mind and are meant to be non-interactive. Their primary use is in landscapes and during decision meetings.

An example information radiator is presented in Fig. 8.9. The main purpose of the radiator is to spread the current status to as wide an audience as possible. The radiator, therefore, is supposed to be easy to overview and require minimum time to

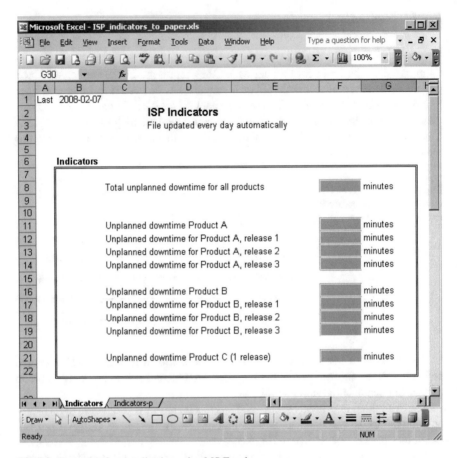

Fig. 8.3 Example of a visualization using MS Excel

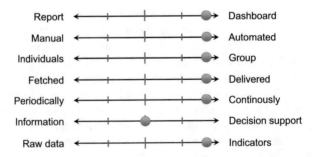

Fig. 8.4 Dashboard selection model—classification of gadget

Fig. 8.5 Example of a gadget

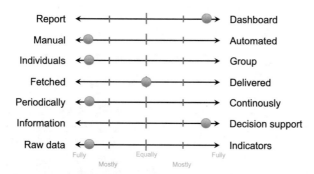

Fig. 8.6 Dashboard selection model—classification of Tableu

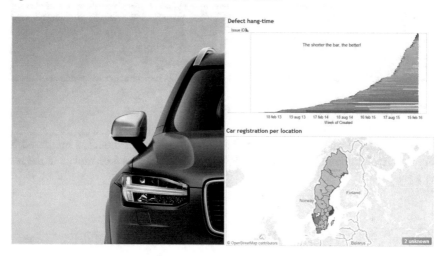

Fig. 8.7 An example dashboard in Tableau

comprehend the information. It is also meant to be rather static, i.e. no drill-down in the data and no interactive features.

From our experience, the information radiators should be used for places where project teams often meet during stand-up meetings and daily briefings, and at coffee areas and near entry/exit to their workspace.

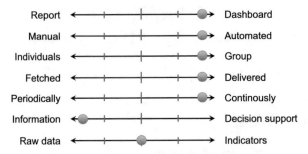

Report   ←——+———+———+—●→   Dashboard
Manual   ←———+———+———+—●→   Automated
Individuals   ←——+———+———+—●→   Group
Fetched   ←———+———+———+—●→   Delivered
Periodically   ←——+———+———+—●→   Continously
Information   ←●—+———+———+———→   Decision support
Raw data   ←—+———●———+———→   Indicators

Fig. 8.8 Dashboard selection model—classification of information radiators

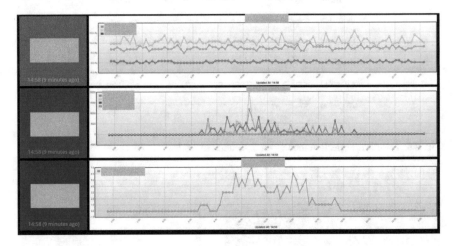

Fig. 8.9 An example information radiator

The graphical representation of the dashboard selection model is presented in Fig. 8.1. Each line represents one dimension, and each dot can be moved to the left or right.

8.3.2   Designing the Measurement Infrastructure

A measurement infrastructure must be characterized by a simple and generic structure, transparency and automation. These three aspects must always be present when designing and/or updating the measurement infrastructure. This means:

- **Simple and generic structure**—Limit the levels of depth of the hierarchy of the infrastructure, and the variety of storage places of raw and derived data. Re-use base and derived measures. Establish naming conventions that relate to specific places of the infrastructure. It must be easy for new entities to fit in, in the existing structure. Also, the architecture must be designed in such a way that it does not have to be re-designed every time there is e.g. an organizational change, or new products are developed.

- **Transparency**—*All* stakeholders, at *all* companies we have worked with, have stressed the importance it has to them, to see how data flows, and that the integrity of the data is kept, from data source to information product. Remember, transparency gives trust!
- **Automation**—Automation is a key prerequisite for the successful function and efficiency of a measurement program. The goal should be to have all operations involved, from fetching the data, to the update of the information products, *fully* automated.

8.4 Maintaining Measurement Programs Cost and Time Efficiently

In Chap. 3 we talked about how to design and deploy measurement programs. The focus of this section is to describe how to, cost efficiently, maintain measurement programs. Shortly, maintenance is about:

1. Monitoring the successful update of information products. This means that the metrics team must control that every information product is updated successfully. If this is not the case, then the metrics team must fix this, as stakeholders and measurement users must always have access to correct information products.
2. Updating information products according to new requirements from stakeholders. It is more of a rule than an exemption that throughout the lifetime of information products, stakeholders will need to make (mostly) minor adjustments to them. One such example can be to change the values of the thresholds of the analysis model.
3. Ascertaining that information products still address the information need of stakeholders. Both the metrics team and the stakeholders must continuously ascertain that information products still address the information need of the stakeholders.
4. Decommissioning information products and measurement systems that are not used. It is important for the effective and efficient function of the measurement infrastructure that it not contain unused information products and measurement systems.

Maintenance is usually perceived to be boring and non-creative, something that *has* to be done. Fact of the matter is that if listed recommendations in this section and Chaps. 3 and 4 are followed, maintenance will be cost- and time-efficient.

Following the set-up of Sects. 3.3.1 and 3.3.2, we go through all five measurement program components one by one, talking about what to consider in general, and listing hands-on checklists afterwards.

8.4.1   Maintaining Measurement Systems

Maintenance of measurement systems is about monitoring the execution of measurement systems and fixing those measurement systems that have not been executed correctly. Maintenance of measurement systems comprises also monitoring that all data transitions from data sources to information products have been executed successfully, and that the integrity of the data through all transitions has not be compromised. When errors in executions are detected, the metrics team must fix them.

We recommend that the metrics team keep statistics about which measurement systems fail the most. This is useful, since measurement systems that fail most often usually have a systematic error that causes them to fail. We recommend also that the metrics team keep statistics about the frequency with which the measurement systems are accessed. This gives a good picture about the most "popular" measurement systems, information that can be utilized in different ways, e.g. to understand which measures are mostly used in the organization, or to know which measurement systems to make (if needed) more efficient (i.e. to run faster).

The following checklist, Table 8.1, is applicable to the metrics team.

8.4.2   Maintaining Information Products

The correct performance of information products is of the utmost importance for the trust of the company or organization towards the metrics team and the measurement program. If, despite all precautions, information products are not updated correctly, it is important that (a) the stakeholders and the measurement users be notified and (b) that the error be corrected as fast as possible.

Mechanisms must be in place to warn both stakeholders and measurement users, *and* the metrics team, about erroneous information products. The reason for this is that no one can check *manually* the correctness of even a relatively small number (e.g. twenty) of information products.

These mechanisms must notify the stakeholders and the measurement users automatically, e.g. by having a dot that turns from green to red in an MS gadget. The metrics team must also have mechanisms in place that notify them about erroneous status of information products. This, so that they can fix the problem fast, preferably immediately! Examples of such mechanisms is to have e-mails sent to them automatically, when e.g. a data table in a database has not been updated correctly.

Having self-healing mechanisms in place provides valuable aid to the metrics team of course, since they reduce the number of errors that the metrics team has to deal with.

Maintaining information products is also about making minor changes to them. Stakeholders want often, after the information products have been deployed for

Table 8.1 Maintaining measurement systems—checklist

Questions	Explanation
Is extraction from all data sources automated?	If extraction of all data is not automated, actions must be taken to automate it!
Is monitoring of *all* measurement systems automated?	If monitoring of *all* measurement systems is not automated, actions must be taken to automate it!
Have *all* data transitions, from data sources to information products, been executed successfully?	Mechanisms must be in place to check that *all* transitions have been successful
Has the data integrity been kept, during *all* transitions, from data sources to information products?	Mechanisms must be in place to check that the integrity of the data is kept, through *all* transitions
Have *all* measurement systems been executed successfully?	Mechanisms must be in place to check that *all* measurement systems have been executed successfully
Is the execution of #1, #2 and #3 activities fully automated?	*Automation* is a key success factor for an effective and efficient maintenance of measurement systems. Effort should therefore be put to automate the execution of all steps in the update of measurement systems
Is the monitoring of #1, #2 and #3 activities automated?	Monitoring of *all* steps, of the update of measurement systems, must also be automated
Are self-healing mechanisms part of the measurement infrastructure?	Self-healing mechanisms save much maintenance time, and should therefore be in place for all measurement systems. See [SMT⁺17] about how to design and use a self-healing mechanism
Is the metrics team notified, automatically, when errors occur?	When errors occur, the metrics team must be notified by automated means, e.g. via mails, or web-pages
Can all members of the metrics team work with maintenance?	*All* members of the metrics team must be able to work with maintenance. This serves two main purposes: all members have (at least) an overview of all measurement systems that are in place, and it is easy to fill in for each other, during e.g. vacations and sickness
Is there a contingency plan in place?	A contingency plan *must* be in place. The plan must be able to be executed by *all* team members

some time, to make minor changes to them, e.g. change the thresholds defined in the (analysis) model. This is very usual, and the metrics team must be aware, and prepared for this. A well-structured measurement system enables fast changes to deployed information products!

Effort must also be put to ascertain that all information products are being used by stakeholders and measurement users. To avoid creating a "cemetery" of information products (compare with "dead code," in software products), it is important that the metrics team asks, at least twice a year, if the information products are still used.

The following checklist, Table 8.2 is applicable to the metrics team.

Table 8.2 Maintaining information products—checklist

Question	Explanation
Is monitoring of *all* information products automated?	If monitoring of *all* information products is not automated, actions must be taken to automate them!
Have all information products been updated successfully?	*All* information products must be checked, that they have been updated successfully
Is monitoring of all information quality indicators automated?	If monitoring of all information quality indicators is not automated, actions must be taken to automate them!
Have all information quality indicators been updated successfully?	All information quality indicators must be checked, that they have been updated successfully
Is the metrics team notified when something is wrong with information products?	Automated means should be in place that will notify the metrics team, if information products are not updated, or if they were updated erroneously
Can stakeholders and measurement users access their respective information products?	The metrics team must check, from time to time, that the stakeholders can access their respective information products. Just because the metrics team can access them, does not mean that the stakeholders can also access them
Are stakeholders and measurement users notified when they cannot trust their respective information product?	Automated means must be in place to notify stakeholders and measurement users if they can or cannot trust information products

8.4.3   Maintaining the Measurement Experience Database

Maintenance of the measurement experience base is basically about (a) monitoring its proper function, and (b) securing that adding data in the (immediate/far) future will not limit or hinder its performance. Table 8.3 is developed for the metrics team to help the team to set-up the measurement experience base that fulfills these goals.

8.4.4   Maintaining the Measurement Infrastructure

Once designed and built, it is important that the measurement infrastructure be attended to. If it is left unattended, the measurement infrastructure sooner, rather than later, decays, making it unfit to host existing and new data, measures, and information products.

In order to keep the infrastructure up-to-date, the metrics team must frequently assess its fitness to comply with current and near future needs. It is imperative that new ways of working, re-organizations, or new products in the company or

Table 8.3 Maintaining databases—checklist for the measurement experience base

Question	Explanation
Is the integrity of the measurement experience base intact?	Integrity of the measurement experience base must be controlled regularly, at least on a daily basis
Is it possible to access the measurement experience base?	Checks must be done regularly, that access from both the metrics team and the rest of the company or organization is possible
Is the measurement experience base secured for near future expansions of the data stored?	Measurement experience base will always grow, so it is important that the technical/architectural solution allows for data expansions in the near future
Is the measurement experience base secured for future expansions of the data stored?	Measures must also be taken to secure the long-term performance of the measurement experience base. "What if..." scenarios should be carried out, at least once a year, to see if measures need to be taken
Is the measurement experience base secured for organizational changes?	The set-up of the measurement experience base must be such that it can cope with changes in the company or organization. Examples of such changes can be: bigger or smaller organizational changes, changes in the ways of working, evolution of products, and changes of business plans

organization not affect its stability and function. It is advisable that the metrics team assess the functionality and fitness of the measurement infrastructure at least twice a year.

8.4.5 Maintaining the Measurement Organization

The software world is far from static. It evolves constantly, and for the time being, it is evolving at a high pace. This is applicable for software products, software equipment and software-related ways of working.

With this in mind, both companies and organizations, *and* metrics teams, need to maintain the knowledge they acquire over the years. When it comes to companies and organizations, it is the responsibility of the measurement sponsor and the metrics team to ascertain that the measuring competence of companies and organizations is not deteriorating.

The following checklist, Table 8.4, can be used by *both* the measurement sponsor and the metrics team. The list should be used at least once a year.

Table 8.4 Maintaining the measurement organization—checklist

Question	Explanation
Is all documentation related to the measurement program, still up-to-date?	All documentation related to the measurement program, must be kept up-to-date
Are courses, seminars and presentations related to all aspects of the measurement program still up-to-date?	Courses, seminars and presentations must be kept up-to-date
Is the knowledge of the members of the metrics team still up-to-date?	The metrics team must maintain its knowledge regarding all aspects of measuring, over time
When was the last time the measurement sponsor and the metrics team informed the company or organization, e.g. via mail or meetings, about themselves and ongoing measuring activities?	Both the measurement sponsor and the metrics team should inform the company or organization about themselves and the ongoing measuring activities. This should be done at least once a year
When was the last time the measurement sponsor and the metrics team assessed the measuring needs of the organization?	The measurement sponsor and metrics team should assess the measuring needs of the company, and see that these are met. This should be done at least once a year

8.4.5.1   Maintenance Phase: Checklist for Stakeholders

During this phase it is important that the stakeholder re-assess the function and importance of the indicator, e.g. "Is the indicator still needed?", "Does the organization still understand the reasons behind the indicator?" Table 8.5 lists questions relevant to the maintenance phase of the measurement system and information product, from the perspective of the stakeholders.

8.5   Keeping Up with Technological and Organizational Evolution

We have seen a continuous, never-ending technological evolution of both the software as such (e.g. new software languages) and its fields of application in most aspects of our lives (e.g. mobile phones). To cope with this fast and vast evolution, new ways of working have been developed, e.g. agile [Coc06, SMP12b].

Thus far we have talked about how to develop, deploy and maintain measurement programs. But this will only take us so far; to truly succeed, measurement programs need to evolve to keep the pace up with the evolution of technology and ways of working.

Table 8.5 What to think of, as a stakeholder, during the maintenance phase of a measurement system, including information products

Question	Explanation
Is the indicator still relevant?	This is a question that the stakeholder should ask regularly, e.g. once every other month. It is de-motivating, for a company or organization, to have indicators that are not relevant anymore, but are still fully accessible/visible to everyone
Is the indicator still valid with respect to: (a) the (analysis) model, and (b) its interpretation?	The stakeholder has to check regularly that the (analysis) model and the interpretation are still valid. If this is not the case, adjustments must be made, e.g. lower the threshold of "red," or change the actions to take when the indicator shows "yellow"
Is the technical performance of the information product correct?	Even if the answer to this question is the responsibility of the metrics team, the stakeholder needs to check this from time to time
Does the stakeholder still have the mandate to act upon the status of the information presented by the indicator?	This question is applicable when changing to a new role within or outside the company or organization
If my indicator affects the company or organization, (a) does the indicator still drive the desired behavior, (b) do they still understand the purpose behind the indicator, and (c) can the company or organization still read and understand the information product?	A stakeholder needs to check regularly that: (a) the indicator does not burden the company or organization, (b) the company or organization still understands the reasoning behind the indicator, and (c) the company or organization still reads and understands the information product as intended

The purpose of this section is to present concrete examples of what it means to evolve, with regard to all components that build up the measurement program.

8.5.1   Evolving Measurement Systems

Measurement systems are technical systems that collect data, perform calculations and present results. The most basic steps in evolving measurement systems are about making them able to handle more data, and perform calculations faster.

Handling more data is necessary due to a number of reasons. For instance, the size of data sources increases with time, so measurement systems need to cope with this. Stakeholders and measurement users will eventually require more complex and advanced measures, which will (among other things) require us to combine data from (many) different data sources. For instance, once measures regarding defect backlog and testing are in place, it will not take long before the company or organization wants to know how many defects there are, per test case. Shortly after, they will like to know how many requirements have been successfully tested, and which defects relate to which requirements. To that, one can add the (average) cost of a defect, to ascertain how much design and testing will be affected, and so on and so forth!

Handling more data requires usually new technical solutions, because there is a limitation on how much data a technical solution can handle. For instance, using MS Excel worksheets to store data is limited to the number of rows and columns, and to the size of the file. To handle more data than MS Excel can handle, one has to use e.g. data marts in a server.

Efficiency, in every aspect, is of essence for the successful function of measurement programs. Calculations in measurement systems is common, and a significant bottleneck in measuring. Effort should therefore be put in making the calculations faster. Some examples for improving the execution time of calculations can be to choose more powerful programming languages, to use smarter algorithms, and to re-use base and derived measures.

8.5.2 Evolving Information Product

Today, with the introduction of e.g. advanced business intelligence tools and machine learning, information products are expected to provide much more than just a number (e.g. number of defects "17"), or color, e.g. the situation is "yellow."

One way to achieve this is to have information products that have filtering possibilities. Presenting measurement users with the possibility to filter the information that is presented is essential. The main gain is that measurement users themselves can manipulate the data, to study additional or other aspects than the one that is presented. By doing this, measurement users become better in measuring, since they learn that data can be manipulated in (many) different ways; they learn to perform analyses (other than the one presented), to compare and correlate data, and more. By the end of the day, they will become (much) better in defining "What to measure," which will help them to be (more) effective when measuring.

The same reasoning is valid for graphical manipulation, i.e. that the measurement users should be presented with the possibility to elaborate with different views on how information is presented. Let us take a simple example; compare a table with data with e.g. number of sold products per country in a worksheet, in MS Excel, and the same information presented on a world map. It is obvious that figures in countries on world map gives a far better (and immediate) overview than a table. To that, it is easy to add color coding to e.g. highlight number of sold units, e.g. have the countries that meet and exceed sales goals in green. This is something that most modern Business Intelligence tools provide nowadays.

Another aspect that information products must cope with is frequency of updates, i.e. how often they should be updated. There is a demand today to have as fresh data as possible. This puts extra pressure on smart technical solutions of measurement systems and information products. E.g. during function or system testing, there are thousands of test cases executed. Employees cannot have data being updated once a day, or even once an hour. Information should be updated more often, e.g.

every tenth minute. Another example is when presenting the defect backlog for the software development project or team—once a day will not be sufficient! The information should be updated every other minute or so. This, both to capture new defects reported, and to see the change of status of existing defects, e.g. a defect going from state "assigned to an engineer" to the state "closed."

There are times when frequent updates of information products are not enough; measurement users need to be able to update data on demand, by e.g. pressing a button. This type of update requires of course a certain type of technical solution. If this is not present, this is something that the metrics team should learn!

Another aspect to take under consideration is to make information products easily accessible. This means that the measurement users should not have to spend time looking for information. One way to do this is to focus on "pushing" information. To "push," as opposed to "pull," means that the information is presented on e.g. monitors, or sent to the measurement users automatically by e.g. e-mails, or by notifications on their mobiles, to look at in an app.

8.5.3 Evolving the Measurement Experience Database

Except for making the measurement experience base easy to access and search in, effort should be made to include additional information. For instance, the base can include information about what other, similar, companies and organizations measure. This will enrich and expand the knowledge of companies and organizations in measuring.

8.5.4 Evolving the Measurement Infrastructure

Evolving the measurement infrastructure means making it more effective and efficient, in order to meet new requirements. The new requirements derive from new technologies, new products, new ways of working, and (of course) more advanced measuring-related requirements from companies and organizations. These new requirements come at a never-ending, and frequent, pace.

New solutions, like cloud services (Software as a Service, SaaS, Infrastructure as a Service, IaaS, and Platform as a Service, PaaS), big data analyses, and use of advanced algorithms, as in Machine Learning, push the boundaries for what a modern measurement infrastructure should be able to handle.

We present here an example from real life of a measurement program that is based on the cloud services (i.e. Software-as-a-Service, Platform-as-a-Service, and Infrastructure-as-a-Service), namely the Measurement-as-a-Service concept. The example is taken from [SM14], and shows the many benefits that such an advanced technical solution provides.

Measurement-as-a-Service is a measurement licensing and delivery model, in which measures and information products are licensed on a subscription basis, centrally hosted, and delivered on demand; see Fig. 8.10. This model provides the following benefits:

- Higher quality of measures, since the knowledge base is shared easier and faster through the centralized storage.
- Lower maintenance costs, since the centralized storage is optimized towards handling of large quantities of data.
- Faster adoption of new measures, since the metrics team has the possibility to quickly assess the quality of measures, has access to the relevant data sources, and can re-use measurement systems among different parts of the company or organization.
- Clear separation of competence in the organization, i.e. stakeholders focus on their business processes, whereas the metrics team is the main point of contact for the measurement competence.
- Limit the number of non-used measures in the organization, since stakeholders and measurement users subscribe to specific measures and indicators, for as long as they need to.
- Access to measures offline.

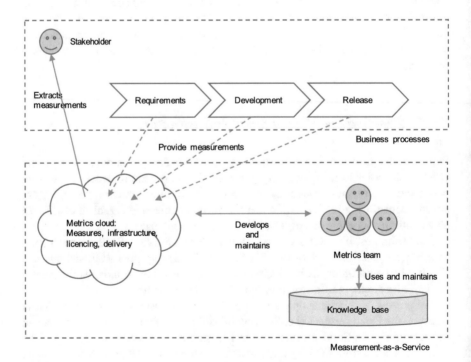

Fig. 8.10 Conceptual model of a cloud-based measurement program

Except for the benefits listed above, there are other, equally important needs that companies and organizations address, e.g. the need for fast and broad distribution of information. Also, the need to have different ways of accessing and distributing information, e.g.:

- there are stakeholders that want to use existing infrastructure for their own measurement systems
- there are stakeholders that want to distribute their own measurement systems within a limited circle of employees, e.g. a team leader to his/her team
- stakeholders and measurement users like to have access to data and information products even offline

The above requirements can be easily addressed by e.g. using the *cloud*-based solution Infrastructure-as-a-Service (IaaS). We present here an example from real life, namely [SMN08, SM14], that is based on this solution.

Using "classic" ways of storing, updating and sharing measurement systems provides a number of limitations, e.g. storage is centralized (regardless of if it is a folder area or a server solution), and all measurement systems have to be maintained by the metrics team.

By combining IaaS and the Dropbox (www.dropbox.com) solution, see Fig. 8.11, the stakeholders and measurement users can develop self-managed measurement systems, to share them as they see fit, by using the existing measurement execution infrastructure. For the metrics team this solution means that they do not need to develop all measurement systems needed, and reduces the need to keep the folder or server solution constantly live.

The benefit presented in Fig. 8.11 is that the cloud solution separates the concerns of storage/execution and information provisioning. The architecture of such a solution can be as shown in Fig. 8.12, where the cloud uses the storage server to provide network access to measurement systems and the execution server updates all measurement systems.

The solution means that we can have the following types of measurement systems:

1. *Public*: i.e. everyone in the company or organization can access these measurement systems, even if some of them were developed for dedicated stakeholders and/or measurement users
2. *Private*: i.e. measurement systems are designed by stakeholders or measurement users and managed by them, which means that updates are done locally. The measurement systems are visible only to them.
3. *Shared*: measurement systems which are private, but their owners have shared with others, e.g. defect backlog of a team.
4. *Locally updated public*: i.e. public measurement systems that are updated by a single user. An example can be features delivered by a team to a dashboard, available to the whole project, which shows the total status of features delivered.
5. *Centrally updated private*: i.e. measurement systems which are private for one stakeholder, but are maintained by the central storage and execution server. These

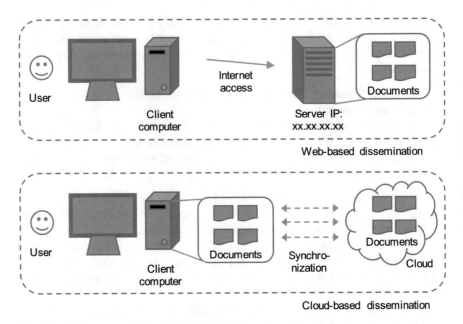

Fig. 8.11 Web-based and cloud-based dissemination

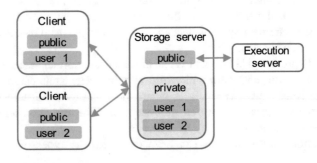

Fig. 8.12 Cloud infrastructure

can be dedicated measurement systems with company-sensitive information, e.g. budget.

The synchronization principles are as follows; see also Fig. 8.13:

1. *Public*: measurement systems are always updated from the server to the client.
2. *Private*: measurement systems are always updated from the client to the storage server.

3. *Shared*: measurement systems are always updated from the owner to dedicated clients.
4. *Locally updated public*: measurement systems are always updated from the client to the storage server.
5. *Centrally updated private*: measurement systems are always updated from the storage server to the dedicated client.

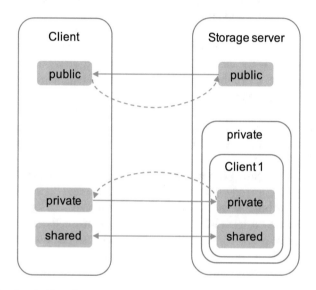

Fig. 8.13 Synchronization of measurement systems

8.5.5 *Evolving the Measurement Organization*

When we talk about "measuring organization" here, we refer to the *whole* company or organization. It is imperative that the *whole* company or organization be involved in the evolution of the measurement program.

This is important for three reasons. The first reason is that, if there are measuring "inequalities" in the company or organization, it may lead to difficulties in communicating (measuring-wise), and/or in the alienation of the group of employees that advances measuring-wise, and the group of employees that have a limited understanding of measuring.

The second reason is that measurement programs can always be better. For instance measurement systems can be faster in executing calculations and handling more advanced algorithms.

The third reason is that companies and organizations must keep up with the constant evolution of technology and ways of working, to constantly keep with up and surpass their competitors.

Given these three facts, we list below several recommendations that can help companies and organizations to evolve, *both* their measurement organization and the rest of the employees. The bullets below are not listed in a priority order.

- Use of measuring related standards—The metrics team must keep up with update of existing standards, and introduction of new standards.
- Expanding knowledge in metrology—Metrology is a vast discipline, and the metrics team should, continuously, expand their knowledge in this area.
- New technology—The metrics team must understand, and, whenever applicable, incorporate new technologies that support measuring, e.g. cloud solutions, machine learning, and new business intelligence tools.
- New ways of working—The measurement organization should always assess its way of working, to see how it can keep up with the new ways of working that are introduced in the world of software, in general, and at their company or organization, in particular.
- Elevating the measuring competence of the company or organization—This can be done by e.g. giving courses, seminars, and presentations. These activities should include both theoretical aspects, e.g. standards, and practical aspects, e.g. how to use a business intelligence tool. Furthermore, these activities should include, not only existing solutions and practices, but also introduce new concepts, and shade some light on what's to come.
- Involving all employees—Broaden the focus outside the existing stakeholders and measurement users. The goal has to be that *everyone* in the company knows something about measuring; that *everyone* in the company *knows something more* this year, compared to last year!
- Helping the employees that want to become independent from the metrics team— This means educating them to become equally good in measuring as those in the metrics team.
- Expand your measuring network—It is important to expand one's measuring network, from one's company or organization to e.g. other units of the company, other similar companies, and academia. Knowing *and* understanding how others measure will significantly improve your measuring competence!

8.6 Summary

When designing measurement programs, measurement designers often focus on rapid delivery of the first measurements. However, experience shows that it is better to spend more time on designing the measurement infrastructure so that it can evolve over time, with the evolution taking least resources possible.

In this chapter, we described how to design the measurement programs for sustainability, i.e. to ensure that the measurement programs will sustain over time. Based on our experiences, we designed a number of checklists that can be used by the measurement designers. These checklists show which elements one needs to have in place, to have sustainable information products, a sustainable database and all other elements of the measurement program. This chapter complements the previous chapters by focusing on organizational aspects of the measurement program.

In the next chapter, we continue by summarizing what we have learned from this book. We also provide a set of practical recommendations for the designers of the measurement programs.

8.7 Further Reading

One of the ways of decreasing the cost of maintenance is not to do it at all, or at least to automate it. In the context of measurement systems, we can recommend using mechanisms of self-healing [SM14] in Chap. 4. The mechanisms can be applied to existing measurement systems, which we describe in our previous work [SMT$^+$17]. Self-healing can reduce the operational maintenance effort significantly by allowing the measurement infrastructure to take care of such problems as restoring non-functioning measurement systems to their previous state.

Using cloud-based measurement infrastructure is also a way of decreasing the cost of maintenance, as it is centralized and we can use the same competence across different measurement areas. In our previous work we provided the example of such a framework [SM14], where the concept of cloud computing was used to distribute the execution of measurement systems and increase robustness of their dissemination.

We recommend the works of Atkins et al. [AMVP03]. One of the aspects important in the use of cloud-based solutions internally at companies is the understanding of how an information product spreads—i.e. the internal communication channels and the reusability of metrics. Another work in this area is the work of Jorgensen [Jor99]. This is not an easy task due to the potentially different definitions of measures. Jorgensen shows contrasting definitions of measures depending on whether quality is defined as "a set of quality factors," "user satisfaction," or "software quality related to errors."

The current cloud system is an evolution of the previous work on ensuring information reliability done together with Ericsson [SM09a]. In this work we address the problems of ensuring that information is available throughout the enterprise and its understanding [KS02, SKT05, MS10, MST12].

For the readers interested in keeping the measurement data secure throughout the enterprise, we propose exploring the work of Yoon et al. [YOL13], who showed how to establish security in cloud computing. Another approach to modelling and implementing cloud-based systems is presented by Zhang and Zhou [ZZ09] in their

CCOA framework. Although a very elaborate framework could be used in our solution, we preferred to use a simple approach and focus on the ease of use. It is the ease of use and performance which are important for similar cloud systems as described by Gong et al. [GLZ$^+$10].

Farooq et al. [FKDW06] presented an approach for structuring the measurement process (ISO/IEC 15939-based) using web services in order to increase scaleability and reuse of metrics. Sakamoto et al. [SMSN13] have developed a tool for mining software metrics and storing them in a web service environment. Their study is a good complement to our work as it addresses the question of metrics acquisition from large software repositories.

Umarji and Emurian [UE05]: the study describes the use of technology adoption theory when implementing metric programs with a focus on social issues. One of the important results from that study was the importance of the factor "ease of use."

Gopal et al. [GMK05, GKMG02]: these studies present results and conclusions from a survey about metric program implementation conducted with managers at various levels (over 200 data points). The results indicated the importance of such factors as management commitment and the relative low importance of such factors as data collection.

Finally, we also recommend exploring the factors needed for longevity of the measurement program as we present in [SM11]. In that work we explored the technical aspects that are important for making a sustainable measurement program.

References

[AMVP03] Kenneth L. Atkins, Bredt D. Martin, Joseph M. Vellinga, and Rick A. Price. Stardust: implementing a new manage-to-budget paradigm. *Acta Astronautica*, 52(2-6):87–97, 2003. TY - JOUR.

[Coc06] Alistair Cockburn. *Agile software development: The cooperative game.* Pearson Education, 2006.

[FKDW06] Ayaz Farooq, Steffen Kernchen, Reiner R Dumke, and Cornelius Wille. Web services based measurement for it quality assurance. In *Proceedings of the International Conference on Software Process and Product Measurement (MENSURA 2006)*, pages 241–251, 2006.

[GKMG02] A. Gopal, M. S. Krishnan, T. Mukhopadhyay, and D. R. Goldenson. Measurement programs in software development: determinants of success. *IEEE Transactions on Software Engineering*, 28(9):863–875, 2002. 0098-5589.

[GLZ$^+$10] Chunye Gong, Jie Liu, Qiang Zhang, Haitao Chen, and Zhenghu Gong. The characteristics of cloud computing. In *Parallel Processing Workshops (ICPPW), 2010 39th International Conference on*, pages 275–279. IEEE, 2010.

[GMK05] A. Gopal, T. Mukhopadhyay, and M. S. Krishnan. The impact of institutional forces on software metrics programs. *IEEE Transactions on Software Engineering*, 31(8):679–694, 2005. 0098-5589.

[Jor99] M. Jorgensen. Software quality measurement. *Advances in Engineering Software*, 30(12):907–912, 1999.

[KS02] Ludwik Kuzniarz and Miroslaw Staron. On practical usage of stereotypes in uml-based software development. In *Forum on Design and Specification Languages*, 2002.

[MS10]   Niklas Mellegård and Miroslaw Staron. Characterizing model usage in embedded software engineering: a case study. In *Proceedings of the Fourth European Conference on Software Architecture: Companion Volume*, pages 245–252. ACM, 2010.

[MST12] Niklas Mellegard, Miroslaw Staron, and Fredrik Torner. A light-weight defect classification scheme for embedded automotive software and its initial evaluation. In *Software Reliability Engineering (ISSRE), 2012 IEEE 23rd International Symposium on*, pages 261–270. IEEE, 2012.

[PSSM10] Kosta Pandazo, Arisa Shollo, Miroslaw Staron, and Wilhelm Meding. Presenting software metrics indicators: a case study. In *Proceedings of the 20th International Conference on Software Product and Process Measurement (MENSURA)*, volume 20, 2010.

[SKT05] Miroslaw Staron, Ludwik Kuzniarz, and Christian Thurn. An empirical assessment of using stereotypes to improve reading techniques in software inspections. In *ACM SIGSOFT Software Engineering Notes*, volume 30, pages 1–7. ACM, 2005.

[SM09a] Miroslaw Staron and Wilhelm Meding. Ensuring reliability of information provided by measurement systems. In *Software Process and Product Measurement*, pages 1–16. Springer, 2009.

[SM09b] Miroslaw Staron and Wilhelm Meding. Using models to develop measurement systems: A method and its industrial use. 5891:212–226, 2009.

[SM11]   Miroslaw Staron and Wilhelm Meding. Factors determining long-term success of a measurement program: an industrial case study. *e-Informatica Software Engineering Journal*, pages 7–23, 2011.

[SM14]   Miroslaw Staron and Wilhelm Meding. MetricsCloud: Scaling-up metrics dissemination in large organizations. *Advances in Software Engineering*, 2014, 2014.

[SMH+13] Miroslaw Staron, Wilhelm Meding, Jörgen Hansson, Christoffer Höglund, Kent Niesel, and Vilhelm Bergmann. Dashboards for continuous monitoring of quality for software product under development. *System Qualities and Software Architecture (SQSA)*, 2013.

[SMN08] Miroslaw Staron, Wilhelm Meding, and Christer Nilsson. A framework for developing measurement systems and its industrial evaluation. *Information and Software Technology*, 51(4):721–737, 2008.

[SMP12a] Miroslaw Staron, Wilhelm Meding, and Klas Palm. Release readiness indicator for mature agile and lean software development projects. In *Agile Processes in Software Engineering and Extreme Programming*, pages 93–107. Springer, 2012.

[SMP12b] Miroslaw Staron, Wilhelm Meding, and Klas Palm. Release readiness indicator for mature agile and lean software development projects. In *Agile Processes in Software Engineering and Extreme Programming*, pages 93–107. Springer, 2012.

[SMSN13] Yuta Sakamoto, Shinichi Matsumoto, Sachio Saiki, and Mitsutoshi Nakamura. Visualizing software metrics with service-oriented mining software repository for reviewing personal process. In *Software Engineering, Artificial Intelligence, Networking and Parallel/Distributed Computing (SNPD), 2013 14th ACIS International Conference on*, pages 549–554. IEEE, 2013.

[SMT+17] Miroslaw Staron, Wilhelm Meding, Matthias Tichy, Jonas Bjurhede, Holger Giese, and Ola Söder. Industrial experiences from evolving measurement systems into self-healing systems for improved availability. *Software: Practice and Experience*, 2017.

[SNM15] Miroslaw Staron, Kent Niesel, and Wilhelm Meding. Selecting the right visualization of indicators and measures – Dashboard selection model. In *Software Measurement*, pages 130–143. Springer, 2015.

[UE05]   M. Umarji and H. Emurian. Acceptance issues in metrics program implementation. In H. Emurian, editor, *11th IEEE International Symposium Software Metrics*, pages 10–17, 2005.

[YOL13] Young Bae Yoon, Junseok Oh, and Bong Gyou Lee. The establishment of security strategies for introducing cloud computing. *KSII Transactions on Internet and Information Systems (TIIS)*, 7(4):860–877, 2013.

[ZZ09] Liang-Jie Zhang and Qun Zhou. CCOA: Cloud computing open architecture. In *Web Services, 2009. ICWS 2009. IEEE International Conference on*, pages 607–616. IEEE, 2009.

Chapter 9
Summary and Future Directions

Abstract There are two statements that strongly relate to the content of this book. "You can't control what you can't measure," by Tom DeMarco, and "In the future, all companies will be software companies," by George Colony. The first one relates to the need that all companies and organizations have, i.e. to be able to control everything that happens during the development and the maintenance lifecycle of software products. The second quote relates to the undisputed fact of the technological evolution we are witnessing, i.e. that software is becoming a natural part of more and more products. In this last chapter, we take these two quotes under consideration, as we discuss trends and future directions that will impact the software measurement programs.

9.1 Introduction

In the last few years we have seen an explosion of new software related technologies and tools, e.g. cloud, virtualization, machine learning, micro data services, IoT, autonomous IoT, big data, virtual/augmented reality, Elasticsearch, Kibana, and more.

This is also a trend that has impacted the world of software measurement programs. Software development companies have started using measurements to a larger extent, something that previously was more the case for business, financial and market analytics (consulting) companies [Abr10]. The role of metrics engineer is starting to be established, as software development companies realize that handling of (big) data, statistics and information products must be handled by professionals.

After almost 20 years working with measuring, we start to see a paradigm shift, from "everybody can measure," to having dedicated roles and teams for measuring-related activities. As we showed in Chap. 3, software development companies, to a larger extent today, formalize the handling of data, and the development and use of measurement systems and information products. Today, to take one such example, it is important that information be presented in a succinct and reliable way, i.e. the information must be presented in an easy-to-understand way, and it must include information about whether what is presented can be trusted or not, as we present in Chap. 5.

Another important trend shift we have seen is the entry of ethical aspects in measuring. Measures such as "How many lines of code did you produce today?", or "How many defects does your code have?", are consigned to the cemetery of "bad" measures, as we discussed in Chap. 8. We see time and again, from our many visits to software-intensive companies, that measures are used to get a better understanding of the organizational and product performance, with the purpose to support/help the employees in their everyday work.

We would like to exemplify this new trend with an anecdote. A few years ago, we were visiting a company. While walking among software development teams, who were sitting in an open landscape, we stopped by one of the dashboards (on monitors) that each software development team had. This dashboard was showing widgets, most of them in red (i.e. they indicated problems). So, we asked "Aren't you afraid showing this openly, that you have so many problems?". They looked a bit surprised at us, and answered, "No, because when a manager or a senior engineer passes by, they will ask what they can do to help us!"

Using measurements more professionally today than 20 years ago has revealed the complex and vast world that is comprised of measurement programs. Companies and organizations stand hesitant or indecisive as to what to start with or focus on. The purpose of Sect. 9.2 is to present companies and organizations with a limited, yet important number of areas that they must focus on. For that, we give concrete examples of what to start with, paving the way towards a successful implementation and use of measurement programs [SMKN11].

Section 9.3 glances at the door into the future, "revealing" some of the trends that will impact the way we perceive and use software measurement programs. Some of those trends are micro data centers and autonomous AI-based measurement systems.

9.2 Measurement Program: Recommendations on How/Where to Start

In this book we have shown what a measurement program is; we have described the components that build up a measurement program, and how to design, deploy and maintain a measurement program.

Going through this book, as well as other related books, standards and theory, one comes to realize the vastness and complexity of measurement programs. There is a risk that the reader (companies and organizations) will feel intimidated to take upon the journey to set up or improve/evolve measurement programs, or, they may get frustrated and give up after some initial, fruitless, initiatives.

The purpose of this section is therefore to present a few key success factors that must be in place for the successful introduction and continuity of a measurement program. Based on our experience we urge companies and organizations to focus on establishing a metrics team, to start studying selected parts of measuring-related standards, to automate key measuring activities, to consider cultural-specific aspects of their companies and organizations, and finally to focus on management information needs.

For each of these areas we explain why they are so important, and give also concrete recommendations on what to start with, enabling thus the smooth journey towards a successful measurement program.

9.2.1   Metrics Team

The first thing that must be in place in a measurement program is a metrics team, which we discussed in Chap. 3. To illustrate this, we repeat some of the responsibilities/activities of the metrics team:

- coordinates measurement-related activities in the company or organization,
- provides the platform for the experts in the different areas of measuring to discuss and exchange experience,
- supports its company or organization with measuring-related questions, such as "What should we measure?", or "How do we set up a measurement system?",
- gives measuring-related courses, seminars and presentations,
- collects data, systematically and frequently,
- builds up, maintains and evolves the measurement infrastructure,
- designs, deploys and maintains measurement systems and information products,
- stores measuring experiences of the company or organization,
- maintains knowledge database of how to combine data from different data sources,
- provides orderly and easy access to raw data, and
- provides orderly and easy access to measures and indicators.

Despite the many activities that take place in a metrics team, the team itself can be small and cost-efficient. From our experience, a team of four can support a company or organization of up to fifteen hundred employees.

Our recommendation is to start up a metrics team with just one employee. The criterion is that the employee should have this job as a full-time assignment. The team can then expand, as the measuring maturity of the company or organization, and the demand for more (and more advanced) information products, increases.

9.2.2   Standards

All jobs are governed by rules. Some of those sets of rules are put together into standards. Standards exist to help companies, organizations, and roles in their daily work. Standards give guidance and provide, many times, concrete examples, e.g. ISO/IEC 25023, in Chap. 8, where we list performance measures.

Standards provide a measuring-specific language that enables easy and precise communication. They limit dramatically the time measuring activities take, since they define the roles that are included in the measurement program, including their respective "authority and responsibility." They limit also drastically the number of measures in companies and organizations since they define how and when to use measures. In our experience, the use of measurement-related standards by companies and organizations helps them to build up and have successful measurement programs over time [Sta, SMH$^+$14].

Our recommendation to companies and organizations is to start with the ISO/IEC 15939 standard, which we describe in Chap. 2. The reason for this is that the standard describes the process of measuring, including the definitions of concepts needed for this process. We highlight the following important concepts from this standard:

- Measurement Information Model: describes what a measurement system looks like, i.e. it lists the main components that build up a measurement system and how they relate to one another.
- Stakeholder: a group or a person with the mandate to act upon the status of the information that is presented by an indicator. Stakeholder is a role of the utmost importance for the successful function of a measurement program. Understanding and using the definition of this role properly ensures, among other things, that the number of employees that *claim* to be responsible for this or that measure diminishes.
- Information Need: the "insight necessary to manage objectives, goals, risks and problems." We have experienced time and again the impact this notion has had, once understood, on drastically reducing the number of measures used in companies and organizations.
- There are three different types of measures: base measures, derived measures and indicators. Base measure is a simple measure, such as number of lines of code or McCabe complexity. Derived measure is a measure that is built up by two or more base measures. Indicator is a measure (base or derived) that has the following attributes tied to it: a stakeholder, an analysis model (e.g. when the indicator should become red), and the interpretation (e.g. what the stakeholder should do when the indicator shows red).

The process of the establishing of the measurement program, including operationalization of the above definitions, is described in Chap. 2.

9.2.3 Automation

Automation is the very foundation for a well-structured and efficient measurement program, a crucial prerequisite for coherent and consistent collection of data, execution of calculations, and updating of information products [SMN08, SM09], as described in Chaps. 4 and 5.

Good practice shows that many activities that take place in a measurement program can, and should, be automated. For instance, the collection of data from data sources as described in Chap. 5. Having the data collection automated saves a lot of time, since export of data may take long time, especially when we talk about large quantities of data. Collection of data can take place at night, so that (a) the metrics team has access to the latest data when they come to work, and (b) evening the access load on the data sources, over day and night.

Storage of data can also be automated [SM14b]. Experience shows that frequent and structured manual storing of data is a time- and effort-intensive activity. Raw data is usually stored in (many) different places, depending on their product and organizational belonging, and (in many cases) depending on whether the raw data relates to development, maintenance, support, tools or something else. Storage of data comprises also derived data, i.e. data that is the result of calculations (i.e. combination of raw data).

Another time- and effort-intensive activity is the calculations that must be performed for every measurement system and the update of its corresponding information products. Keeping in mind that even simple measurement programs can have hundreds of measurement systems, it is intuitively easy-to-understand that this is an area that, if automated, saves substantial time for the measurement organization.

Completeness, correctness and timelining of data and information products (i.e. information quality of measurement programs, described in Chap. 4) is another area that needs automation. The reason for this is simply the vast number of things that must be checked. For instance, measurement users must know that data integrity was kept throughout the data flow, from data sources to information products, and that every single calculation was performed accurately. "Multiplying" every information quality check with the number of measurement systems and information products gives a number so high that the use of automation is necessary.

The last example that we present here, that can be automated, is the orchestration of all the activities described above, i.e. collection of data, execution of calculation, update of information products and control of information quality [SM14a, SMT$^+$17].

Our experience shows that companies and organizations should start with automating the collection of data from data sources firstly. Once this area is automated, companies and organizations should move on to automating the execution of calculations in the measurement systems [SMT$^+$17, SMNS16].

9.2.4 Company/Organization Specific Cultural Aspects

If we look at the large picture, software development companies share many common ways of working and goals. For instance, modern software companies and organizations follow (more or less) the principles of lean and agile. All of them strive to have products with high quality; all of them want to have short development cycles [SMP12].

Though there are many common things that characterize companies and organizations, there are also some things that are unique.

In our experience, from visiting, interviewing and working with many companies, we have observed some small, yet significant differences among companies and organizations. Sometimes, those characteristics, if you like, are stated clearly, e.g. in this company we focus on speed, or in this organization we put extra focus on documenting our code [SM16, Sta17]. Other times those characteristics are subtler, e.g. engineers put pride in carefully reviewing the code of their colleagues, or senior designers and testers are always available to support/help their colleagues, whatever the question/need is.

Our experience shows that it is of the utmost importance that established measures in companies and organizations capture these company- or organization-specific characteristics. Employees must recognize in measures these specific "cultural" characteristics.

For instance, if an organization is characterized by having high focus on code reviews, then there must be measures that relate to this, e.g. average number of reviewers, average time it takes to perform a review, average number of errors found per review, and percentage of successful reviews. If an organization has an outspoken focus of lean, then measures that address queue and throughput must be in place.

Identifying and developing these types of measures is something we recommend that the metrics team start with, *after* basic areas of the measurement program are in place, e.g. infrastructure and automation.

9.2.5 Management Focus

Managers are a measurement-intensive user group. They use measures in their everyday work. They need measures to e.g. take decisions, to know the performance of their organization, to understand the market situation, and to set up strategies for their future organizational goals. Given the impact of managerial decisions and strategies, measures play a major part in the successful performance of companies and organizations [SM11].

Measuring is a time- and effort-intensive activity, so managers must put substantial time into measuring. We have observed over the years, in our contact with many companies and organizations, that managers put a lot of time into verifying both the input data, and the result from the calculations. This is of course not strange, since their decisions can/may have (severe) negative impact on companies and organizations.

The metrics team can play a decisive part here, i.e. they can reduce substantially the time managers put into measuring and controlling the results of measurements.

Our recommendation is therefore that the metrics team start supporting firstly the management in developing measures that address aspects that are important to them. The metrics team has the competence to help the management in collecting data, performing calculations, and designing and updating information products. The metrics team has also the competence to set up a controlling mechanism for information quality, and make that available to the company and organization.

Once major parts of the management-related measurement needs are in place, we recommend the metrics team to move on to support project/program management teams. As for the management, projects/programs are also big consumers of data and measures.

After the metrics team has established handling of measures for these two groups, the team can start addressing the information needs of leading roles, e.g. senior architects and designers, and individuals.

9.3   Future: Autonomous AI-Based Measurement Systems

The technologies, methods, standards and practices presented in this book are applicable for variety of types of projects and organizations. They provide the possibility to make the measurement program efficient and cost-effective.

However, we can see that this is not enough today. Measurement programs are valuable assets, but they are not as valuable as the products of the companies. The products of the companies bring in the revenue and therefore keep the companies in the market, whereas the measurement program contributes to the products being better, cheaper, of high quality and more valuable to the customers. So, their contribution is indirect.

In the nearest future, we perceive the measurement programs to increasingly consist of Autonomous, AI-based, measurement systems. These systems can replace such roles as those of the measurement designer and the measurement librarian by automating many of their tasks. These autonomous measurement systems can utilize the modern machine learning algorithms to change their behavior—for example they can notify the stakeholders that the trends in the data changed and therefore they need to change their focus to another indicator. These measurement systems can also adjust the rules of counting/measuring entities, their measurement instruments, in order to align more closely with the information needs of their stakeholders.

This book helps us to move in this direction by presenting how we can combine a flexible design of measurement systems with the machine learning algorithms. Chapter 2 presented the way in which we can structure the measurement systems based on the ISO/IEC 15939 standard and Chap. 7 presented how we can utilize machine learning for that purpose (see also [RS15] and [RSH$^+$14]).

We hope that this book will help the reader to move towards the direction of cost-efficient measurement by utilizing the techniques and the knowledge available in it.

References

[Abr10] Alain Abran. *Software metrics and software metrology*. John Wiley & Sons, 2010.

[RS15] Rakesh Rana and Miroslaw Staron. Machine learning approach for quality assessment and prediction in large software organizations. In *Software Engineering and Service Science (ICSESS), 2015 6th IEEE International Conference on*, pages 1098–1101. IEEE, 2015.

[RSH+14] Rakesh Rana, Miroslaw Staron, Jörgen Hansson, Martin Nilsson, and Wilhelm Meding. A framework for adoption of machine learning in industry for software defect prediction. In *Software Engineering and Applications (ICSOFT-EA), 2014 9th International Conference on*, pages 383–392. IEEE, 2014.

[SM09] Miroslaw Staron and Wilhelm Meding. Ensuring reliability of information provided by measurement systems. In *Software Process and Product Measurement*, pages 1–16. Springer, 2009.

[SM11] Miroslaw Staron and Wilhelm Meding. Factors determining long-term success of a measurement program: An industrial case study. *e-Informatica*, 5(1):7–23, 2011.

[SM14a] Miroslaw Staron and Wilhelm Meding. Industrial self-healing measurement systems. In *Continuous Software Engineering*, pages 183–200. Springer, 2014.

[SM14b] Miroslaw Staron and Wilhelm Meding. MetricsCloud: Scaling-up metrics dissemination in large organizations. *Advances in Software Engineering*, 2014, 2014.

[SM16] Miroslaw Staron and Wilhelm Meding. Mesram–a method for assessing robustness of measurement programs in large software development organizations and its industrial evaluation. *Journal of Systems and Software*, 113:76–100, 2016.

[SMH+14] Miroslaw Staron, Wilhelm Meding, Jörgen Hansson, Christoffer Höglund, Kent Niesel, and Vilhelm Bergmann. Dashboards for continuous monitoring of quality for software product under development. *System Qualities and Software Architecture (SQSA)*, 2014.

[SMKN11] Miroslaw Staron, Wilhelm Meding, Göran Karlsson, and Christer Nilsson. Developing measurement systems: an industrial case study. *Journal of Software Maintenance and Evolution: Research and Practice*, 23(2):89–107, 2011.

[SMN08] Miroslaw Staron, Wilhelm Meding, and Christer Nilsson. A framework for developing measurement systems and its industrial evaluation. *Information and Software Technology*, 51(4):721–737, 2008.

[SMNS16] Miroslaw Staron, Wilhelm Meding, Kent Niesel, and Ola Söder. Evolution of the role of measurement systems in industrial decision support. In *Handbook of Research on Global Supply Chain Management*, pages 560–580. IGI Global, 2016.

[SMP12] Miroslaw Staron, Wilhelm Meding, and Klas Palm. Release readiness indicator for mature agile and lean software development projects. In *Agile Processes in Software Engineering and Extreme Programming*, pages 93–107. Springer, 2012.

[SMT+17] Miroslaw Staron, Wilhelm Meding, Matthias Tichy, Jonas Bjurhede, Holger Giese, and Ola Söder. Industrial experiences from evolving measurement systems into self-healing systems for improved availability. *Software: Practice and Experience*, 2017.

[Sta] Miroslaw Staron. Dashboard development guide how to build sustainable and useful dashboards to support software development and maintenance.

[Sta17] Miroslaw Staron. *Automotive software architectures: An introduction*. Springer, 2017.

Printed in the United States
By Bookmasters